Norwegian
Cooking

Odd Ivar Solvoll

Ingebjørg Moe

Heidi Birkrem

Liv Leira

Anna-Karin Lindstad

Britt Kåsin

"Norwegian Cooking"

Norwegian edition: «Mat på norsk»
English translation: Melody Favish

Publisher:
Kom forlag as
Postboks 865
6501 Kristiansund

Project leader: Svein Gran

post@komforlag.no
www.komforlag.no

Photographer: Espen Grønli

The food photographed by Espen Grønli was prepared and styled for photography by Odd Ivar Solvold

Recipe editors:
Ingebjørg Moe, Export Office for Fish
Heidi Birkrem, Information Office for Meat
Liv Leira, Information Office for Eggs and White Meat
Anna-Karin Lindstad, TINE (Norwegian Dairies)
Britt Kåsin, Information Office for Fruit and Vegetables

Other photographers: See page 288

Graphic design: Unniform AS, Kristiansund
Printer: TiTrykk, Skien

Norwegian edition: ISBN 82 90823 959
English edition: ISBN 82 90823 967

Norwegian Cooking

Editor

Bjarne Håkon Hanssen

Senior photographer

Espen Grønli

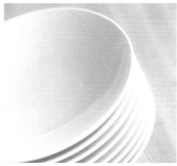

Preface

I really like food. I always have. But especially when I was minister of agriculture, I came into contact almost daily with different aspects of the Norwegian kitchen. And everywhere I went, people knew that I like food, and I got to talk about it and taste all kinds of food from all over Norway.

That has inspired me, both in my own kitchen, and to spread the word about Norwegian food and Norwegian traditions. I am especially interested in everyday food. I want good Norwegian ingredients to be part of the meals we eat every day.

I have really enjoyed working with a very well-informed panel of recipe editors on this book. They have helped to make it what I had hoped it would be: a well-written, inspiring book about the food we eat in Norway in 2003. The recipes are based on our own traditions, with some impulses from abroad. A living culture is not static – it develops through impulses from outside.

The Norwegian farmer is proud of the agricultural products produced here. Norwegian agriculture has been spared any huge food scandals. That's because of the ethics of our farmers. Norwegian agriculture gives us good, safe food.

And Mother Nature has given us a fantastic coastline that provides the basis for fishing and aquaculture. Natural conditions and experienced fishermen and fish farmers have turned the ocean into our largest pantry.

Norwegian cuisine rests on a solid tradition, based on good, pure ingredients, in which the flavor of the ingredients dominates the finished dish. That's one reason why Norwegian food has also managed to win favor internationally. It's so gratifying to see how Norwegian chefs win so many international competitions.

Countries with a strong food culture have certain similarities that are not accidental. The everyday meal is prepared from scratch, with its basis in relatively reasonable, often locally produced, fresh ingredients that take some time to prepare. The meal is a gathering point for family and friends, and being together around the table is just as important as the food served. These elements are also important in the development of the Norwegian kitchen.

"Norwegian Cooking" has emphasized everyday food, though holiday food and weekend food are also included. The book encourages more extensive development of local produce with more focus on regional cuisine.

Throughout the past few decades, the different information offices have worked hard to spread product information in a responsible, informative manner. This information has stood for quality and creativity by giving consumers the best possible basis. The recipes in this book have been developed by the information offices – in line with available ingredients, our own tradition plus those impulses from abroad.

My heartfelt thanks to Heidi Birkrem at the Information Office for Meat, Britt Kåsin at the Information Office for Fruit and Vegetables, Live Leira at the Information Office for Eggs and White Meat, Anna-Karin Lindstad at TINE (Norwegian Dairies) and Ingebjørg Moe at the Export Office for Fish, for their traditional and tasty, exciting and creative recipes.

Thanks also to Reidar Helgesen at Bread Facts, for important contributions of recipes for good and healthy breads.

In working on this book, we have also been helped by different professionals who have contributed articles on Norwegian cuisine. Many will recognize the name of researcher Runar Døving, who has been a breath of fresh air in the debate about Norwegian food. Runar Døving, a researcher at the State Center for Consumer Research, wrote the chapter on Norwegian food culture.

Some readers might feel that wine has been emphasized too much over other drinks. That may be the case when one takes into consideration Norwegian traditions regarding food and drink. When Thor Richard Teien from the State Wine and Liquor Monopoly paid so much attention to wine, it is to satisfy the enormous interest expressed by Norwegians regarding wine in recent years, as well as to give practical advice in an area where many of us still find ourselves on shaky ground.

Norwegian cooking features healthy food. The fresh ingredients that are the basis for many recipes - whether meat, chicken or fish, are all low in fat. Treated right and served with vegetables, potatoes, rice or pasta, they are the healthiest foods you can eat, along with fruit, bread and other whole grains and a number of dairy products.

To delve more deeply – which is of course very important – Knut-Inge Klepp wrote the chapter: "What is healthy food?" Klepp is professor of nutrition at the Institute for Nutritional Research at the School of Medicine at the University of Oslo and is leader of the National Council for Nutrition and Physical Activity. We feel safe with his recommendations.

"Norwegian Cooking" is a book you can use – and I hope it will help you to develop Norwegian cuisine in your own kitchen. Preparing food is a labor of love, both for yourself and for those who are fortunate enough to dine at your table.

Bon Appétit!

Contents

Part 1 Introduction

Part 2 Recipes

Norwegian Cooking
– contrasts in the kitchen

It's early Saturday afternoon, but gray clouds make it darker than usual for October. The doorbell rings! Our guests have arrived. We're glad they brought the kids, and we're looking forward to an enjoyable Saturday evening for both big and small. It's autumn and chilly, so we prefer to stay inside.

I began making dinner earlier today. First I went shopping. I like to check out the meat counter in the fall, when it's filled with fresh Norwegian lamb, one of my all-time favorites.

Our friends have brought chanterelle mushrooms. They like going for walks in the woods and they are also good at taking advantage of everything nature has to offer. I bought garlic, potatoes, cream and broccoli. That's the way we like our leg of lamb. Nothing makes a gray day in October brighter than the aroma of lamb and garlic.

In addition, I have made a delicious starter. I bought Serrano ham from Spain and flavorful arugula. I found a bottle of good cold-pressed olive oil at the shop, and I bought a bottle of good Italian wine to drink with it all. Norwegian and imported ingredients and products – Norwegian lamb, Spanish pork, Greek olives and Italian wine. That's the way we eat in my Norwegian kitchen on a Saturday evening in October.

When we have guests, we prepare the food together. The banter around the kitchen counter is just as important as the conversation around the table. One person peels potatoes. I like to bone the lamb before roasting it. Stock made from lamb bones makes the best sauce, and scalloped potatoes add a special touch.

That kind of meal gives me the strength to deal with a tight schedule on weekdays. Good friends become even better friends. The kids get to help out and like to try their hand in the kitchen. We have enough time for once. There are no deadlines, the food will be ready whenever, and we have enough to talk about. Before anyone has even thought about dessert, the evening is well on its way to night.

What a contrast to that same kitchen on the following Tuesday!

Luckily, I managed to come home from working at the Norwegian Parliament at 4:30. That meant that I would be able to fetch our little boy at the daycare center. We had to pop into a shop to buy fixings for dinner. There was exactly one hour before one of the other boys needed driven to his guitar lesson.

There's a big food industry in Bergen, and all Norwegians know about the Toro brand. Every year, one hundred million packets of dehydrated soups and sauces are produced for hungry Norwegians. Today we will do our part to keep them in production. Two packets of soup with macaroni. Quick, simple and cheap, and the kids like it!

We run a yellow light and pull into the driveway. Within minutes, the packets and some water turn into soup. Our littlest guy really likes it. And then it's back into the car once more. There will still be soup when we return, and the dirty dishes can wait.

No Serrano ham, no garlic, no chanterelle mushrooms, just dehydrated tomato soup. Or pasta with meat sauce. Fish sticks. Frozen pizza. Frozen pizza? That's right, frozen pizza is a popular dinner dish in Norway, not because it's so delicious, but because it's quick, simple and cheap. Just shove it into a hot oven for 15 minutes and dinner is served. Come on and eat, kids!

That's the way we live, and the way many other Norwegians live on a Tuesday in October. Traffic at a standstill. Soccer practice. Parent-teacher meetings. Working overtime. Not much cold pressed virgin olive oil and fancy trimmings here. We can just dream about next weekend and leg of lamb as we stumble into the kitchen with our dehydrated soups and wet children.

But does it really have to be tomato soup and ready meals to keep food on the table during the week and the budget from breaking by mid-month? Is there time to begin at the beginning, to cook from scratch, on a Monday? Can we start at the fish counter and end up with pan-fried fish on a Thursday? Does that take longer than cooking frozen fish sticks right from the carton into the pan? And does it cost a lot more?

I think it's more about imagination and inspiration than time and price alone. We want to inspire you with this book, give you ideas and explain how you can make simple, tasty and healthy meals in your home kitchen every single day of the week.

I have participated in countless discussions about the quality of Norwegian ingredients. I feel that product labeling, especially of meat, has been needlessly poor. We can buy beef at every meat counter. But what kind of beef? Cow or steer? Is it a new breed of cattle?

Other meat comes from sheep. But what kind of sheep? From inland or along the coast? Does that matter? Of course, it does. A sheep that has

This is the way vegetables should be displayed at the supermarket. There should be both abundance and quality. A selection this good is a source of inspiration for any cook.

Norwegian lamb is among the world's best. Norwegian sheep graze on salty grasses, and that adds flavor to the meat.

grazed by the sea tastes different from one that has grazed on a mountain slope.

Even though I as a consumer feel that we don't have enough information about the food we buy, we can at least feel safe that Norwegian ingredients are of consistently high quality. We are getting better and better at handling fresh foods. That's one reason why I think people should be encouraged to make food that enhances the quality of the ingredients.

I think it's great that Norwegian chefs have been so successful. I have met many who have done well in cooking contests both at home and a-broad. They have their own opinions about the quality of Norwegian ingredients, and they have high standards. By emphasizing these high standards, they have managed to get Norwegian ingredients that satisfy their needs and their high demands.

People often ask me which is my favorite foreign cuisine. That has changed and will probably change again. But for now, I am tempted to say Japanese. Why? Because of its simplicity. The Japanese are good at emphasizing individual ingredients. They use very little seasoning. Sushi is raw fish and rice. The seasonings elevate the flavor of the ingredient. I don't make much Japanese food in my home kitchen. Raw fish is not exactly food for small children. But I feel that it's both exciting and challenging to prepare food that brings out the flavor of the individual ingredients. Simple food, where the flavor is not drowned in gravy and seasonings. And in many ways, this is also the foundation of the Norwegian kitchen.

But of course, I also like real spicy food that gives my taste buds another kind of challenge.

My food

I come from Namsos, a little town by the mouth of a river. It is the main city in Namdal valley, near both the coast and the sea, but also the mountains and forest. It's not far from the ptarmigan in Lierne to the cod in Vikna.

My mother came here from a little place called Bangsund, not far outside of town. Her father worked both in the forest and at a sawmill. She moved the 15 kilometers (10 miles) into Namsos so that she could attend business school.

In town, she met the son of a fisherman from Herøy in Helgeland. He also came to town to attend business school.

And that resulted in me. I was born at Namdal hospital on a cold November night in 1962. I cried so much as a baby that my parents didn't dare produce any more children. At any rate, I am an only child.

Namsos in the 1960s was a good place for children, and I think it still is. My childhood was safe and good. The framework was known and predictable. I got a lot of care and attention, and a lot of good food.

I have always liked food. The food served in the kitchen of my youth reflected the background of my parents. It was a varied diet. Fish, game, fruit, berries. Traditional Norwegian country cooking. My mother worked outside the home, but she still had time and energy to serve my father and me good food. When Papa and I made dinner, we never got any further than fried blood sausage with syrup. Today that is not my favorite dish…

Gathering food was important in my family. It still is for my parents. Every summer, from the time I was seven or eight, we used to travel north to my father's home town, the little fishing village of Sandvær in Herøy. There we hardly ate anything other than fish. And no matter what time we docked, even if it was two in the morning, we still cooked small pollock with their livers. Sometimes we didn't have to go farther than the pebbles on the beach. We cooked fresh pollock

in seawater and ate it with our fingers, on flatbread. It was a little more civilized when we prepared the fish inside the house, but the ingredients were the same. Freshly caught pollock, new potatoes, flatbread, liver and liver stock. Sometimes my mother or grandmother served a kind of sweet and sour fish soup alongside.

I remember vacations at Sandvær as endless summers with good weather and good fishing. We caught huge cod weighing over 20 kilo (44 lb) with a Swedish jig, redfish with a sneak. I can still see in front of me those strange red fish with the huge eyes that floated up on their own and formed a stripe over the water. Salted redfish is still one of my favorite dishes.

For the most part, the fish was salted. Pollock, cod, redfish – all were placed in barrels and sent by boat to Sandnessjøen. I was happy to be an

Norwegians have good access to fresh fish and they love to go fishing. Cod is a wonderful ingredient, and Norwegian fish are also in demand abroad.

Then it was time for picking berries in the woods. The marshes in Aursundlia near Bangsund were golden with cloudberries. I still feel that the cloudberry is the most beautiful of all wild berries. And it tastes wonderful right from the marsh, as jam, or mixed with cream on Christmas Eve. We used to find blueberries in the same area, or in Vemundvik farther out in the Namsenfjord. Then Papa and I went out on the fjord and raked herring. It was served fried, poached and cured. Cured herring kept until Christmas and was served as tomato herring for Christmas breakfast.

The grand finale of all this food-gathering was a half pig and a whole lamb. They came from the Farmer's coop shop in Namsos and were brought home in the back seat or trunk of our car. Then, the real circus began in the kitchen. The sharpener came out of the drawer and the knives were sharpened, and the saw was placed on the table. The lamb was placed on its back and partitioned with experienced hands, and the pig's head stared wide-eyed at us. But now we knew there would be lamb and cabbage stew on the table, there would be lamb roll for Christmas, and the pig's head would be made into headcheese.

That was the kitchen of my childhood. Does any of that exist in my kitchen today?

I have to admit that I don't forage for food much these days. I don't fish a lot and I'm not much of a berrypicker. It's true that fish from Sandvær frequently find their way from Namsos to our house on Hoffsveien in Oslo. But active food-gathering, as my parents once did and still do, is just not part of my lifestyle.

The dishes of my childhood, however, live on in my kitchen today. I want my children to enjoy traditional Norwegian food, as I did. That's why I want them to eat fresh salt cod, fried pollock, lamb and cabbage stew, salt meat and creamed cabbage, light and dark sailors' stew, beef soup and good old-fashioned Norwegian Christmas food.

Cloudberries are delicious – and beautiful! By combining a hike in the mountains with picking berries, you can experience the landscape and enjoy homemade jam in the winter.

only child. The trunk was filled with salt fish. There was just barely room for me alongside all the baggage. The roof rack was like a tower on top of the car. When freezers became popular, there was less salt fish and more frozen fillets. The car is still heavily loaded on the return trip from Sandvær.

After we returned from Helgeland, we started gathering and harvesting. We picked strawberries for jam. I was always on hand for taste-testing, first from the pile of cleaned berries, then with a finger in the jam jar. I can still taste that sweet flavor of summer.

Why? It sounds banal, but for me it's all part of being Norwegian. This is our culture. This is part of our tradition. And it's part of a healthy diet. I believe that many agree with me, that it's a means of honoring those generations that came before us. When the food of our mothers and grandmothers is placed on the table, a little part of them is there, too.

Our identity as a people and as a nation is determined by more than just the language we speak. It is determined as much by the cultural aspects that separate Norwegians from other nations, those customs and traditions that have survived through the generations. A great many of them pertain to food and meals. Food is culture and identity. It is roots and connections.

Norwegian food is more than just Norwegian recipes. It's also Norwegian ingredients. Dried ribs of mutton with meat from New Zealand is just not the same.

When I was minister of agriculture, I traveled throughout Norway and often spoke about food. That a secretary of agriculture talked about food, and not about cows, probably was a surprise for many, but no one seemed to mind. After the introduction, during the coffee break, we talked just as much about food as we did about traditional agricultural politics. I met many people, especially parents of small children, who were interested in Norwegian food. That has been my inspiration in working on this book. I am lucky that I can still call my mother and ask her for a recipe. Not everyone is that fortunate.

I eat and serve more than just the food of my childhood. As years passed, even pizza came to Namsos. I remember the first time we had it at home. My friends had told us about this great culinary experience, and Mama was encouraged to find a recipe. And she did. Out of the oven came a bread with ground beef and cheese on top. We hadn't quite understood that the crust was supposed to be thin and crispy...but that opened the door, if ever so slightly, for new experiences.

While I was in high school, we heard that a Chinese restaurant had opened in Trondheim. With my new driver's license and a borrowed car, we zipped down one Friday night, 200 kilometers (120 miles) each way. That was our introduction to even more exotic flavors. Sweet and sour sauce. Sautéed vegetables. And I was one of the first people from Namsos to try frog legs. I have never been afraid to try new foods.

In my youth, I was very active in the Social Democrat youth organization and eventually became the leader for North Trøndelag. Later, I was on the board of the national organization. That enabled me to travel to Egypt, Israel and Nicaragua. And during the summer, I traveled all over Europe by train. I tried French, Spanish and Italian food, and I found out that food was more than fried herring and roast moose, even more than pizza and Chinese food. The sum of all those experiences on the path to adulthood has

shaped my version of the Norwegian kitchen today. For me, Norwegian cooking is both the traditional and tacos and pizza.

I can't lie about enjoying food. You can see it on me! I love to taste, I love to eat. I like most things and enjoy my food. But a meal is more than food. Putting something in your mouth and sensing the flavor on your tongue is not enough. Good food never tastes as good alone as it does with friends. The sum of the flavor and the company equal the experience.

Dinner is the highpoint of the day for many families, and we remember gatherings around the dinner table for our entire life.

A meal is more than food and flavor. It's company and togetherness.

If I can be a little pompous: Dining together helps the cause of peace. International leaders often meet over a meal. I believe that the best peace agreements are those with gravy spots!

After a tough match, teams meet again at a banquet with a good meal.

And when my wife and I have had a quarrel in the afternoon, we can still go to bed as friends after a good meal.

A meal is an exercise in being together, and group meals provide an important framework for communing together. At work. In the family. Meals together strengthen bonds. If they disappear, the group is weakened.

Fresh sweet rolls are peacemakers. How can you hate someone if you have shared a roll together? Especially when the other person baked it himself.

Food with a dialect

In 1991, I met a man from Røyrvik, Svein Håpnes. He was elected to the county government from a party other than my own and was a breath of fresh air in local politics. We soon became friends.

Svein was and is a goat farmer. He took over the family farm in 1981. Skånalisæter is in the northernmost part of the county, with Sweden to the east and Børgefjell national park to the North. Here, up in Kjølen, between Norway and Sweden, the houses are far apart with lots of open space. The large farms have traditionally been along the lake. Skånalisæter was originally a mountain dairy that was part of one of these large farms.

Skånalisæter has been in the family since before 1900. It was a typical farm for this district. A few cultivated fields, a lot of grazing pasture, and goats for producing milk. Svein and his wife Eli Kristin were proud to deliver goat milk of high quality. But it didn't matter much. Because after the milk was transported 156 kilometers (95 miles) to Namdal dairy, it wasn't used in goat milk products. Instead, the goat milk from Skånalisæter and other producers in the area was mixed with cow milk that had been rejected as food for humans and sold as animal fodder.

Svein felt that it wasn't right to put his soul into milk that would end up as animal fodder. He wanted to put his soul into milk for human beings. First class ingredients should be made into first class food. And what was even more frustrating, Svein was often contacted by people who wanted to buy goat cheese.

There was one specific product that the mountain folk and South Sami of the area wanted. Coffee cheese.

Coffee cheese?

That's right! It is unsalted white goat cheese. Along the river Kjølen, from Røros to Finnmark, this has been a familiar, popular product. The contents have been the same everywhere. Pure goat milk. The methods of conservation used

have varied. In Inner Namdal, the cheese is traditionally dried. In other places it is smoked or fried.

Life in the mountain area has consisted of hard physical work since time immemorial. There were many long trips up the mountain to herd goats and pick berries and mushrooms. Any load carried in a backpack had to be light. Food had to be nourishing. The climate was harsh. The coffee pot has always been a good hiking companion. A fire and a cup of coffee supplied warmth to a chilled body. And dried meat or coffee cheese was added to the coffee for an extra boost. A kick, as Svein says.

The dried cheese was shaved into the cup where it melted. This coffee cheese was difficult to find in the Namdal valley in the 1980s. That's when the idea started to form in Svein and Eli Kristin's minds. Maybe there was a market for this cheese, as there used to be for Svein's grandparents a long time ago at Skånalisæter.

In Sweden, cheese-making on the farm was still quite common in the 1980s, so the couple went there on a study trip in 1985. That made them even more enthusiastic about producing their own cheese at Skånalisæter. New buildings had to be constructed on the farm anyway, so they just built one more room than they needed. That would be the cheese factory. In 1986, everything was ready, but they didn't open the factory until 1995.

Coffee cheese

Real feta cheese made from 100% Norwegian goat milk.

During those intervening years, they made a long, hard journey; not in the mountains of Namdal, but from office to office, from hope to disappointment – and then to new hope. The buildings needed a certain minimum standard. The water needed to maintain a certain quality. They had to learn about the profession. They had to finance equipment. And they had to establish partnership with TINE, Norway's dairy coop.

To make a long story short: Today you can go to Skånalisæter and buy coffee cheese. And brown goat cheese. And soft white cheese, salty white goat cheese, different herb cheeses, and brown goat cheese spread and gomme, another traditional Norwegian cheese. The next study trip was not to Sweden but to France. The result was a blue cheese called "Blåmann" (blue man).

Even feta cheese, made in the authentic way, is produced at Skånalisæter. With goat milk. The feta sold commercially has very little in common with Greek feta. It's made of goat milk, sheep milk – or a blend. What we buy is usually Danish, made with cow milk.

Today Svein and Eli Kristin use their entire milk production to make cheese. The limiting factors today are production capacity and availability of milk. The room from 1986 is too small and needs to be expanded. The neighboring farms are going to start delivering goat milk to Skånalisæter farm dairy. And as long as they are adding on to the cheese factory, they have decided to start their own restaurant. Soon it will be possible to taste your way through their entire assortment of cheeses – with wine! But that's not produced at Skånalisæter…

This is one positive story from a profession that clearly is faced with challenges. For the Håpnes couple, the market is not a problem. They have to say no to shops at home and abroad that want to market their cheese. Svein and Eli Kristin and other farmers are good at marketing their profession. They meet many people. They are in direct contact with customers and get direct responses regarding the products they make. They are having fun. And they are earning good money. A lot has to be reinvested back into the plant. But still, their hourly wage is twice as high when they produce cheese as when they just produced milk.

Fish in cages

I have had the pleasure of visiting the National College of Agricultural Engineering at Ås on many occasions and I have gotten to know Per Olav Skjervold. When we first met, he was associate professor.

Through Per Olav, I heard the exciting story of how Norwegian fish farming began. Per Olav's father, Harald Skjervold, was professor of animal husbandry at the College. Early in the 1950s, he worked intensively to improve the productivity of livestock through systematic breeding. Animals were needed for that project. It was Skjervold's idea to use salmon, because they produce enormous quantities of eggs, and because these eggs are fertilized externally.

Breeding fish through artificial insemination was already an established technology. As early as 1900, there were ponds for farming trout at Ås. The fish was later set out in rivers and lakes. But no one thought of doing this on an industrial scale.

In 1963, purely by chance, Skjervold met a Swede who produced fodder for trout in artificial ponds. They decided to work together, and in 1965, Skjervold placed the first fish pen in a shallow (2-3 meter) pond on the grounds of the College at Ås.

In 1967, NLH and others built a fish farm at Dal farm near Eidsvoll. At that time, Skjervold realized that it was possible to farm salmon systematically, not just experimentally, but as an independent product. In June of 1968, an article in the main Bergen newspaper told of remarkable

Salmon pens in Hardanger, a frequent sight along the Norwegian coast.

results. After only one year, Skjervold discovered that the best fish grew 60% faster than average. They sorted and systematized the stock and selected the fastest growers for commercial production.

This discovery led to the establishment of a breeding station on Sunndalsøra island, and that formed the basis for the fantastic Norwegian aquaculture industry.

Today, Norwegian farm-raised fish are one of our most important exports. Who would have imagined that when Skjervold began his experiments? That we would grow fish for food in cages seemed too unbelievable to be possible. Today we eat more salmon and trout than ever. Salmon now appears on the weekday dinner table. It's inexpensive, nutritious food.

The development of Norwegian salmon production has been nothing less than sensational. In 1982, 10,000 tons were produced. In 2001, the total production had increased to 415,000 tons. Of this amount, around 350,000 tons were exported. Salmon is raised at 848 production units all along the coast.

And these new "farm animals", salmon and trout, have become much larger in production volume than traditional farm animals. In 2000, the total production of meat in Norway was 259,000 tons, while that same year, we produced 470,000 tons of salmon and trout.

The European Union is our largest market for salmon and trout. Of all countries in the Union, we export the most salmon to Denmark, primarily because salmon is processed on a large scale in Denmark. Other large markets in the Union are France, Germany and Great Britain. Japan is also a big consumer of Norwegian fish.

Today, Norway is the world's leading salmon exporter, and Norwegian farm-raised salmon is consumed in more than 100 countries. And the industry is still developing. Exports are rising in Asia – China, Singapore and India – and in Russia and Poland.

Other species than salmon and trout are also being farm-raised in Norway, and commercial production of mussels, cod and halibut is already underway.

Farming of new species such as mussels is a growing industry. In 2000, nearly 1000 tons of mussels were produced in Norway. The industry has great potential.

Today, Per Olav Skjervold works for TINE, the Norwegian dairy cooperative, which has branched out into the fish business. It's a question of taking advantage of opportunities and experience in land and sea-based food industries. And Per Olav is a very active player in this work, in the true spirit of his father!

A taste of Norway

Norway is an attractive vacation destination. Every year, thousands of foreigners make their way here. Foreign tourists visiting Norway are generally affluent. Most know that Norway is a high-cost country before they arrive, but they come anyway. They come because Norway is a beautiful country and they want to experience nature. They want to see mountains and fjords. They want to breathe clean air and feel the elements. They also come to experience the Norwegian cultural landscape, created by Norwegian agriculture.

Many tourists come by car. They drive over Svinesund Bridge and drive all the way through Norway up to the North Cape. If they choose to stop at local roadside restaurants or cafés hoping to try local specialties, they will most likely be disappointed.

Even though the dialect varies from one part of the country to another, there's not much variation in restaurant food. Wiener schnitzel, hamburger platter, pizza, celery cabbage with thousand island dressing. We need more food with dialect in Norway.

My vision as minister of agriculture was that in addition to reveling in the beautiful Norwegian countryside, they should also be able to taste the flavors of the landscape. Nature, history, traditions. These vary greatly from East to West, North to South. They give each area of the country its own special character. Together, they could add to the total experience of our guests from other countries.

In addition, Norway is our own closest vacation destination. We need to become more familiar with other parts of our country. The food from

Tourists in Norway should be able to enjoy good food as well as magnificent sights on their trip through the country.

different areas can be just as exotic as that of other countries. More Norwegians have probably tried Chinese food than *smalahovud.*

Norway exotic? When looked at from a foreign tourist's point of view, it can be quite unusual to eat old salted pollock, preserved with its entrails intact and full of blood, and left half-forgotten and alone for years, only to be brought into the kitchen and served as a delicacy with mashed potatoes and fried bacon. Fermented fish? Half-rotten trout that smells, well, unique and tastes unique, too? *Boknafish?* Half-dried fish, cooked and eaten as if there hadn't been time to wait for it to dry completely. *Lutefisk?* Cod in lye?

Hmm…Try to explain this to an Englishman! Once upon a time, Norway was different. There was a time when food was produced and sold on most farms. There was a small cheese factory in most farming communities and local slaughterhouses dotted the landscape. That meant variation and abundance.

The world looks different today, for many reasons. The last decades have resulted in significant centralization and streamlining in the Norwegian food industry. Local cheese factories are gone and industrial production has taken over. This has been a natural development, and most cheese production will be produced indus-

trially in the future as well. But there is a new market - those who want to return to their roots. Small-scale food production, local foods with local flavor. Food with a dialect.

France is the greatest tourist nation in the world, visited by more foreigners than any other place in the world. What attracts tourists to France?

Paris, of course, the city of lights that everyone has heard about and dreamt about since they realized that there were other countries out there to visit. The Eiffel Tower. But I feel that Norwegians have gotten to know France through its food.

In many places, goats are efficient gardeners! No animals graze more thoroughly than goats.

Roquefort cheese, Bordeaux wine, Camembert, Champagne, Brie, Cognac, French cuisine, French food, French flavors.

Food production in France is also industrialized. But many small cheese factories and some small slaughterhouses, like those that were closed down in Norway, are still alive in France. They don't even try to compete with the huge factories that supply French supermarkets. But for the French, they provide an important supplement to industrial production. How have they managed to do this? What has the French minister of agriculture done that we haven't been able to do?

Wine has been produced in Bordeaux for centuries. Not as a commercial mass product, but as wine for drinking at home, when inviting neighbors over for a drink and for enjoying at local festivals. The wine producers of Bordeaux began to market themselves commercially during the 1800s. Bordeaux got a reputation for being of good quality. That reputation spread quickly, both in France and over to England. To increase production, new high-yield vines were imported from North America around 1850.

That was a big mistake. Along with those imported vines came an insect that had never been to Bordeaux before, the Phylloxera vastarix. It nearly destroyed the original Bordeaux. In a desperate attempt to save at least some of the original growth, twigs were grafted onto resistant vines, including those from North America.

Through this intricate process, it was possible to rescue wine production in Bordeaux. But for a while, there was a shortage of Bordeaux wine.

Some less conscientious producers took advantage of that and labeled wines from other areas as Bordeaux. Even apples and pears found their way into the vats along with grapes.

In 1892, a new law specified exactly how and where Bordeaux wine should be made. The new limit was strictly enforced. In that way, the concept of Bordeaux wine was created. Wine from a specifically limited geographical area. And word spread that it was a wine of particularly good quality. Demand increased. Eventually it was impossible to satisfy demand within the designated geographical borders. Having been burned earlier, the growers did not attempt to increase production. In fact, they limited it even more. That resulted in an interesting market phenomenon that is relatively unfamiliar to Norwegian farmers – much greater demand than production resulted in a major price increase. Bordeaux wine became an exclusive product. Astute business-men realized that what started out as a health measure to save the vines proved to be excellent market strategy. A brand with global format was born.

This market strategy had to be tested in other areas. Other alcoholic drinks: burgundy wine from Burgundy, champagne from Champagne, cognac from Cognac, armagnac from Armagnac. Sparkling wine and brown liquor is produced all over Europe, but only grapes from the Champagne district can be called champagne in their liquid form. Cognac is not cognac unless the grape is grown in Cognac. In fact, all pro-duction also has to take place in those designat-ed areas, too.

The range was expanded to include other agri-cultural products: cheese from Roquefort, chick-en from Brest. White meat, red meat, potatoes. Every aspect of gastronomy and agriculture got its "product of origin" marking.

This is called AOC: "Appellation d'Origine Controlée. In other words, the geographical and historical identity of the product has been checked by the authorities and given a stamp of approval. Today, this system is used throughout the European Union, and we will soon find such products in many countries. Parma ham and Parmesan cheese are two such products.

I would love for this idea to be implemented in Norway.

We are not members of the European Union, and we don't need to approve any statutes through our economic agreements with them. But, as a cabinet minister, I took the initiative to draw up a recommendation for such a procedure in Norway, identical with that used in the European Union. It is now in place, and the foundation Matmerk (foodmark) will approve Norwegian products on behalf of the Norwegian authorities.

Do we have any good candidates?

I don't know whether these will be approved, but I do have a few ideas about which products might be candidates.

Peas from Ringerike. Fermented fish from Valdres. Thick milk from Røros. Innherredssodd (soup). Voss sausages. Kviteseid butter. Misvær cheese. Bidos (Sami meat soup). Ringerike pota-toes, Fjell almond potatoes. The product must have a clear historical and geographical connec-tion. It has to be part of a strong tradition and made according to specified, local, traditional recipes, or cultivated within a limited geographi-cal area.

There are three levels of such labeling. A "Norwegian AOC" is the strictest. The lower levels are a little more liberal. But all are an-chored in tradition, history and local culture.

That's my dream. I think it can become a reality. I really believe that this is the way to go, not for everyone, but for some, for many more than today – even in Norway.

Local specialties are produced at a number of farms all around Norway. One example is Fausko farm, an ecological mountain farm in Hemsedal valley. Beef from the farm, fish, game and berries from the mountain are turned into gourmet meals served at an old coaching inn. "Local products for global palates" is the philosophy behind Fausko.

Local meat-processing is increasing. One local firm is Jens Eide's Slaughterhouse, outside of Lillesand. Jens Øystein Eide fetches the animals himself, and they are slaughtered at his own plant, and in the factory store, there are over 200 products.

Local sales of vegetables are also increasing. Farmers' markets can now be found in Norway, and their numbers are increasing. Local produc-ers sell their products on the street. The old vegetable markets are experiencing a rebirth! TINE, Norway's dairy coop has established Ostecompagniet (The Cheese Company) to help local producers market their cheeses. They want to increase access to good cheese in Norway.

Fjordland, owned by the three large coopera-tives, TINE, Prior (Norwegian poultry) and Norsk Kjøtt (Norwegian meat), has been very successful in recent years. Fjordland produces fast food. Through the "sous vide" (vacuum pressure) tech-nique, they are able to preserve the flavor of the

Norwegian poultry production is a quality industry.

ingredients better than in the past. The food is lightly heat-treated in a vacuum. The food is almost completely cooked, ready to be reheated at home. The selection includes traditional Norwegian dishes, such as meat cakes and mutton and cabbage stew, as well as international dishes.

Consumers want a good selection and high quality. We want to know where and how the food is produced, and we want to know who produced it. New products are being developed all the time. One of the biggest challenges, for both producers and customers, is how the products are marketed. How can I buy local specialties? In Denmark, Internet shopping for food is a great success. Through the Internet, the customer has access to an unusually large selection of goods and can buy from home, any time of day or night. In Norway, www.kaupa.no is becoming a modern meeting place between the producer and the consumer. At that website, we can find out all about the origins of products, and many well-known cooks contribute recipes and tips.

The Norwegian kitchen can never be as big, popular and rich as the French or Italian. But it

can be bigger than it is today. We can offer visitors more local and exotic color on their plates than we do today. If we set high goals, we have to have high expectations. My ambition is that in 15 years, when German tourists, as they return home, are stopped at Svinesund and asked what they will remember about Norway, they mention both the beautiful landscape and great gastronomic experiences, as well as a strong feeling of having experienced all of Norway: unforgettable impressions, the strong scent of fresh air and salty sea – and the flavor of unique Norwegian delights.

From field to table

Mad cow disease has existed in Britain for many years. Most people felt that it would remain there. The Britons had been careless in their production of animal fodder. But by the spring of 2000, there were reports of the disease on the European continent. By the end of the year, cases had been reported in France, Germany, Netherlands, and even in Denmark.

As minister of agriculture, I couldn't guarantee that the disease would not come to Norway. But I still felt quite safe that it wouldn't happen. Why?

If the food is to be safe, we have to have full control from field to table.
If the food is to be safe, the animals have to eat the right fodder.
If the food is to be safe, all slaughtering has to take place according to stringent regulations.

That's how it is in Norway.

Every animal has to be inspected by a veterinarian. Every pig that is slaughtered in Norway is still tested for trichina. In addition, the final check has to make certain that the meat is treated correctly until we take it home from the supermarket. It's all about cutting, packing,

Smoking meat in an old-fashioned smokehouse. Old, local traditions are the basis for many interesting products.

marking, storing and cooling. Cooling is important! Too many refrigerated cases are not nearly cold enough.

Every link of the chain, from the cow grazing on the farm, to the steak served on our dinner tables, is decisive for the safety of our food.

We need to exercise our strength as consumers. We should speak out if we are dissatisfied, and we should take our business elsewhere if we aren't satisfied with the quality at shops where we normally purchase food.

But I don't feel that we as consumers should be responsible for the safety of our food. That is a job for the authorities. The government has to make certain that our food is safe. As consumers, we should be able to buy fresh and frozen food, both imported and domestic, secure in the knowledge that the food is safe to eat.

It is against the law to sell unsafe food. And there shouldn't be any dangerous food in the shops. I have worked extensively with this problem. And the best that I can say to Norwegian consumers is that with all the experience I have gained in this area, I feel very safe when buying Norwegian food, both from the land and from the water. And Norwegian farmed fish are nutritious, good food.

Kitchen politics

The kitchen needs to be given more attention in politics! It isn't enough just to organize this work sensibly. Enough money has to be invested each and every year on these important tasks.

Food is important. It takes up a lot of our time, whether we are eating, planning the menu, or shopping for what we are going to eat. It also consumes part of the household budget.

We have a policy for everything in this country. For salting the roads, for driving snowmobiles, and for fishing herring. For electric power supplies, for asthma medicine and for taxes on music cassettes.

Agriculture in Norway is important for several reasons. Of course, it yields excellent products, but farming also helps to keep the population in an area stable, and it maintains the cultural landscape. This is a typical farm landscape in Trøndelag.

We have directives from the European Union that regulate the sizes of eggs and the curvature of cucumbers.

But we have no food policy. We have no unified policy regarding something that is so important in our lives.

I was very proud to be called the minister of food when I was a cabinet member. That the department of agriculture was called the department of food pleased me greatly. The kitchen has to become part of party agendas.

It's important to retain Norwegian food production even in the global society, where everything moves freely over borders. We live in a peaceful part of the world, and war and catastrophes seem rather remote. But there can be times of crisis here too, and if only for that reason, it is important to maintain food production in Norway.

We should be able to combine the need for protective tariffs for certain Norwegian products with the wishes of Norwegian consumers to be able to buy Spanish ham without blowing the food budget entirely. We don't have to protect ourselves against all imports, but we need to protect the most important Norwegian products.

When Spanish farmers are able to produce fantastic Serrano ham, it should inspire us to political action to create a Norwegian rival for such quality products. Why don't we develop a wonderful, tender dried leg of mutton that Spaniards will want to buy from us? We have to learn from the example of Skånalisæter and develop more unique products based on Norwegian agriculture.

We have to establish a policy in which the consumer can be assured reasonably priced, simple and good raw materials and products, and at the same time be able to select special quality products at a high price. Norwegian consumers have

to use their power. We don't do enough of that today. We have to speak our minds about prices, but also about selection of goods. Many say that we are too few to support such a wide range of products as in the rest of Europe. But when I want to buy a new car, I can choose from the same wide selection as a Frenchman or a German. We need to practice a tariff policy that stimulates diversity, at the same time that the consumers demand it.

These and many other basic questions need to be answered. My ambition with this book has been to call attention to some possibilities and to hint at the answers.

Above all, this is a cookbook with a wealth of good recipes. But maybe it will also inspire you to think a little about food politics.

A lot of food on the table, a little food for thought.

Bon Appétit!

Norwegian Food Culture

– Norwegian food in time and place

What we put into our mouths is important. When, where and especially what we eat is a fundamental cultural phenomenon. The eating habits of other cultures may seem strange to us, just as those people wonder about our diet. Norwegians don't regard insects as edible, but someone from Uganda might feel the same way about shrimp. It is difficult to understand and accept that eating pork for some people is just as disgusting as eating dog is to us.

Food is often used to describe people of other countries. Swedes refer to Norwegians as cod-eaters, while Norwegians have nothing positive to say about sweet Swedish bread and fermented herring. The French describe Englishmen as "roast beefs", while the English call their neighbors across the Channel "frogs". All cultures have a framework for the types of food they eat, how it is prepared, and with whom and when they eat it.

Norwegian food culture is arranged according to the categories "everyday" and "holiday", and our traditional dishes usually can be classified as everyday and holiday food. There are fairly explicit rules regarding the types of food that belong in those two categories. A Thursday dinner is ranked differently than a Sunday dinner, and it's definitely different from a Sunday breakfast. Saturday sweets (marketed as such in Norway) are to be eaten only on Saturday.

Food is also grouped according to the hours of the day, and the names of many meals reflect this. The Norwegian word *frokost* comes from the German *frühstück* and means the first meal of the day. *Middag* comes from midday, *kveldsmat* (*mat* means food in Norwegian) or *kvelds* is food eaten in the evening (*kveld* in Norwegian). *Nattmat* is eaten at night (*natt* in Norwegian). Even the names for meals in Latin and Old Norse refer to the times when they are eaten. *Dugurd* (the daily meal) comes from *dugr* (day), while *non* means the ninth hour.

That meals were eaten at specific times made them important as meeting places. The family can be spread out during the day, but they gather around the dinner table. Most Norwegians agree on mealtimes. Dinner is eaten at around 5 pm, when everyone comes home from work (most Norwegians finish work at 4 pm). That a family dines together is important both for family members and for society.

People who work together often eat lunch together, all at around the same time.

The order of meals and the foods served are also fairly clear, though most of us hardly give that a thought. We want to have breakfast before dinner, and bread is considered breakfast or lunch food, but not dinner food. We don't start with dessert and end with a fish dish either. At a buffet, people stand in line to serve themselves appetizers, while it's empty around the cheeses and desserts. We don't think about this until we see a foreigner with chocolate pudding on the same plate as shrimp and roast pork. Our food rituals are really rather strict, though we regard them as completely normal.

Traditional food is important at Christmas. Pork ribs with all the trimmings is still the most popular Christmas dinner.

Everyday food is supposed to be filling but somewhat boring. Holiday food is exciting and lavish. Fish sticks with rice, take-away rotisserie chicken, fish casserole and meat cakes with stewed cabbage and potatoes are typical Norwegian everyday dishes, and no Norwegian would ever serve them on a festive occasion. To serve a fish casserole at Sunday dinner shows an unfamiliarity and lack of understanding for Norwegian food customs – even though it may taste delicious.

Everything is turned upside down on weekends and holidays. What was forbidden on weekdays is required at the weekend. Mealtimes are also different. We eat a later breakfast and dinner. Saturday stands out particularly from weekdays, because the cheap and healthy give way to the expensive and possibly less healthy. Sunday is more correct, more exemplary, with a roast in the dining room, nicer clothes and cleaner hands.

Most holidays feature special food that contrasts greatly with everyday food. This food is often called "traditional" and that means traditional both for the family and the country. Christmas and Easter in particular, but also autumn, winter and summer vacations, feature many special dishes that have become popular favorites, as well as those that are reserved for the specific holidays. The expression "the aroma of Christmas" refers to the food we eat at that time of year. As with all other rituals, what, how, when and with whom we eat is also regulated at Christmas. Christmas dinner is not eaten with colleagues from work, though it's fun to enjoy a Christmas buffet before the holiday with them.

For most people, Christmas is the most important family ritual, and all the preparations and expense in connection with the holiday show just how strong the family unit is in Norway. Food is an important part of the celebration. There are special cookies, seven different kinds that are not made during the rest of the year. The food served on Christmas Eve is very important. If mother and father have brought with them different traditions from their respective parents, what they serve at Christmas will play an important role in the establishment of the new family's Christmas customs.

The packed lunch
During the last 100 years, very few new food products have been adopted for regular use. Cucumber, tomato, broccoli, pizza, bell peppers, pasta and rice are the most important, though pasta and rice both have a long history. Foods such as chili, coriander, monkfish, sushi and oysters are given a lot of attention in the media, but they don't appear on any statistics. Food habits change very slowly. An important exception is the packed lunch. The Norwegian lunch is rather unusual in the scheme of things. A packed lunch, made at home, usually consists of whole grain bread with margarine and something on top – cheese, liver pate or salami. It is usually eaten with milk and followed by fruit. This "dish" is really quite new, and it is the biggest change in Norwegian food customs over the past 100 years.

We usually eat our packed lunch with others, in the canteen at work, in the classroom, or while walking in the country. We unfold the paper and eat our slices of bread without dishes or tableware – we eat with our hands. The packed lunch is required at schools, and because it is so widespread, all Norwegians have a relationship with it. For that reason, it is one of the most common daily food reference points.

The history of the packed lunch can be directly connected with the "Oslo breakfast", an arrangement initiated by Professor Carl Schiøtz, head of school health services at the time. The Oslo breakfast, which was served in the capital as part of an experimental project in the 1920s, consisted of whole grain bread, milk, raw vegetables and fruit. It was served in rooms with open windows under the motto "for the right lifestyle" and "for physical and mental health". The goal was "to fight the hypochondria that plagues so many people unnecessarily" Helped by the combination of foods in the Oslo breakfast, Norwegians were supposed to become healthy and "natural". The Oslo breakfast contrasted with the boiled vegetables that doctors at the time felt made Norwegians a weak people.

People now prefer low-fat milk with their packed lunch of simple open-face sandwiches. Otherwise, things are pretty much the same.

The opposition toward cooked food led to a comprehensive change in attitude regarding nutrition. At the turn of the last century, Norwegians ate hot food at breakfast and lunch, but this practice disappeared almost completely in the years between the two world wars. Toward the end of the 1900s, only 13% of us ate hot food for lunch. Schiøtz recommended "real food, the pure food that nature has given us – raw food, milk products, raw fruits and vegetables". It is amazing that Schiøtz's recommendations still live on after all these years.

The Oslo breakfast was a national nutritional plan for a poorly nourished people, but it was difficult to implement and it was expensive. Local governments lacked the economic resources to carry out the reform. Country doctor O. L. Lien found a solution to the problem. He launched an "Oslo breakfast" but with a packed lunch in Sigdal, his district. Mothers were supposed to pack foods recommended by Schiøtz in their children's lunches, and in that way, parents were under scrutiny, too, so the entire population learned to eat nutritious food. This kind of school lunch became known as the "Sigdal school breakfast", though later it was just called matpakka (food packet). Both breakfast, which was eaten at home, and what is now lunch, followed the same pattern. Lien's suggestion led to the greatest change in modern Norwegian culinary history. The midday meal in Norway is entirely different from that eaten in the rest of Europe. There have been a few more gradual changes, but Lien's recommendation led to a complete change in the nation's eating habits. The packed lunch is proof that individuals can change food and meal patterns.

The ingredients in packed lunches are still seen as part of a "healthy Norwegian diet" or "pure Norwegian food". A hot lunch has no status at all, and it is seldom given a thought. Most Norwegians seem to think that milk and whole grain bread have always been part of the Norwegian diet.

Our relationship with the packed lunch runs throughout our entire lives, and it is marked by certain stages, including growth, defiance,

This is the way Norwegians enjoy life! The packed lunch is very important. And chocolate is the best dessert…

independence and responsibility. It goes like this: During kindergarten and primary school, our mother places the food in a plastic container decorated with a picture. Then we want the food packed in paper, first with drawings from Mom or Dad, then plain. Eventually we make our own lunches. In high school, we don't want a packed lunch, so we throw it away and buy sweet rolls instead. We move away from home, make our own living and make our own lunches, until we have children and buy a plastic container decorated with a picture. Then we have come full circle. There is only one very short difficult period in life when young people feel that the freedom to buy a hamburger means tearing themselves away from the family.

The packed school lunch is an element in socialization. If the lunch is too nice, it has to be hidden from others, and the same is true if it contains unusual food. The packed lunch is regarded as typically Norwegian and is a kind of ethnic food, and its frequently ascetic nature has become part of our culture. As with all other ethnic

markers, it is watched with a "nationalistic" eye, and people can feel morally affronted if noodles or chocolate are substituted for it. There are even those who consider calling child welfare authorities if children do not bring a packed lunch to school.

The packed lunch is eaten alone but with others in a kind of community, because one eats a meal with others, yet alone because everyone does not eat the same thing. Very seldom is a packed lunch shared with others. This is a very intimate act. If a child in kindergarten or elementary school forgets lunch, the kindergarten or school provides one. Adults who forget their lunches usually go out and buy food. If they have forgotten money, they borrow from a colleague – it's easier to lend money than share a packed lunch. The packed lunch is a symbol of the closeness of the family unit, so it is fully acceptable to share a packed lunch with another family member. You just can't give such a "gift" from mother or wife to someone outside the family.

The packed lunch is far more than an ethnic marker and a moral barrier for the expansion of lunch restaurants. It also makes a statement that eating in public also belongs to the family, and vice versa. From this, one can interpret that the family has a very strong position in Norway, even though many say that the family unit is weak here. Foreigners who have experienced a Norwegian Christmas or the celebration of Constitution Day on May 17 know just how important family is for Norwegians.

When a commercial packed lunch was launched by professional lunchpackers, it was given the nationalistic name, *Ola-pakka* (*Ola* is the most common name in Norwegian) and decorated with a red, white and blue paper band like a May 17 ribbon. The choice of colors, those of the Norwegian flag, was not a casual one. May

17 is a day for family celebration. When wrapped in a May 17 rosette, the lunch celebrates both the family and the country in public. The contents of the *Ola-pakka* are no less interesting: whole grain bread with bologna, cheese, brown cheese, *nøkkelost*, salami and ham. The lunch is spare and ascetic, just as Schiøtz recommended in 1926. In this way, it fits right into the story of "the healthy Norwegian and the proper family".

The fight against the demise of the packed lunch is therefore a noble battle against the degeneration of a nation. To withdraw and say that everything is as it always has been, and that new generations will follow old is to destroy even the central myth of the apocalypse. In our fellowship as a nation, we need more than specific examples of national culinary traditions such as mutton and cabbage stew. We also need real and practical traditions worth fighting for: dry slices of bread with yellow and brown cheese or a single slice of salami that gets moved around a larger slice of bread to accommodate every bite. Tasty it isn't, but it is worth fighting for.

A situation in which the packed lunch is not appropriate, yet one is expected to bring along homemade food, is volunteer work on a project outside the home. If parents are expected to spend a Saturday fixing up a sports clubhouse, or if everyone living in an apartment building gets together to clean the grounds, coffee and cake, or even beer and pizza, is often served. These are not what we would call everyday food. The packed lunch brings the kitchen to work, while the voluntary project brings the living room. Eating a packed lunch during a group project is an insult to the others. As an example, a young girl invited a friend to participate in a mission youth group for the first time and she was told to bring something to eat. She packed a lunch, but when she got there, she saw that the others had brought both hot and cold dishes that were served on platters. She hid her packed lunch and said that she had forgotten to bring food.

You've got to start young!

Myths and facts about Norwegian food culture

There are many ideas regarding Norwegian food customs. Some say that we hardly have any food culture, that we are world champions in consuming frozen pizza, and that we don't even have time to eat breakfast anymore. If we look around at our circle of family and friends, we can form a picture of the typical Norwegian meal pattern, and that pattern is supported by the facts and figures. Let us take some of the statements and look at the naked facts:

"People don't eat meals anymore"

Breakfast
We often hear that breakfast is the most important meal of the day from a nutritional point of view. Breakfast is regarded as an important beginning to each day. What we eat is more important than how we eat. Most family members eat as they get up. It's not important that everyone eat together. Half of all Norwegians eat breakfast at home alone. The other half eat it at home with others. Weekend breakfasts are more social. Two-thirds eat breakfast with others on weekends.

Most people eat breakfast every day. The oldest age group eats breakfast most frequently (96% of those over 60 eat breakfast every day), while the youngest women often drop breakfast. Only 73% eat breakfast every day.

It is widely imagined that most Norwegians are so stressed that they eat breakfast on the way to work, but in reality, nine out of ten eat breakfast at home, and most of the rest eat breakfast at work or at school. Only a tiny percentage of the population eat breakfast in the car, on the bus or train, or at a gas station or snack bar.

The Norwegian breakfast is an individual and practical meal. That one chooses to eat alone poses no problems. How one eats is a matter of practicality. Most people eat breakfast after they are finished in the bathroom and before they have to leave home. Work, childcare and school determine how breakfast is eaten. For those who live alone, breakfast can be peaceful and quiet. On weekends, the social aspects of breakfast become more important. Many prefer to eat brunch instead, and the usual slice of bread with brown cheese is replaced with bacon, eggs and rolls.

Lunch

Fewer people eat lunch than breakfast. Lunch is often dropped at weekends, when sleeping late and eating a late breakfast is morally acceptable. Most people eat lunch, but 15% eat lunch fewer than three times a week. In contrast with breakfast, it's the youngest boys who drop lunch most frequently. Naturally, those who do not have a job are the least concerned with lunch, and they tend to follow weekend breakfast and lunch patterns all week. In "institutional" life, such as at work and at school, there are scheduled lunch breaks, and one is expected to bring a packed lunch.

There is a notion that Norwegians have adopted continental eating habits, but as with breakfast, bread dominates lunch both at weekends (88%) and weekdays (65%). On weekdays, only 25% of Norwegians eat salad, vegetables and fruit for lunch, and only 13% eat a hot lunch. That increases to 25% at the weekend.

It has also been stated that the packed lunch is on the way out, but still more than 60% of Norwegians bring a packed lunch to work or school at least three times a week. Only 20% state that they purchase lunch at a canteen, and fewer than 3% buy lunch at a snack bar or gas station.

Childcare, school and work regulate Norwegian lunch habits. Over 50% eat lunch together with colleagues or school friends, 25% eat alone, and 20% together with the family. Lunch is much more social than breakfast, and it is usually eaten at school or at work. 1% eat lunch in the car. Eating at snack bars, gas station and other places where food can be purchased is still quite unusual in Norway.

The traditional breakfast is still a favorite.

Dinner

There are many myths associated with dinner. All refer to divorce statistics and the demise of the family. In reality, eight of ten children under the age of 17 live with both biological parents, and the dinner meal is alive and well and is the most important meeting place for the family. It's about flavor, company, enjoyment of food and being together.

According to statistics, 81% eat dinner every day, and 96% eat dinner more than three times a week. Eating dinner is still the norm. Dinner is a social activity. Young single women drop this meal most frequently, but 82% of them still eat dinner more than three times a week. Dropping dinner may mean eating soup, pizza, cereal or a fried egg, and those foods do not qualify as a "proper" dinner meal.

73% eat dinner with other family member, 6% eat with friends, colleagues and fellow students, and 20% eat alone. 18% of singles eat dinner at home with others, and that rises to 45% at the weekend. Dinner is generally eaten at home –

91% eat dinner at home, 3% eat dinner at a snack bar or fast-food restaurant, 3% eat at work or at school, and 2.5% eat dinner at a restaurant.

The dinner habits of single women change considerably when they get a partner, marry and have children. 91% of women living in a relationship without children eat dinner more than three times a week, while 99% of women living in a relationship with children eat dinner more than three times a week.

Dinnertime has changed over the past 15 years. In 1985, we ate dinner between 3 and 5 pm on weekdays. Today, many of us eat between 5 and 7 pm. Rather than splitting dinner, we choose to eat later so that as many as possible can dine together. Dinnertime at weekends hasn't changed, and we still eat between 3 and 7 pm.

There are many impressions regarding changes in the Norwegian dinner, and that pasta and pizza have become part of the Norwegian kitchen. Hot food is the main component in a Norwegian dinner. 96% eat hot dishes on weekdays, and 93% on the weekend. Salad, fruit and vegetables are also important ingredients. Around 41% of Norwegians eat these at dinner. Many say that we are becoming a fast-food nation, but really, only 7% eat that kind of food during the week and 11% at the weekend.

Dessert, however, is on its way out. Paradoxically enough, the "dessert generation" has stopped eating dessert. But still, 21% eat dessert during the week and 32% at the weekend.

Meat is the main choice for dinner in Norway. Fish is served much more frequently during the week than at the weekend. The traditional ways of serving potatoes (boiled and mashed) are the most popular all week, and potatoes are served with every third meal. Pasta, pizza and hamburgers are also familiar dishes on the Norwegian dinner table. But the traditional dinner plate, with meat or fish, boiled potatoes and vegetables is still the most widespread.

Skinless, boneless fish, chicken or pork are often just as quick to prepare as ready-made food.

"Ready-made or prepared food is replacing traditional meals"

Some maintain that Norwegians have lost the ability to prepare food, that we eat only ready-made food and are world champions in eating frozen pizza. The average Norwegian does not

Sausages are popular, fast and good everyday food.

regard ready-made food as a "proper" dinner. Most add a few extra ingredients to prepared food to make it seem more homemade and personal. On its own, ready-made food is considered an emergency solution. Packet soups are used as a base, and other ingredients, such as cream, mushrooms or vegetables, are added. Only a few follow the directions explicitly, except for perhaps the very first time.

All cultures have rules for how meals are supposed to be. For Norwegians, the rules for a proper dinner are as follows: The food should preferably be made from scratch. It should be eaten in the kitchen and be prepared by mother or father – in any case not by McDonald's. It should be eaten with a knife and fork and as many as possible family members should be there. Dinner should be hot and consist of red or white meat or fish plus a heavy carbohydrate – preferably potato, but also rice or pasta are acceptable. In contrast with breakfast and lunch,

dinner should consist of different dishes throughout the week.

For the average housewife (yes, women still prepare most of the food in Norway), it is important for the family to be together. But often that is not possible, and then the demands are lessened. If many cannot eat dinner at home, it's all right to eat a frozen pizza in front of the TV. Socially split meals more often consist of ready-made food or quick and easy food than meals in which everyone can attend.

Everyday food and holiday food, as described earlier, are the most important categories in Norwegian food culture. Almost all dishes and foods can be classified either as everyday food or as holiday food. An everyday dinner often consists of food that is nutritious yet quick and easy to prepare, such as fish cakes with boiled vegetables or fried sausages with pasta. Labor-intensive dishes that start with raw stew meat or a whole fish, and so-called gourmet food, are reserved for weekends and holidays.

Those ready-made or prepared foods regarded as morally problematic tend to change over time. Bouillon cubes, bread and canned fish products are no longer considered prepared foods, but packet soups and noodles still are. If you eat "fancy" food on a weekday, it is to celebrate something, if not, then you are a snob. On the other hand, you are not regarded as particularly normal if you don't splurge on weekends.

Different studies indicate that there is a stable and permanent course of action regarding Norwegian meals, and this is social. Those who live alone eat fewer meals than those who live with others. When one lives alone, there is a greater likelihood of choosing something simple and cold rather than preparing a proper hot meal. For many who live alone, especially younger people, that will not be a lasting situation. Studies show that dining habits change considerably throughout a lifetime. The transition from living alone to living as a couple or to becoming parents seems to be the most important reason for changing dining habits. Establishing a home means establishing a group to eat together.

Think about the gift table at a wedding. When people marry, and more than 20,000 couples do this each year, they receive many gifts. Most of these gifts are connected with preparing and serving food, such as dishes, coffeemakers, mixers, pots and pans, bases and silverware. Many of the gifts end up at the back of a cupboard, but most are used in the couple's home during the week and on weekends.

When new dishes enter the Norwegian diet, they are accepted in a previously established meal pattern. Pasta and rice are served with dinner according to the rule for variation. Pasta and rice are heavy carbohydrates that are regarded as healthy, and they can be considered obligatory side dishes for different fish and meat dishes during the week. Pizza, however, breaks most rules and therefore fits perfectly into the weekend – and for young people. As young people become adults and have children, they will do as others have done – they call their mothers and ask how long to cook a pork roast.

Young people prefer skinless, boneless fish.

"Restaurant meals are replacing meals at home"

The huge increase in the number of restaurants and cafes may lead some to think that we don't eat at home any more, that we eat out most of the time.

Studies show that it is still not a daily affair for Norwegians to eat at a café or restaurant. It's something most people do only occasionally. Of all meals, only one in fifty is eaten at a café or restaurant. Around 25% of Norwegians eat out less than once a year! Those with high incomes living in Oslo dine most frequently at restaurants,

Young people like to meet at cafés, but the home is still the most popular meeting place.

Grazing is a very small part of the Norwegian dining pattern. Fewer than 5% eat "along the way" once a week or more, and close to 50% never eat that way. 2% eat at a gas station once a week or more, and 50% never eat at a gas station. The problem is that those who buy a hotdog at a gas station are very visible. If we could look into all the kitchens and register all the meals eaten there, we would see that the extent of "grazing" is inconsequential to the big picture.

"People have no time to eat"

Many have gotten the impression that we don't have enough time, and there are probably many who feel that way. Parents of small children have a lot to do, and when both have full-time jobs, the hour around picking up the kids from day-care and making dinner is very hectic. But if we think about it, we realize that parents of small children have always had a lot to do. Even though most mothers stayed at home in the past, their days were no less busy. Back then, a family with five children might live in 40 m^2 (420 square feet), and father worked 50 hours a week with only Sunday off. The likelihood of father coming home for dinner was small. Without an electric stove, dishwasher, refrigerator, freezer, microwave oven and blender, making food took a lot longer time.

Statistics clearly indicate that we have more and more free time. And there is a certain pressure associated with the use of that free time, but we can use it to do whatever we want. And there aren't many who would choose to turn the clock back 100 years. Statements such as "I have so little time" and "we live in stressful times" show a lack of historical reference points.

Surveys regarding use of time conducted by the National Bureau of Statistics indicate (not surprisingly) that women use increasingly more time working for pay and less time on housework. For men, the reverse is true. Statistics show that we use more time for social events and only a little less time for meals. For Norwegians, meals are important, and we prioritize them as best we can.

and often the youngest eat out the most. For most other people, eating at a café or restaurant is something they do to celebrate a special event or to give themselves a treat.

It is, however, quite normal to eat at a snack bar/hotdog stand or fast-food restaurant, but it is still not done very often. In this category, there are naturally great differences according to age groups. While around 7% of those between 15 and 24 eat at a snack bar/hotdog stand once a week, almost no one over 40 does that as often (only 1%). Over 40% of the youngest surveyed very seldom or never eat at a snack bar, while among those over 40, around 86% never eat at

that kind of an establishment. The meal most frequently eaten at a snack bar is Saturday evening – does that surprise you?

A great deal of negative attention is paid to food consumption that breaks all the rules regarding meals – "grazing" – as if we were animals. "Meals" of this kind have very low status. Eating a hotdog at a gas station breaks all the rules for how a meal is supposed to be: wrong place (on the street or in the car), wrong time (between meals), wrong way (standing alone, without a knife and fork).

"The youth of today love luxury. They have bad manners, they have only contempt for authorities, they disrespect the elderly and talk about silly things instead of working. They contradict their parents, talk too much, gorge on food, put their feet on the table and annoy grown-ups."

Socrates said that more than 400 years BC. That older people feel that youth are ill-mannered is nothing new. Every time a child is born, a new person becomes a parent, and every new 50-year-old worries about the next generation. As far as eating habits are concerned, no one is born with them, they have to be learned, and they are learned. It is highly likely that the youth of today, the girls with their bare navels and the boys with their baggy jeans, will become responsible parents, and they too have to learn to prepare food.

Young people go out a lot with other young people, that is what grown-ups call breaking away. Rejecting proper, healthy family food is an important part of this breaking-away process and is nothing new. When young people toss their packed lunches into the trash bin and buy sweet rolls and French fries instead, it's all about showing their independence from their parents – "I don't want to eat your food out there – I am ready to live my own life" In the youngest age group, 8% eat at a snack bar more than once a week, but 40% seldom or never eat there. Frequent visits to snack bars and hotdog stands require a fatter wallet than most teenagers have.

After a few years of rebellion, most establish their own households and have children. And when Christmas is just around the corner, many feel obligated to prepare traditional family food, and to learn about how to do it.

Etiquette books show that the rules for formal dining have changed very little over the past 100 years. The rules concerning everyday meals are implicitly understood. We don't think so much about washing our hands before we eat, or that we teach our children to finish the portion if they have served themselves.

There has been a change in the way children are reared, from "learning to obey" to "learning to be independent". Children play a greater role in deciding what the family will eat, and father is not longer the most important person at the table. The most important thing is that children get nutritious food. But at the same time, it is important to have rules, and by enjoying a common meal, the participants have to control their impulses and desires. If people don't teach their children how to behave if the king drops by for an unexpected visit, they will not have done their job right.

We consumers are bombarded constantly with ads telling us to try new dishes and new flavors. Trend researchers tell us that our food habits are changing "faster than the satellite signals from MTV". In great parts of society, familiarity with stylish food is a sign of culinary cultural competence, but for others, it's less important.

Empirical research indicates that food habits change slowly. It's true that fewer eat boiled potatoes for dinner now than in the past, but potatoes are still the most popular side dish. The boiled potato is central in the description of a proper meal. When foreign dishes come to Norway, they are adapted to our food culture. We make pizza with ground meat and Norvegia cheese rather than with pepperoni and mozzarella. Oil often replaces butter, because it is seen as healthy and easy to use. Flavors are being adjusted constantly, but there are very seldom any revolutionary changes in eating habits. Some changes can be described as historic, but

most deal with habits changing throughout the course of a lifetime. It is easy to use examples of the food habits of youthful city-dwellers to predict future changes on a national basis. Some foods, such as pizza, do become a reality, while others, such as sushi, hardly have a chance at achieving status in the Norwegian meal pattern. Fish is too well established as healthy everyday food for what some call cat food to become a hit on the Norwegian dinner plate. When people say that back in the 1950s, Mom made proper meals, it's easy to forget that people had less money and less selection at the supermarket than they do now. The belief that everything was better in the past implies a criticism of the working woman, that Mom has stopped being a housewife. It is, however, a fact that the working woman prioritizes food and meals before other traditional activities such as dusting and mending. She is the protector of meals in the home,

From Theatercafeen in Oslo

and she still cooks, even though she also works outside the home. Around 80% state that the woman of the house generally prepares the food, while 6% say that they share in the activity. Only 8% report that the man of the house does most of the cooking. Social pressure regarding being a good protector of meals is very strong among women.

Food and meals are important subjects, both morally and socially. It is all about pleasure and enjoyment, medicine and health, manners and socializing, and it is part of our national identity. The meal as a social, moral family institution is very strong in Norway. It has probably never been stronger. That is due to our increased wealth, a greater selection of food, more information and focus on food, as well as more free time. And don't forget the parsley – bon appétit!

The taste of nature

Hunting and fishing, picking mushrooms and berries are important leisure activities in Norway. In contrast with the rest of Europe, where hunting and fishing are the preserves of the upper class, in Norway, these are quite normal activities for everyone. Norway is a big country with a small population, and it has a long coastline, so it's easier for us to have access to common land than elsewhere in Europe.

Quite a few Norwegian households have fishing equipment, and nearly half own or have use of a boat. A third own or have access to a cabin or vacation home, and as many as a fifth have or have use of a shotgun. 90% of Norwegians enjoy vacations in the country, staying at cabins. 85% like a cabin by the sea, and 60% spend their vacations in Norway.

It is difficult to calculate the amount of foraging for food. We all know about fishermen who brag about landing such huge fish, and what isn't sold over the counter is difficult to track. Mushroom-picking is widespread, but we don't know how much is picked. Hunting is easier, because the hunter has to report what he bags. Depending on how one calculates, game represents just below 5% of the meat we eat, and somewhere between 20 and 30% of the fish we eat are caught by sports fishermen. These are significant amounts and represent considerable value. In addition come mushrooms, berries, herbs and gardening.

Norway is a long country, and the different regions include different animals in their fauna. In East Norway, people eat auk (even though it is forbidden) and pike-perch; in the northernmost counties, they collect seagull eggs; in the inland regions, people fish for trout; and in West

On the average, every Norwegian goes berry or mushroom picking twice a year.

Bring out the boiled potatoes, cucumber salad and white wine!

Norway, they hunt deer. In this way, the different regions have different local dishes.

Foraging and leisure activity
The use of the public land is important for vacations and leisure activity. Hunting and fishing are primarily leisure activities, and the food itself is no longer the primary goal. On a fishing trip, you are supposed to relax and have fun, charge your batteries – without being obligated to supply the household with food. Vacation is a time when everyday norms do not apply.

Those who work during vacations are regarded as sick, workaholics. Even though leisure time is supposed to be used for relaxation, foraging is accepted "work". Quite large amounts of food can be gathered in this way, and it can have considerable economic value. In July, for example, over 50% of all fish that end up on the table,

are self-caught. The corresponding figure for the winter months is under 10%.

Foraging is ideologically important and should be done in the correct way. Norwegians are generally against the practice of "catch and release" that is common in the US and England, where people catch fish only to throw them back into the water. That the catch is eaten as food is an important part of the identity of the Norwegian sports fisherman. That also means that people learn how to prepare fish and game. We learn to gut, prepare, smoke and cook fish and to clean mushrooms at an early age. We like to select from nature's pantry. Eating a fish you caught yourself is a part of the Norwegian identity, even though many mothers are less than overjoyed when their teen-age sons come home with buckets of small pollock.

Foraging and sex
Even though women are treated as equal to men and to a great degree do the same things as men, there are still very few women hunters – only 5% of active hunters are women. Hunting and fishing are primarily "boy things". Fathers take their children fishing, no matter what the sex, and that's why most Norwegians have been on a fishing trip. Almost 100% of all boys and almost 80% of all girls between the ages of 11 and 16 say that they have been on fishing trips. Participation declines with age, fastest among girls. By the time they are 67, only around 10% of all women fish, as opposed to 60% of men. Boys are socialized into fishing through their fathers, while women drop out.

Fishing and hunting are part of being a male. Fishing terms are used to describe the relationship between the sexes. A common expression

Salmon is no long the luxury food it used to be, but it still tastes luxurious.

for checking girls is to "cast a line". There is a story to this picture. If the "fisherman" is lucky, he gets a "nibble" or she "takes his bait". Boys call girls chicks or fair game. Excitement and sexuality are associated with the wilderness. Another expression among boys is that "you never bring along fish on a fishing trip". The double meaning in this sentence refers to an area where women aren't welcome, and which functions on the men's terms, while at the same time, men say that the reason they get together is to hunt as a group. Men hunt for the "fish" (both the fish and the woman). He doesn't want the woman to tag along – neither Mama (the boss) or the girl (the booty). That means that he does not have to shower or brush his teeth, and he can get up when he wants. Hunting is a male thing and takes place in a male environment. That's why it can be uncomfortable for a woman to participate in these activities. In order to be accepted, she nearly has to change her sex and become "one of the guys".

Picking berries and mushrooms are more feminine things, but not to such a great degree. Mushroom and berry-picking are family activities. Excursions such as these are more common among city dwellers and those with higher education.

Foraging can be important for the grown-ups in a family, but for the children, its really a game. Children fish for pike and perch, but grown-ups are more interested in trout and whiting. Children are more interested in the catch and less interested in the food – they feel no responsibility for the budget or for family dinners.

Gifts from foraging

Those who live by the sea, especially in North and West Norway, catch fish in significant amounts. It's the men who fish, and it's the men who give fish away, often tens of kilos of fish per man. In the country, many more deer are felled that most families can eat. Fish, game and mushrooms are distributed in an entirely different way than over the counter – they are presented as gifts.

When someone has caught fish, shot an animal or picked a few kilos of cloudberries, he has to find a recipient for the products. The principles for exchanging gifts are that the recipient is obligated to the giver. This obligation is not paid back immediately, nor is it paid back in kind, and after a time, it becomes unclear just who is obliged to whom. One doesn't think consciously that something has to be given in return, but it should be done. If someone has given away a case of fish, he usually gets more than just a cup of coffee in return – perhaps a service of some

kind, a sack of potatoes or a bottle of red wine. The recipient knows that by accepting the fish or the meat, he has to give something in return, but that debt is undefined, both with regard to when it shall be repaid, and with what. The aspect of sometime in the future is implicit in the principle of giving, and no one knows exactly the amount of the debt. In this way, both parties may feel at the same time that they have an outstanding debt and that they owe someone something.

Taste and identification

Hunting and fishing are an important part of the Norwegian identity. Participation in hunting and fishing is part of a specific lifestyle, and we have a special relationship with food that is caught in the wilderness. It fits into specific contexts – we like to serve game at special occasions such as weddings, confirmations and christenings. And we may soak in brine the fish we caught in the mountains last summer and serve it at a fermented fish party in the winter. We maintain that what we catch ourselves tastes extra delicious. We emphasize the gamy flavor, and 60% of all Norwegians feel that wild salmon tastes better than farm-raised. Only 1% feel that farm-raised is better. There are examples of people preferring farm-raised salmon, but they believe that it is wild.

Why don't people want to eat nutritious, good food like farm-raised salmon when it is so cheap? It is because of cultural notions that Norwegians are people of the wilderness and resistance to change. According to industry representatives, when people farm fish, they are not doing anything different from what farmers have been doing for centuries with farm animals. And they are correct – it is completely natural, but it will take a long time before it is perceived as natural.

The wilderness and the field are two separate places, with similar separate notions of how one should use the food from each. While the pig is culture and is led to the slaughterhouse, food from the wilderness is nature. The fisherman or hunter is supposed to take his equipment out into the wilderness and catch or kill the food, which symbolizes a battle between man and beast. Hunting has to take place in the right way, at the right time and in the right place to satisfy Norwegian ideals. Shooting a moose in the forest is hunting, shooting one in the field is slaughtering, in the park is killing, and in the garden is close to murder. And ideas about the taste follow those same categories – a moose shot in a field tastes like beef.

Through fish farming, the salmon moved from the wilderness to the farm – the categories mesh and the relationship between them becomes problematic. The expressions "wild fish" and "tame fish" for salmon reveal that these categories are important, which in the next step results in different concepts of the fish, from flavor to

appearance. The tame salmon is given the attributes of a farm animal, while the wild salmon has those of the wilderness.

The salmon has always had an air of mystery and exclusivity and has traditionally been characterized as a delicacy. If you ate salmon or trout, you either knew someone who fished, or you belonged to the social class that could afford such expensive ingredients – just as it is for lobster and ptarmigan today. Through farm-raising, salmon has become cheaper and accessible to everyone, but it is no longer exclusive game.

It would be like cursing in sacred wilderness to say that chicken tastes better than ptarmigan. But in all probability, farm-raised fish taste better than wild, even though people don't believe it.

The flavor is probably better because it is possible over time to cultivate the best fish and have better control of the product. Fish are starved right before slaughter to avoid bad flavors. You are guaranteed not to get a salmon that's ready to spawn, and the amount of fat can be regulated. And the journey from slaughter to fish counter is far better monitored than with traditional catches. Norwegians eat their fish with the heart, and the wild animal and ideas of untouched wilderness add to the flavor. The more expensive the food, the better it seems to taste.

The king of the forest is an impressive sight – and moose and other game is served on many a Norwegian table.

Food and Drink

– you get to decide

How we combine food and drink can vary greatly, because the possibilities are virtually endless. Tradition, availability and budget usually enter into our choices. The cheapest drink of all, water, is delicious and plentiful in Norway. And there is tradition assosiated with it, too. It is an exellent thirst-quencher and increasingly a natural and important accompaniment to another drink, as noted below.

Over time, particular combinations are viewed as successful, and they have entered into the culture of food and drink as the correct choices. But there are many different opinions concerning what is successful and what isn't. That applies to specific countries, specific cultures and specific societies. There is, however, something in our physiology that makes us react in similar ways toward most combinations. We are all created relatively alike, with basically the same ability to perceive flavor and aroma, and we all react in similar ways. Education and adaptability also play a role. We can get used to combinations that seem hopeless in the beginning, but they improve considerably over time. Certain individual characteristics can also influence our preferences. The amount of stomach acid a person has can determine his reaction to acidic food and drink. People with a low level of acidity can enjoy half a grapefruit, while others might have to sprinkle tablespoons of sugar on it just to get it down. But these are only minute details in the big picture. Most of us grow up in relatively similar conditions, and we like the same combinations. Sometimes we force ourselves, because it's easier to conform to others, but in general, we share our preferences with the world around us.

Most of us prefer a glass of cold, fresh milk with whole grain bread and sweet Norwegian goat cheese to a glass of lukewarm juice. And there are better combinations of food and drink than roast beef and cranberry juice. But to what extent are we willing to search for the right

combinations. Coffee or tea? Milk or juice? Sparkling or still water? What will we drink at breakfast, at lunch, and at dinner? Are some sandwich fillings better with tea than with coffee, or with juice rather than milk? Perhaps, but most of us are very tolerant. Those who prefer coffee choose it irrespective of accompaniment. Interest in pairing food and drink is usually greater for special occasions, evening meals and get-togethers with others. The selection of wine poses the greatest challenges. Red wine with shrimp or port with big game are not our first choices, and generations of experience at home and abroad have taught us that certain combinations are better than others. Many of these combinations probably were not immediate successes, but they are a result of adaptation over time. The Norwegian palate has received impulses from abroad, though many specifically Norwegian combinations are not found anywhere else in Europe.

Changing drinking customs

The yearly wine consumption per person in Norway is 14-15 liters (3 ½-4 gallons), while the figure for beer is 55 liters (around 14 gallons), so the number of meals accompanied by alcoholic beverages is relatively low. And since we know that beer and wine are often consumed without

food, that number is even smaller. And the authorities regard that as positive. Consumption is, however, rising, and with the high cost of both food and drink in Norway, it should be the goal of every consumer to combine them in the best possible way. And even though the average Norwegian enjoys wine with dinner only rarely, it still happens more frequently than it did even 15-20 years ago, and much more attention is paid to the enjoyment involved in pairing food and drink. Wine is served primarily at the weekend and on special occasions, though an increasing number of people can afford to serve it more often. There's really no chance that we will reach consumption comparable to that of the big wine-producing countries, France and Italy, a generation ago – 130 liters (around 33 gallons) per capita per year. But today it is not unusual to enjoy a glass of wine or two with an ordinary workday dinner, whereas in the past, water, soda or juice were the beverages of choice. It's only natural to drink simpler wines with simpler meals. And price is important. Typical workday meals, whether fish, meat, pasta or pizza, tend to go better with simple red wines, and sales of just these wines have increased greatly over the last few years. Two groups in particular have expanded rapidly – light, soft Chilean wines with a certain French air about them, and "bag in a box", cheap light European wines from low-cost countries. This type of wine is also good without food, and because it is light and easier to understand and appreciate, more complicated wines such as Bordeaux have lost ground.

Important meals, with many courses and more complicated food, present the greatest challenges in pairing food and wine.

Wine bottles should be stored on their sides. In that way, the natural cork retains its original texture, remains damp and does not allow air to enter. Bottles with caps or plastic corks can be stored standing. The correct temperature for storing wine is 10-12°C (50-55°F).

Wine with food

The different styles of wine

An understanding the flavor and aroma components of the different wines is needed in order to combine them with food. It's also equally important to know the different characteristics that give wines their identities. When you pair wine with a particular kind of food, you should be familiar with a number of the wine's properties, such as sweetness, freshness, body, oak, bouquet, concentration and depth of flavor in white wines; oak, fruitiness, freshness, tannin, concentration and aftertaste in red; freshness, sweetness and fizz in sparkling wines; color, freshness and sweetness in rosé wines; and sweetness, freshness and alcohol headiness in fortified wines.

Both here in Norway and otherwise in the world of wine, it has been normal to group the wines according to the country or region of production, but there are times when this doesn't work as it should. A young, fruity, light Bordeaux is very different from an older, heavier wine from Pauillac, even though both are from Bordeaux, and according to many, they should go well with the same type of food. Because of this problem, many authors of basic wine books have made new groupings unlike previous ones.

According to Englishman Oz Clarke, these are the correct groupings. Food to match the wines in these groups will be discussed later.

1. *Juicy, fruity red wines*
   Fruity wines with little tannin are often characterized as modern. These wines often come from the "new world", but European wine regions are now producing them as well. Chilean Merlot is the prototype. Characteristic European wines are Beaujolais, Valdepenas and Bardolino.

2. *Soft, strawberry-like red wines*
   Charming, soft wines with a berry-like fruitiness, with a touch of raspberry, strawberry or
   cherry. Good red Burgundies based on Pinot
   Noir grapes are the prototype for these
   wines. Other examples are Rioja, Navarra and
   Cotes du Rhone Villages.

3. *Intense, black currant red wines*
   Complex red wines with heavy tannin, often
   made completely or partly with Cabernet
   Savignon grapes, preferably with a touch of
   vanilla and cedar after long aging in the
   barrel. The most famous are the expensive
   Bordeaux wines; other examples made from
   the same grape come from California,
   Australia, Chile and South Africa.

4. *Spicy red wines with an especially warm
   character*
   Full-bodied rich red wines redolent of black
   pepper and chocolate, often with a smoky,
   tannic character. Wines from the northern
   part of the Rhone, based on the Syrah grape,
   are the prototype. Australian Shiraz is another good example, as is American Zinfandel
   and Chilean Carmenere.

5. *Thirst-quenching sweet and sour red wines*
   Red wines with a fruity flavor of cherries and
   plums, often a bit herby, with a moderate
   touch of vanilla and tannin. Almost always
   Italian. Chianti wines are the most characteristic, but also wines from Piemonte and
   Salentino.

6. *Delicate rosé wines*
   Aromatic, refreshing and delicately dry rosé
   wines can be made of several different types
   of grapes, but the best are made with
   Grenache. They often have a strawberry
   aroma and are wonderfully thirst-quenching.
   From France, Italy, Portugal and California.

7. *Bone dry, neutral white wines*
   Crisp, refreshing wines that are seldom rich
   in character, but they are the best accompaniments to shellfish. This is a large group
   with Muscadet as the prototype. Other
   examples are Chablis that has not been aged

in oak and northern Italian wines such as
Soave and Chardonnay from Alto Adige and
central Italian Frascati.

8. *Green, full-flavored white wines*
   Sharp, full-flavored white wines that are
   always engaging, often with a hint of goose-
   berry. The most prominent representative of
   this group is Sauvignon Blanc from New
   Zealand. Other good examples are Sancerre
   and Pouilly-Fumé from the Loire valley in
   France, also made of Sauvignon Blanc, in
   addition to Rieslings in three weight classes,
   from Mosel, from the German Rhine and
   from Alsace/Austria. The Rieslings often have
   a trace of sweetness combined with honey
   or a mineral character.

9. *Intense, nutty white wines*
   Rich, juicy white wines with a nutty or oatmeal flavor. These dry wines are often aged
   in oak barrels. The best known are
   Chardonnay-based French Burgundies. Other
   typical examples come from Australia and
   South Africa. Oak-aged Graves/Pessac-
   Léognan wines from Bordeaux also belong in
   this group.

10. *Mature, toasty white wines*
    Modern wines with the aroma of peaches,
    apricots and other tropical fruits, ideally full-
    bodied and juicy, represented by Chardonnay,
    most often from Australia, but also from the
    US and South Africa. Chardonnay from
    Penedes in Spain is also a good example.

11. *Aromatic wines*
    Perfumed white wines with the distinct char-
    acter of exotic fruits and spring flowers, with
    Gewürztraminer from Alsace the most promi-
    nent representative. Other characteristic
    representatives are worldwide Muscatell,
    Viognier from the northern Rhone and
    Torontes from Argentina and Spain.

12. *Sparkling wines*
    Sparkling wines should have a clean, refresh-
    ing style in addition to the bubbles.
    Champagne is, without a doubt, the best
    representative, but competition from the
    Loire, Spain, Italy, Germany, Australia and the
    US is increasing.

13. *Golden, sweet white wines*
    Rich sweet wines that make you sip and
    smack your lips, but seldom tempt beyond a
    single glass. Honey is often the most domi-
    nating flavor, often accompanied by peach
    and apricot. The most famous are the
    Sauternes wines, in competition with the
    best German and Austrian wines, in addition
    to sweet variations from the Loire, Alsace
    and Hungary. The great strength of these
    wines is their rather high acidity, which adds
    freshness.

14. *Warm fortified wines*
    Wines with the rich flavor of raisins and
    burnt sugar, characteristic of full-flavored
    ports, but also in competition with the
    Madeiras, the marsalas, and the sweet oloro-
    sos from Jerez and the Malaga wines.

15. *Full-flavored fortified wines*
    Bone-dry wines with an individual style that
    are an acquired taste, but which can be
    served with or without food. The most
    prominent representatives, fino and manza-
    nilla sherry, come from southern Spain.
    Competitors come from Australia, South
    Africa and Cyprus.

The Wine Commandments

The Norwegian Institute of Gastronomy in Stavanger developed a list of commandments for matching food and wine, and for the order in which the different wines are served. Originally there were ten commandments. Now there are twelve.

1. *The food should not overpower the wine – or vice versa.*
    A natural rule. To get the most enjoyment from food and wine, no single ingredient should dominate. A heavy, tannic red wine will trample a delicate ingredient like chicken.

2. *Fatty food needs a wine with tannin or acid.*
    Acid cleanses the palate and adds life to a combination. Wine without acid tastes flat, and wine lacking in tannin also lacks body. Beef is best with a tannin-rich red wine.

3. *Bitterness in food and wine amplify one another.*
    Bitter flavors remain on the palate for a long time. That has to be considered when pairing food and wine. A wine rich in tannin brings out the bitterness in food. Brussels sprouts and Bordeaux are not a good combination.

4. *Warm spicy food calls for a wine with some sweetness.*
    Dry wine and highly spiced food cancel each other out. On the other hand, wine with some residual sweetness will buffer the spiciness. Don't be afraid to serve German semi-dry white wine with an exotic, spicy meat dish.

5. *The wine should be just as sweet and rich as the food.*
    Wine changes its character when combined with sweet or rich foods. The choice of fat or butter in the food also influences the choice of wine. Dessert wine should be sweeter than the dessert itself. Red Merlot wine marries well with meat in cream sauce, while port wine is lovely with chocolate mousse.

6. *Wine should complement the food.*
    The food and wine should harmonize by going in the same flavor direction. Mild wine with mild food, simple wine with simple food, and robust, hearty wine with richly flavored food. In other words, don't serve an expensive burgundy with meatloaf.

7. *Wine can contrast with the food.*
    A traditional challenge is sweet wine with salty food. The combination is challenging and it doesn't always work. Smoked and cured meats are good with semi-dry German white wine, and Sauternes is good with slightly salty Roquefort cheese. But be careful.

8. *Avoid very sweet or heavily alcoholic aperitifs.*
    Sweet or heavily alcoholic aperitifs reduce our ability to appreciate the fine nuances in the wine and food that follow later in the meal.

9. *Dry wine before sweet wine.*
    Sweet wine leaves a film in the mouth, and if it is served early in the meal, it can easily spoil further flavor sensations.

10. *Light wine before full-bodied wine.*
    If a light wine is served after a full-bodied one, it will taste thin and watery.

11. *Wine with a low alcoholic content should be served before a wine with a high alcoholic content.*
    If a low-alcohol wine is served after a high alcohol wine, it will taste thin and watery.

12. *A young wine should be served before an older one.*
    Older wines are usually more complex than young wines. If a young wine is served after an older one, it will give the impression of being of lower quality.

Since the original ten commandments eventually became twelve, there is little reason to believe that it will stop there. Some rules seem to be increasingly more important in the "wine with food world" and will probably be elevated to new commandments. These include:

– Cold food harmonizes better with light wine than hot food made of the same ingredients.
– Grilled food requires a heartier wine than the same ingredients prepared in the oven or microwave.
– Food that is cooked for a long time requires a heavier wine than the same ingredients cooked for a shorter time.
– Food with intensely flavored garnishes requires a heavier wine than the same food with less intensely flavored garnishes.

The classic meal

A classic Norwegian meal is composed of appetizer, main dish and dessert. There are, however, many exceptions. Frequently both the starter and the dessert are dropped, or at least one of them. Sometimes we serve a little cheese between main dish and dessert, like central Europeans, and at other times, we serve many small dishes instead of the traditional appetizers and main dishes. There are endless variations.

Now we will focus on traditional meals as well as on the many different "tables" that have become so popular in Norway.

It is worth noting that sweet, highly alcoholic aperitifs are served much less frequently than in the past. We now know that both sweet and strong flavors hinder the palate from registering small nuances in food and wine, and that benefits no one. Serve dry white wine or sherry (fino or manzanilla) instead, or even a dry sparkling wine. For special occasions, dry champagne is perfect. Avoid salted peanuts, which have some of the same disadvantages as sweet, strong aperitifs.

The wine groups mentioned below can be found in "The different styles of wine" on page 40.

Chicken and sparkling wine – a good duo for special occasions. Both champagne and more reasonably priced alternatives can be served. The wines can be both dry and semi-dry.

The Appetizer

Serve light wine with the starter. A dry white wine, not aged in oak (group 7 and 8), is usually best with shellfish and light fish dishes, while shellfish and fish served with sauce or mayonnaise, such as seafood salad and marinated salmon, are better with a richer wine with low acidity or a trace of sweetness (group 10 and 11).

Salads are best with light, fresh white wine (group 7), shellfish and vegetables with dry rosé wine (group 6) or a light, fresh young red wine with no trace of oak, and chicken with wines from groups 1, 2 and 5. Melon with cured ham

is hardly a typical Norwegian starter, but it is very popular. Pair it with a dry, neutral white wine, or with a slightly sweet white. Port is also a popular choice.

If pasta is served as a starter, the wine should complement the ingredients in the sauce, such as shrimp in cream sauce, veal, pesto, etc. The wines are often as light as those served with salads.

Vegetable dishes are often combined with richly flavored white wines (group 9 and 10). Be careful with raw onions and fresh tomatoes – both

are enemies of wine. Lightly sautéing vegetables before serving makes selecting wine easier. Don't use vinegar in vegetable dishes or in salads. Lemon juice is much more amenable to wine. Olive oil, which is often used in vegetable dishes, will help make the combination of food and wine more successful.

Mushroom dishes are often made with cream. Use an aromatic white wine (group 9 and 10).

Soup is often served as a starter. For many, sherry is the natural accompaniment. Fino or manzanilla are often served with clear soups, while

A wine that's full of flavor but lacking in tannin goes well with game. Burgundies and Rhone wines from France, Rioja from Spain, Chianti and Piemonte wines from Italy and Zinfandel from the US all are good with game.

Game is often rich in flavor, but it is relatively lean. Use a rather complicated wine from Burgundy (Pinot Noir), the northern Rhone (Syrah) or Piemonte (Nebbiolo). American Zinfandel is also good (groups 1, 2 and 4). If the game is served with a rich, creamy sauce, a wine with heavy tannin, made with Cabernet Sauvignon grapes (group 3), is a good match.

Beef is often marbled with fat and goes well with tannin-rich wine made with Cabernet Sauvignon grapes. Cabernet Sauvignon grapes are grown both in Europe and overseas. Aged Bordeaux is excellent with aged roast beef (group 3). Veal is lighter and can be combined with a full-bodied dry white wine – preferably a burgundy – but it's best with a light red wine from Chile, Italy or the southern Rhone (groups 1 and 5). Lamb is aromatic and goes well with a mature Rioja, Pomerol or St. Emilion. Serve a full-bodied white wine with lamb fricassee.

oloroso is better with creamed soups. A rather full-bodied white wine, such as Chardonnay that has not been oak-aged, is a good choice for all soups, as is dry Madeira.

As can be noted in the recommendations, white wine is the usual accompaniment to appetizers, but rosé wine is also suitable, and light, fresh red wines can also be good alternatives.

The Main Course

Fish
As a very general rule, poached fish goes well with white wine, while fried fish is best with red wines. Make certain that the wines do not have an oaky character, even if there are a few exceptions to that rule.

Norwegians are especially fond of red wine with poached cod and other white fish, and the combination is excellent, if the wine bears no trace of tannin or oak. Wines in groups 1, 2 and 5 are best. If the poached white fish is served with a creamy sauce, the white wine can have a trace of sweetness, as in many German wines. Fried white fish can also be matched with a full-bodied white wine (Chardonnay without oak)

but they are still best with red wines from groups 1, 2 and 5.

Mackerel is a difficult fish to match with wine. Many prefer beer with fried mackerel and a moderately full-bodied Chardonnay with poached.

A wine served with poached red fish should be white, dry and full-flavored (groups 8, 10 and 11). Choose the same wine, even if the fish is fried.

Bacalao is popular in Norway, and there are endless variations. The most popular recipe features a sauce based on tomato paste and is therefore best with a flavorful white wine (groups 8, 10 and 11) or a light red wine (groups 2 and 5). Many however prefer beer and aquavit.

Meat
Most people prefer red wine with meat. But there are wide variations in meat, from light white meat to heavy red meat, from neutral to flavorful, from lean to marbled, and from spiced, salted or smoked to almost unseasoned. In addition, sauce and garnishes can vary greatly and give the dish a different style or character.

Flavorful wine from "the new world" goes well with spring lamb. Good choices are Shiraz and Cabernet Sauvignon from Australia and Merlot and Cabernet Sauvignon from New Zealand

Poultry often means chicken or turkey. A light red wine or a dry white wine go best (groups 1, 2, 5, and 9). Fattier birds such as duck are better with Cabernet Sauvignon. Stews made with poultry are often full of flavor and pair well with Portuguese red wines.

How the meat is prepared is often the key to selecting wine, as is the kind of sauce and side dishes. Smoked and salted meats are usually served with a light red wine (group 5), but they are best with beer, as is our "national dish", sausages.

Grilled meat and stews are often rich and full of flavor – serve with a red Rhone wine and Portuguese red wines.

In an overview such as this, it is difficult to include every imaginable meat dish and the perfect wine for each. As a rule, you should serve a tannin-rich wine with dishes containing a high proportion of fat (either the meat is naturally fatty, or there is added fat) and serve lighter red wines or full-bodied white wines with meat with a low proportion of fat.

Norwegians like to serve full-bodied red wines. There is nothing wrong with the so-called masculine red wines, but a lighter, more delicate red wine often suits the meal better, and it is in no way inferior.

"The Cheese Interlude"

Here we refer to the "cheese board", but remember that the wine served with the main dish should determine which cheese should be included in this little interlude before dessert. In that way, we do not have to serve one more wine with the meal.

The Dessert

Wine with dessert is not a simple combination either. As a general rule, the wine should be sweeter than the dessert. Otherwise, the wine will taste sour. That causes difficulties, because desserts are usually composed of several ingredients. Simple, less complex desserts are easier to complement with wine.

People used to think that all kinds of Sauternes, port and Madeira can be served with "everything" but that is hardly the case. Varying amounts of fruit acids and sweetness in these wines forces us to be more precise in our selections. Fruity acids are the most difficult to handle. If fortified wines are served with highly acidic desserts, there will be a collision of flavors, which doesn't please anyone. Muscatel wine is often best.

The combination of strawberries and Asti Spumante (sparkling northern Italian Muscatel wine) is excellent, but serve cream instead of ice cream with the berries. Ice cream deadens our ability to register flavors. Muscatel wine in different levels of sweetness goes with all berries.

Cloudberries are popular in Norway. These go well with cream sherry or sweet tokay. It's not easy to refer to special wine groups in this case, but the right wines are usually in groups 13 and 14.

Different kinds of ice cream are often best with a sweet Madeira, bual or malmsey. These combinations are at their best when the ice cream is slightly melted.

It can be difficult to find a wine to pair with chocolate, but a really rich chocolate cake is wonderful with red Bordeaux, and chocolate mousse is perfect with a young, red port wine.

Cakes made with milk and eggs go well with Marsala, while those made with nuts are better with port wine or cream sherry.

Traditional homemade caramel custard is usually quite sweet. Comandiere St. John from Cyprus,

Sweet desserts require sweet wines. Here is a small selection of French wines. Muscatell wine is considered best with fruit, while "les vins doux naturels" are best with cakes and nuts.

sweet Madeira and an aged port wine are all good choices.

It is often difficult to find the perfect lowest common denominator among all the dessert wines. The safest choice is a well-aged tawny or vintage port. An aged Sauternes is also a good choice.

Cold Buffet

The traditional Norwegian cold table (which also features hot food) or buffet, as it's often called abroad, consists of many different kinds of food, frequently with luxury ingredients. This multitude of dishes makes selecting wine difficult. Beer is often the best choice, even though more and more prefer wine.

It is nearly impossible to find a wine that works perfectly with all the different ingredients. Some that come close are full-bodied, dry white wines with no oakiness; rather full-bodied, dry, sparkling white wines; dry rosés or rather light red wines.

In selecting wine for a cold table, you might want to follow this advice: Build up the meal as if it were a dinner with many courses. Begin with a little glass of beer or crisp dry sherry with the herring as a starter. If you prefer shellfish, start with a glass of dry white wine. Then select a slightly heavier white wine to accompany the cold salmon. Find the right red wine for the meat using the criteria mentioned earlier, and enjoy that same wine with the cheese. Or you might prefer a little glass of port both with the cheese and the dessert. A little complicated

perhaps, but eminently doable, especially if several agree on the same wines.

Half bottles and single glasses are also a solution, but that's usually more expensive. Another way is to concentrate on one kind of food, fish, shellfish or meat. But most people can't imagine doing anything like that, either because they don't want to appear greedy, or more likely because they don't want to miss any of the wonderful dishes on the cold table.

Open-face sandwiches

As a meal, these have a lot in common with the cold table. The solution has to be the least common denominator, according to the choices mentioned above.

Canapés

These are often served at receptions or in place of a starter. If caviar alone is served, then dry champagne is the almost obligatory choice. Other dry sparkling wines are also suitable. Otherwise, it's a good idea to serve only a few types of canapés to make the choice of wine easier.

Cheese table

In Norway, cheese and wine can be a little meal in itself, especially as a finale to a "meeting" in a wine club, at informal get-togethers, and on Saturday evenings. Often different cheeses are served on a platter garnished with fruit and vegetables. Red wine is frequently the beverage of choice. Farther south in Europe, cheese and wine are part of a larger meal and are served between the main course and dessert. This is not the case in Norway. We drink so much milk that we don't need cheese as part of the evening meal. In addition, we consume cheese at both breakfast and lunch, so our need for cheese is

Cheese and wine go well together, but consider the flavor and richness of the cheese when pairing it with white wine, light and heavy red wine and port wine.

satisfied - except when we invite people over for wine and cheese. We feel that it is natural to eat apples, grapes, celery, bell peppers and tomatoes with cheese and wine. But do these things go together? They really don't. There is a good reason why southern Europeans serve only bread with cheese and wine. Raw fruit and vegetables don't go with wine at all. In other words, be careful how much fruit you serve with cheese, even if the tray looks better with rather than without.

What about the combination of cheese and wine? How successful is it really? To what degree is there harmony when the flavor of the cheese and the wine meet on the palate? Is it really true that the one red wine served goes equally well with 8-10 different cheeses? The answer is often "no". Frequently, a metallic aftertaste ruins the flavor of both good cheese and good wine. More and more who are concerned about the harmony of a meal now prefer a dry, full-bodied white wine, such as a Chardonnay, as the main wine at a cheese meal. The cheese world is so diverse that it is difficult to find one wine, and especially a red wine, that can be combined well with the great range of cheeses.

Experience has shown that the following combinations work best:

- Choose a relatively light white Chardonnay, from Chile for example, or a light German white wine with a little residual sweetness to accompany firm, rather hard mild white cheeses made from cow milk (so-called firm rennet cheeses), such as Jarlsberg, Edam or Swiss. Light red wine (groups 1, 2, and 5), such as Beaujolais, Valdepenas or Bardolino, can also be served. Stay away from red wine with a high tannin content.

- Choose a white wine with more body, such as Chardonnay from Australia, Cote d Or or California, or others in group 9, to go with similar cheeses but with a stronger flavor, such as Parmesan and St. Albray. You can also serve a medium- bodied red from the Rhone, the center of Italy, Bulgaria and Romania (groups 4 and 5).

– Select a Rioja, a mature Bordeaux or Gewürztraminer, or in other words, red wine with some tannin, or a full-flavored white wine to accompany stronger cheeses with a higher fat content, such as Ridder, Port Salut and Münster.

– A tannin-rich red wine made of Cabernet Sauvignon grapes (group 3) is best with soft, rich, aged cheeses with rind, such as brie and camembert.

– Wines with a rich sweetness, such as Sauternes and port, are best with high-fat, aged blue cheeses such as Gorgonzola and Roquefort.

– Port wine is recommended for flavor bombs such as Stilton and the Norwegian specialty, *gammelost*.

How do we solve this problem when we would like to include many kinds of cheese on the table, and of course, we want the combination of wine and cheese to be successful? I recommend serving several wines with a cheese table – ideally, a dry white wine, a fruity red wine and a tannin-rich red wine, and perhaps even a port wine. The easiest thing, however, is to serve cheeses that are similar, then you need only one wine. Such a proposal may be difficult to accept, but you then know that everything tastes good together.

Shellfish table

A well-assorted shellfish table is not as challenging as a cheese table. But even with shellfish, there is such wide a range of flavors that the wine should not overpower the shellfish, or vice versa. And here, too, you need to get down to the basics. From a wine point of view, it's best to choose one type of shellfish and find the best wine to complement it.

White wine is a must with shellfish. Dry, flavorful French or semi-dry German – richly flavored French Chablis, Muscadet or Sancerre, or semi-dry German Riesling both from the Rhine and Mosel valleys.

Frenchmen love their "plateaux de fruits de mer" and they can be an example for our shellfish table. The best presentations are found along the Atlantic coast, in Nantes, Bordeaux, La Rochelle and Bayonne, but the Mediterranean versions in Sète and Marseilles are not far behind. Local wines are often served with these platters, but as a rule, fresh, acidic and neutral white Muscadet is best with the fruits of the sea.

The range of flavor in the shellfish has to correspond with that in the white wine. Be careful with oak-aged whites. They can knock out the subtle shellfish flavor completely. Remember that mayonnaise and lemon, which are served with everything from shrimp to lobster, call for a more full-bodied white wine than shellfish served

alone. Remember that Norwegian crab claws are best with a relatively light white wine, while the rest of the crab is better with a heavier white or even beer. Many also prefer beer with salty, dill-flavored crayfish. Fresh white wine, such as Riesling from Alsace, is also excellent.

Mussels (which taste good when steamed in beer) go well with a full-bodied dry white wine, preferably a Sauvignon Blanc from Sancerre, northern Italy or New Zealand. A comparatively light, neutral wine is better with these mild shellfish than one that is rich and full of flavor. Choose a Muscadet as the French do, Chablis, Pinot Grigio from Northern Italy or a good vinho verde from Portugal.

The herring table

Few white wines can live up to the enormous wealth of flavors in a herring table. Beer and flavored aquavit are much better, however dry sherry – fino and manzanilla in particular – is served more and more frequently.

Grilled food

It is said that the popularity of grilled food is responsible for the increase in consumption of red wine at the expense of white wine. That may be true, but white wine is also good with different kinds of grilled food.

There really shouldn't be any great difference in the choice of wine if food is grilled rather than cooked in the oven. Just follow the general rules for combining food and drink. There is, however, a tradition of using heartier, more robust wines, both red and white, and preferably with an oakier character, with food prepared on the grill. Hearty Portuguese and Argentine red wines are popular, as are overseas whites.

Smoked, salted, dried, marinated and fermented food

These types of food are among the most traditional in Norway. Beer and liquor have always been part of the diet in Norway, while wine is a relative newcomer. For that reason, traditional food is still combined with beer and sometimes aquavit. But there are more reasons for choosing beer and aquavit. Smoked, salted, dried, marinated and fermented foods are much more intensely flavored than fresh foods, and that makes them difficult to pair with wine, even though some new types have made this more of a possibility.

If you want to serve wine with such traditional food, a robust, full-flavored white wine from Alsace is probably the best choice, though it may be difficult to convince Norwegians of that. The combinations of Gewürztraminer from Alsace and gravlaks or marinated reindeer have, however, won acceptance. Other rich Alsace wines are also good, as is dry sherry.

Dried meats are best with an oaky, flavorful white wine. But those who prefer red wine should select lighter varieties, such as those from northern Italy. Valpolicella Classico, which sometimes has the aroma and flavor of cherries, is a good choice. Heavy, tannic red wines should be avoided.

Christmas food

Christmas food is generally traditional, so that the recommendations in the previous section can be followed.

Both *pinnekjøtt* from western Norway and pork ribs from eastern Norway are best with beer and aquavit. But you can try a hearty white Alsace wine or a light Italian red wine for a change. Only tradition makes us reject this alternative.

Follow the same advice with lutefisk, but do not serve it with red wine. Some like it with champagne or sauternes, but that is a subject of debate.

Enemies of wine

As mentioned earlier, certain types of food, garnishes or ingredients don't work with wine. Fortunately, these are few in number, because in the vast world of wine, usually one or two types or variations do work. If nothing seems to work, then serve beer, or use as little as possible of the ingredient in question.

Lingonberry compote is a problem food. Some Norwegians can't enjoy game without lingonberry compote, even though that combination is unfortunate when served with wine. Rowanberry jelly is a better choice, but if you have to serve lingonberries, you can neutralize their sharp acidic quality with potato or a piece of meat before drinking wine.

It's also a good idea to avoid vinegar in salad dressings at meals where wine is served. Olive oil helps neutralize the acidity, but it's even better to substitute lemon juice for vinegar.

Raw tomatoes or onions are not good with wine either. A drizzle of olive oil helps, as does a quick sauté over low heat.

Raw or hardcooked eggs don't go well with wine either, so limit their use.

Beer with food

Even though a wide variety of beer is sold, few ever consider finding the right beer to pair with food. That is a pity, because beer is such a versatile drink that some types are indeed better with certain dishes than others.

One reason may be the dominance of pilsner in Norway. Most pilsner is drunk without food, but there is no doubt that many dishes are much better with a stronger, hearty, robust beer than with comparatively light pilsner.

But this can also be a matter of price and availability. When the alcoholic content of beer exceeds 4.75%, the price increases considerably, and it can no longer be purchased in grocery stores, only at Norwegian government stores.

The matching of beer and food is based on the same principles as those for wine and food. Light dishes made with shellfish, fish and light meat are best with a pilsner-type beer, while salted, smoked or fatty food is best with a stronger beer. Use an especially rich beer with strong cheeses, and try bock beer with cream cakes. It can also be an exciting ingredient in cream cakes, for marinating and as a flavoring in whipped cream. It's a time-honored tradition in Norway to use beer in sauces. Don't forget that a glass of cold, low-alcohol beer is a good aperitif.

Beer has been the drink of the people in Norway for eons, and it is served with many traditional dishes.

The different kinds of beer

There are many ways to group beer. There are two main types: underfermented and overfermented. The former is comparatively light and fresh, like pilsner, while the latter is dark and hearty, with a residual sweetness. English ale and stout are typical of the latter. Both can be found in Norway, but they are consumed in very small quantities. The special designation refers to the production process and type of yeast used.

Beer can also be classified by alcohol content. High-alcohol beer contains from 4.75 to 10% alcohol in Norway, even more abroad. Light beer and alcohol-free beer are other groups. These are similar to pilsner, and because they are aged, some call them light lagers. The main different from pilsner is that they lack some of pilsner's solidity because of their low alcohol content.

The most common types of strong beer are yellow beer, extra and bock beer. The first two are closely related to pilsner, but they are stronger and have a richer flavor. In the past, they were often referred to as export beer. Bock beer is much richer and darker, with more malt flavor, and it is sometimes even creamy. There are lighter varieties of bock beer.

Most beer is made with barley, but it can also be made with wheat. Wheat-based beer has a lighter flavor and texture.

A great deal of imported beer is quite different from Norwegian beer. As a rule, it is strong and flavorful. In addition to those types already mentioned, there is also Hefe-Weissbier, brown, pale, Irish, cloister, Trappist and porter beer.

Popular Christmas beer is usually a strong beer flavored with malt and spices. The color is often red-brown. Christmas beer is also made with an alcoholic content lower than 4.75% and resembles a heavier pilsner.

Liquor with food

Liquor in the form of aquavit is often served with food in Norway, usually with traditional Christmas food, and it's often chased with beer. The combination of liquor and wine is less suitable and not recommended. Genever has long been served as an accompaniment with food, especially along the coast, and in some homes, it competes with aquavit. Cold vodka also is served. But there is no doubt that aquavit is the most popular liquor with food.

The combination of liquor and food beyond aquavit, genever and vodka is unusual in Norway, even though some people may want to try something else during the meal.

Strangely enough, the "trou normand" – calvados – that Frenchmen sometimes drink between courses, has never caught on in Norway.

Aquavit

Until the mid 1990s, the selection of aquavit was relatively stable. Most brands were Norwegian and had been aged in an oak barrel, which often tempered the spicy character of the aquavit, unlike those from Denmark and Sweden. Arcus, which separated from the Norwegian State Wine Monopoly in 1996, produces most of the new brands, but imports from the other Nordic countries have increased considerably.

A good rule for using traditional aquavits is to serve those with the most dominant spicy flavors with heavily salted and smoked foods, while milder and more well-rounded flavors call for longer aged, less spicy aquavit. Quite a few new aquavits have been named according to their uses, such as Opland Rakefisk (fermented fish) Aquavit, Norwegian Lutefisk Aquavit, Ystad's Aquavit for Norwegian Salmon, Good Old Smaladram, and others. These all clearly state when they are to be served. For the other large group of newcomers, the so-called regional

aquavits, you need to know more about the individual flavors to pair them with food.

Here are Arcus' recommendations for combinations with the different aquavits:

Classic aquavits

Gilde Taffel
Fish and shellfish, especially crayfish and crab. Also good with herring, bacalao and other fish dishes.

Oplandske***
Cured ham, dried mutton, herring

Løiten***
Smoked and cured foods, traditional Christmas dishes.

Simers Taffel Aquavit
Perfect for the herring table, excellent with hearty, fatty food, especially dishes served with sauerkraut.

Lysholm Linie
Roast pork, fermented fish and cured meats, a good all-round aquavit for the Christmas table.

Løiten Linie
Salted and smoked meat, rich meat dishes. Excellent with traditional Christmas dishes.

Gammel (Old) Opland
Lutefisk and other traditional Norwegian Christmas dishes

Gammel (Old) Reserve
Traditional Norwegian Christmas dishes, smoked and salted meats, fermented fish.

Gilde Non Plus Ultra
Used primarily as an after dinner drink with coffee or with food.

Regional aquavits
Gammel (Old) Porsgrund
Fish and shellfish, bacalao.

Morsa Aquavit
Traditional Norwegian dishes.

Bergens Aquavit 1818
Herring and other robust Norwegian dishes.

Gilde Maquavit
Hearty and robust meat and fish dishes, after
dinner.

Lysholm Throndheimsaquavit
Hearty meat dishes, Christmas dishes, after
dinner.

Simers Oslo Aquavit
Traditional Norwegian dishes, after dinner.

Skipper Worse Aquavit
Good with beer or as a mixed drink blended
with a little ice or water.

Special aquavits
Gilde Skalldyrs (Shellfish) Aquavit
Crab, crayfish or other seafood, marinated and
smoked salmon.

Løiten Export
Grilled salmon, cured or marinated fish.

Løitens Sommer (Summer) Aquavit
Fish and shellfish, white meat, cured meats.

Norsk Lutfisk Aquavit
The traditional Norwegian *lutefisk* meal.

Lysholm Bacalao Aquavit
Dishes made with salt fish.

God Gamal (Good Old) Smaladram
Pinnekjøtt, *smalahovud* (smoked sheep head),
and other lamb and mutton dishes.

Fru Lysholm Aquavit
Traditional mild to medium-flavored Norwegian
dishes.

Oplandske Rakefisk Aquavit
The traditional Norwegian fermented fish meal.

Gilde Juleaquavit
Pork roast, ribs of pork and other traditional
Norwegian Christmas dishes.

*Linje aquavit is without a doubt the best-known Norwegian liquor abroad. Chased with beer, it's
perfect with hearty foods, but it also goes well with lighter dishes.*

What is healthy food?

– the answer is easier than you think

Many are concerned about diet and nutrition. Food and health are interesting topics and "developments" in the field are widely covered in newspapers and magazines, TV and radio. While in the past, most people agreed on what was a healthy diet, there is often contradicting advice today.

That is because now there are more opinions and more outlets in which to express them than ever before, and some of these messages have commercial interests to back them up. At times, it is indeed difficult to establish a clear connection between food consumption and health. Different studies need to be compared and evaluated against each other. When results from single studies make headlines, contradictory ones are not far behind.

From a nutritional point of view, there isn't much disagreement about what is considered a healthy diet for most people.

All food is healthy food!

Food is important to us in so many ways. Most people in Norway have easy access to a wide range of ingredients, and food is a source of pleasure and enjoyment! It is part of our culture and traditions, our identity and understanding of ourselves. Beyond covering our basic needs, food

is primarily a means of communication, both with respect to who we are (ourselves and others) and our relationships with others.

When we speak of healthy food, we need to evaluate that food according to the World Health Organization's broad definition of health, which includes physical, mental and social health. In such a context, all food can be considered healthy. A fizzy drink with zero nutritional value can help create a mood when enjoyed with friends, aspects that are indeed healthy.

It's not the individual foods that are important, rather the entire picture of all the components in our diet, and how much we consume. In the past, giving children a fizzy drink on Saturday was considered healthy. Now, 25% of all 13-year-olds drink a liter of fizzy drinks every day, thereby replacing nourishing food with empty calories. Total caloric consumption is so high that there is an increased risk of obesity, which can lead to health problems in later life.

That's the way it is with all foods. Too much of any single food is unhealthy. A varied diet is best. And it is possible to compose a healthy diet that takes advantage of many different foods. A healthy diet can be based on all kinds of ethnic foods. It may contain meat, dairy products, and potatoes, but it doesn't have to include any of these foods.

For that reason, we need to differentiate between nutritional guidelines that can be satisfied with many different kinds of foods, and specific recommendations. Guidelines specify which foods a person may eat when considering the existing dietary-related health problems in a society, culture and traditions, as well as the food available.

A specific example is the "five per day" campaign. Today, people the world over are

Ice cream and candy can also be good for you.

encouraged to increase consumption of fruit and vegetables because of their positive effect in fighting heart disease and certain cancers. In many countries, including Norway, this has resulted in "five per day" campaigns in which people are encouraged to consume at least five servings of fruit and vegetables per day. On average, Norwegians eat only two or three servings per day. The "five per day" campaign means a doubling of consumption, an ambitious goal. In Denmark, the campaign emphasizes six a day, in France ten a day. These differences point out differences in both serving size as well as in existing consumption. While we do not know exactly how much fruit and vegetables per day provides optimal effect, there is consensus that everyone should eat more. With such a low consumption in Norway as a base, it would be unrealistic to aim for ten per day. If we achieve the goal of five a day, we will reap great health benefits. At the same time, this shows how we consider culture, traditions and available food in giving specific advice.

The potato also counts in the "five per day" campaign in Norway, though it does not in many other countries. That food has become a "hot potato" in the official nutritional debate because so-called low-carbohydrate diets and the potato's glycemic index (GI) have been launched as a means of fighting increasing obesity (GI is a measure of how much the blood sugar rises after consumption of a food corresponding to 50 grams of carbohydrate). While everyone a- grees that the increase in the consumption of fatty, processed potato products such as chips and French fries is unfortunate, there is disa- greement regarding the plain boiled potato. Norwegian nutritional authorities emphasize the boiled potato's traditional role in the Norwegian diet as a source of nourishment. Since consump- tion of boiled potatoes has plummeted during the past 10 years, it is clear that the increase in obesity cannot be attributed to the boiled potato.

Once again we see that concrete nutritional recommendations are anchored in and to a great degree based on culture and tradition, on avail- able food, and on a change in existing health problems. Otherwise said: The recommendations are based on a normal, balanced and varied Norwegian diet.

Nutritional recommen- dations and consumption

Norwegian nutritional recommendations are based on Nordic recommendations that are updated regularly. The present recommendations were issued in 1997. These are now under revi- sion by a group of Nordic experts and will be ready in 2004. During revision, a systematic eval- uation is made of all recent research surrounding the different nutrients, as well as an evaluation of recommendations made by other countries.

Norway has a good system for monitoring devel- opments in diet and intake of nutrients. The Department of Health and Social Security issues a yearly report "Developments in the Norwegian Diet", that lists food and nutrient consumption as indicated by reports regarding food supplies and in the National Bureau of Statistics' ongoing consumer research. In addition, there are regular nutritional studies of different age groups in the population, from infants through youths to adults and the elderly.

Results of these studies indicate that there have been great changes in the Norwegian diet over time, and on average, the present diet provides enough of most nutrients. At the same time, there are some clear nutritional weaknesses, and behind the averages are great discrepancies be- tween the different groups. As an example, stud- ies indicate that those with higher education maintain a healthier diet, with higher intake of fruit and vegetables and less saturated fats than those with less education. Parallel to that, there are many differences between the sexes and the different age groups.

Consumption of saturated fats (hard fat, primari- ly from animal sources) and sugar is higher than it should be. This is also supported by other data. A high intake of saturated fat is an impor- tant risk factor in heart disease, still the leading cause of death in Norway. A substantial drop in fat consumption, including saturated fat, has

What could be better than fresh berries that you picked yourself?

contributed to the significant, positive reduction in the mortality rate from heart attacks and sudden death in Norway in this same period.

The percentage of energy consumed deriving from sugar has also increased, and the sources of that sugar have also changed. Today we are especially concerned about the marked increase in the amount of sweetened beverages (fizzy drinks and juice products with sugar added) consumed by children and young people. Sweet drinks do not give the same feeling of fullness as food, and the increase in the amount consumed, combined with less physical activity, can explain the increase in obesity and type II-diabetes as a result.

If we look at non-energy providing nutrients, vitamins and minerals, we find that people do not get enough Vitamin D in Norway. In addition, women of childbearing age consume less iron and folic acid than they need. Everyone (beginning as infants) should take cod liver oil or another Vitamin D preparation. In addition, all women of childbearing age, who plan to or may become pregnant, should take a daily folic acid supplement. Beyond that, there are no general recommendations regarding diet in Norway. To the contrary, we recommend that people try to cover their vitamin and mineral needs through food rather than dietary supplements. A varied diet also provides many other important nutrients, and it reduces the risk of consuming too much of certain substances.

Food intake and specific dietary recommendations.

The Norwegian diet is in constant flux. That has been especially noticeable during the last 25-30 years. These changes have been both positive and negative. A positive effect, in line with official nutritional policy, is that consumption of vegetables has increased by 25 kg (55 lb) per person per year, and there has been a decrease in intake of whole milk to the advantage of newer lower-fat alternatives. Consumption of butter and margarine has also gone down. As a whole, reduction in consumption of full-fat milk, butter and margarine has contributed strongly to the reduction of total fat intake during this period.

Consumption of the lean, nutritional potato, however, has gone down by half, while consumption of fatty, processed potato products has quadrupled. Intake of sugar has also increased, more meat is consumed than ever before, and the consumption of cheese is also increasing.

Fish consumption has gone down during this period, but we do not have good enough statistics prior to 1995. In 2000, private households consumed fish corresponding to 31 kg (68 lb) whole fish per person.

While we see a beneficial, long-term increase in the amount of vegetables consumed in Norway, there have been fewer changes in fruit consumption, in spite of the increase in sales of orange juice. Today, we recommend that adults eat around 750 g (1 2/3 lb) vegetables, potatoes, fruit and berries per day, or as mentioned earlier, "five per day". Studies indicate that on the average, we eat only 450 g (1 lb) per day, and only one in ten reach that goal of five per day.

Whole grain breads and vegetables should be the basis of our diet. People consume too many sugary drinks. Water and low-fat milk are much better alternatives, and that is emphasized in government guidelines for school children.

According to nutritional recommendations, public health illnesses and the Norwegian diet, we can give some specific recommendations for a healthier diet:

– Eat more vegetables, fruit, berries and potatoes (at least five servings of fruit and vegetables each day).
– Eat more whole grain bread and other whole grain products.
– Eat more fish, both for lunch and dinner.
– Eat less saturated fat, especially hard margarine and butter.
– Eat low-fat milk and meat products.
– Reduce consumption of sugar.
– Reduce consumption of salt.
– Drink water when thirsty.

In addition, we recommend moderate daily physical activity, corresponding to 30 minutes of fast walking. Increased physical activity, in addition to the above recommendations, is especially important in preventing obesity, but inactivity is also an important risk factor in many chronic conditions.

We have no specific recommendations in Norway regarding coffee other than that filter coffee is recommended over boiled, because the filter removes fat particles in the coffee. Nor are there recommendations regarding alcohol and wine consumption, other than that no more than 5% of total energy intake should come from alcohol. Our evaluation is that we know too little to give concrete advice regarding the healthy consumption of these beverages.

If the diet is changed according to the above recommendations, it should contribute to the reduction in the number of cases of popular illnesses, including heart disease, a number of cancers, as well as obesity and type II diabetes.

The numbers presented here are averages. We know from research that great discrepancies exist between different groups, both according to sex and age, as well as between different social groups (according to education and income).

Norway is also becoming a multicultural society, and food products from the world are now

At the outdoor fish market in Bergen.

available here. As noted earlier, there are many ways to build up a healthy diet. The advice given here is general, addressed to the general population. There are also more specific recommendations for pregnant and nursing women, for infants, for those wanting to lose weight, and for different patient groups.

For more specific nutritional advice pertaining to a particular illness, poor health or weight reduction, contact a dietitian or a doctor. There are many unrealistic diets that can cause health problems. Do not be misled by diets that promise quick considerable weight loss and are not based on a regular diet that can be followed over a long period of time.

Conclusion

The conditions for maintaining a healthy, varied diet based on standard Norwegian products and other foods that are easy to obtain in Norway are good. From a professional nutritional point of view, the main challenges for the future are increasing the amount of vegetables and fruit consumed, choosing whole grain products and low-fat meat and dairy products and reducing the consumption of sugar-added drinks and other products.

Norway exports great quantities of fish. It is one of our best products, and we should consume more of it at home.

Breakfast

– a good start to the day

The alarm rings, work calls. A new day has begun and everyone needs food to live. We need breakfast. Breakfast in Norway is varied, and yet we all do almost the same thing. We get up, go to the bathroom and then down to the kitchen and make breakfast. We eat almost the same thing – bread with something – but with small individualistic touches.

Most Norwegian breakfasts consist of cold food. Norwegians eat a lot of bread – 91% of all Norwegians eat bread for breakfast during the week and 93% on weekends. But there are also many who eat vegetables in the morning. Around 13% eat cereal or porridge. Eggs are a popular weekend breakfast food.

Breakfast is an endless variation of special habits – whether you go back to bed with a cup of tea and a cracker, stay in the kitchen and fry some bacon, or whether you just eat some yogurt in front of the TV. Some people read the morning paper while they eat, while others listen to the radio. Some eat with the family. Some make breakfast for others, while others have it served. Senior couples sitting at the same breakfast table over a long life eating the same meal every day. According to sales statistics, most sleepy Norwegians manage to slice some whole grain bread (virtually no one buys sliced bread in Norway, as it's pre-packaged and by definition stale before it's opened), and they top it with mild cheese, jam, caviar from a tube (it's pink and made from cod roe), salami or liver pate.

Breakfast is not the time for creativity. People may have plenty of time or hardly any at all, but everyone has a morning routine. Some move quickly from bed to bath to kitchen, while others are slow in their tracks. Habits get broken only when it's practical.

We say that breakfast is the most important meal of the day, that it's important for the body to have something to "go on". For those who are hungry when they wake up, it's not a problem, but for those with tired eyes in the morning, it's a never-ending battle to force down a piece of bread.

There's a lot you can do to increase your appetite in the morning. Get up 15 minutes earlier and take everything more leisurely. You can vary the meal with porridge, crispbread or cereal with yogurt or milk, fruit or hot food. It's important to find a routine you can enjoy and which gives the body what it needs. Everyone knows that eating breakfast helps make the day.

Adults are always worried about the eating habits of the younger generation. In a normal family, the children probably eat breakfast together. Mother goes to work before the children eat breakfast, and Father doesn't like food that early in the morning. But both understand that the children need food. Getting

Homemade granola

children to eat breakfast is a headache for many parents. If you read old cookbooks, you will find that this isn't a new problem. You know that you're not alone, and bribing the kids to eat is nothing new, and pretty soon, it's the weekend.

Sunday morning is the day when most Norwegians eat a leisurely breakfast. There's no alarm clock that day, and the kids are happy to watch cartoons on TV. Rolls get warmed in the oven and the table is set with ham, cheese and fresh fruit and vegetables. Now's the time for fresh orange juice, and the aroma of coffee fills the room. Norwegians love herring for breakfast, preferably a variety, accompanied by hard-cooked eggs. It's more like brunch than breakfast.

The packed lunch

Historically, most Norwegians pack their own lunch, and it tends to be simple and traditional. Cheese, liver pate and salami have stood the test of time.

But it's also possible to make a packed lunch more interesting by varying the kind of sandwich filling and adding vegetables, or even a little surprise in the bottom of the box. You can also vary the kind of bread – choose a bagel, ciabatta or other interesting bread and all kinds of possibilities present themselves.

Homemade granola

Instead of buying granola, you can make your own.

Combine two or more of the following: Oatmeal, wheat bran, wheat germ, puffed oats or wheat, sesame seeds, sunflower seeds, chopped nuts, raisins or other dried fruit with a couple of tablespoons of honey.

Place the honey in an oven tray, set the oven temperature at 200°C (400°F). Add the mix, with the exception of the dried fruit, stir and let it bake until dry. Cool and add the fruit.

Store the homemade granola in a tin or glass jar with a lid. It's great with cold milk or yogurt!

Sandwiches

Cheese waffle

1 serving

2 slices bread
1 tablespoon ketchup
1 slice boiled ham
1 thick slice of cheese, preferably Jarlsberg or mild light cheese

Spread one slice of bread with ketchup and top with ham and cheese. Top with the other slice of bread. Place in a waffle iron and press down the lid. Cook until the bread is crispy and golden.

Sandwich cake

1 whole-grain bread, sliced horizontally
1 white bread, sliced horizontally

Filling

135 g (4 oz) cream cheese
3 tablespoons chopped parsley
3 tablespoons chopped dill
1 tablespoon lemon juice
2 teaspoons Worcestershire sauce

Filling

125 g (4 oz) cream cheese
100 g (4 oz) smoked ham, chopped
2-3 tablespoons grated horseradish

Delicate sandwiches made with two kinds of bread

Filling

125 g (4 oz) cream cheese with pineapple and mandarin oranges

Layer the slices of bread with filling to form a loaf. Press down on the top and pack in plastic. Refrigerate under pressure. Cut into thin slices that can be cut in two on the diagonal to form triangles.

Bacon and cheese sandwiches

4 servings

4 bacon slices
4 slices white bread
4 tomatoes
shredded basil
salt and pepper
4 thick slices cheddar

Preheat the oven to 225°C (425°F). Fry the bacon until crispy. Drain on paper towels. Toast the bread and arrange on a baking sheet. Cut the tomatoes into thick slices and place on the bread. Sprinkle with basil, salt and pepper and top with cheese. Bake until the cheese starts to melt. Garnish each with basil and serve hot.

Anne's best sandwich

1 serving

Guacamole

1/2 avocado
4 tablespoons (1/4 cup) sour cream
1 garlic clove, minced
2 teaspoons lemon juice

2 slices bread
butter
1 tomato, sliced
50 g (2 oz) chicken or turkey, sliced
50 g (2 slices) Swiss cheese

Bacon and cheese sandwiches

Anne's best sandwich

Mash the avocado with the remaining ingredients. It can be a little lumpy. Fry the bread in butter. Spread one slice with guacamole. Top with remaining ingredients and the remaining bread. Fry until the cheese is melted. Serve with more tomatoes, chopped scallions, fresh herbs and the remaining guacamole.

Cheeseburger *with salami*

1 large burger bun (see following recipe)
1 teaspoon butter
1 tablespoon ketchup
2-4 lettuce leaves
2 slices spiced salami
3 thin onion rings
cucumber slices
tomato slices
2-3 slices cheese

Divide the bun in two and spread with butter and ketchup. Shred the lettuce and place on the bread with the remaining ingredients. Top with remaining bread. A good lunch with an apple and a glass of milk.

Burger buns

6 buns

25 g (2 tablespoons) butter
1 ½ dl (²/₃ cup) cold water
1 ½ dl (²/₃ cup) 2% milk
25 g (1 oz) fresh yeast
1 teaspoon salt
2 dl (³/₄ cup) finely ground whole wheat flour
4 ½ dl (2 cups) flour

Melt the butter in a saucepan. Remove from the heat and add water and milk. The liquid should be lukewarm, around 37°C (98°F). Crumble the yeast in a bowl and add the liquid. Stir until dissolved. Add salt and flour and mix until smooth and elastic. Use enough flour so the dough won't be sticky. Knead well. Divide into 6 equal parts and form into balls. Roll each ball flat, around 10 cm (4") in diameter. Place on baking sheet lined with baking parchment. Cover with plastic and let rise for around 15 minutes. Preheat the oven to 225°C (425°F). Brush with milk and sprinkle with coarse flour before baking. Bake for 8-10 minutes. Cool on a rack.

Bagel *with cream cheese and turkey*

1 bagel or roll
1 celery stalk
salad greens
3 tablespoons cream cheese
4 slices smoked turkey

Halve the bagel. Wash and slice the celery, shred the greens. Spread cream cheese on both bagel halves. Top with celery, greens and turkey. A great portable lunch.

Bagel with cream cheese and turkey

62

Tortilla rolls with cream cheese

Tortilla rolls *with cream cheese*

This is a good lunch with an orange and some raisins

2 tortillas (25 cm /10″) in diameter
4 tablespoons (¼ cup) cream cheese or fresh chevre
1 red bell pepper

Spread the tortilla with cheese. Clean and chop the pepper and sprinkle the bits over the cheese. Cut into quarters and roll up. Pack each roll separately in plastic. For an easier, less sticky lunch, peel the orange before packing.

Shrimp and salad in pita

Mackerel turnovers

Ciabatta *with egg salad*

Egg salad
2 hardcooked eggs, chopped
1 slice smoked salmon, shredded
3-4 tablespoons sour cream
1 teaspoon mustard
chopped dill and chives

butter
ciabatta
red and green oak leaf lettuce
Combine all ingredients for salad and serve on buttered ciabatta with lettuce.

Turkey and egg sandwich

1 slice country bread
butter
arugula
3-4 slices smoked turkey
4-5 cooked green asparagus stalks
1 hard cooked egg, quartered
chopped red onion
cress

Spread the bread with butter and top with arugula. Layer remaining ingredients in order.

Shrimp and salad *in pita*
4 servings

2 tablespoons mayonnaise
pinch five-spice blend
$^1\!/_2$ teaspoon Dijon mustard
shredded salad greens
2 scallions, thinly sliced
1 carrot, shredded
100 g (4 oz) fresh bean sprouts
1 tablespoon chopped fresh coriander
juice of $^1\!/_2$ lemon
salt and pepper
4 pita pockets
500 g shrimp, shelled

Combine mayonnaise, five-spice blend and mustard. Combine vegetables. Season with lemon juice, salt and pepper. Spread a thin layer of mayonnaise in each pita pocket. Fill with salad mix and shrimp. Serve immediately.

Fishburgers *in pita*
4 servings

4 large fishcakes (see recipe page 140)
butter
4 pita pockets
lettuce
sliced onion
sliced tomato
pickles
dressing or tartar sauce

Reheat the fish cakes in butter. Heat the pita pockets. Stuff each with a lettuce leaf and a fish burger. Top with onion, tomato and pickles. Drizzle over dressing.

Mackerel turnovers

4 sheets (US: 1 package) frozen puff pastry
400 g (14 oz) smoked mackerel
2 hard-cooked eggs
1 dl ($^1\!/_3$ cup) sour cream
beaten egg

Preheat the oven to 225°C (425°F). Partially defrost puff pastry and roll out. Cut out 15 cm (6") circles. Clean the fish and separate into chunks. Chop the eggs. Combine fish, eggs and sour cream. Spoon filling onto the pastry. Fold pastry over filling and press the edges together with a fork. Brush with beaten egg and bake for 15-20 minutes.

Helpful hint
These pastries can also be made with poached or fried mackerel and onion, bell peppers, zucchini, olives, dill and tarragon.

Fishburgers in pita

Eggs

– versatile and indispensable

An egg contains almost all the nutrients we need – in nature's own elegant packaging. It's a wonderful ingredient, so versatile that it can be the main ingredient in every meal. Its role in cooking makes it almost indispensable. Eggs are a leavening agent, they bind ingredients together, they thicken, color and emulsify foods, and they make them shiny. And last but not least, they taste good, too.

The size of a hen's egg varies from 45 to 80 grams. An average egg weighs 65 grams. Broken down into individual components, the shell weighs around 8 grams, the yolk 22 grams and the white 33 grams. A small egg has just as much shell as a large one, because the larger the egg, the thinner the shell. Just as with clothing, egg cartons are marked S, M. L, and XL. Most Norwegian eggs are M or L.

Eggs keep well. According to the "use by" date stamped on the carton, eggs should be used within 28 days after they are laid. Previously, the limit was 45 days. Eggs have not changed, but now Norway has to follow guidelines issued by the European Economic Zone, and those guidelines come from countries with salmonella in eggs. Because they are of such good quality, Norwegian eggs can be stored in the refrigerator long past the "use by" date.

Nutrients in 1 egg

Protein	8 g
Fat	6.3 g
Iron	1.2 mg
Vitamin D	0.9 µg
Vitamin E	1.1 mg
Calcium	31.5 mg
Vitamin B2	0.3 mg
Vitamin A	88 µg
Vitamin B	0.04 mg
Niacin	2.0 mg

In addition, an egg contains selenium, iodine, copper, manganese, fluoride and zinc. An egg had around 90 calories, around the same as a glass of soda pop.

If you are worried about cholesterol in eggs, fortunately that is just a myth. The egg yolk does contain cholesterol, but it is not the kind that affects blood cholesterol. The fat in eggs is primarily unsaturated and does not increase the cholesterol in the blood.

Egg tips

If eggs sit at room temperature for at least half an hour before cooking, they are easier to peel.

Room temperature eggs
– produce greater volume when beaten and in baked goods
– are easier to separate into yolk and white
– do not crack so easily during cooking (you can also stick a hole in the rounded end of the egg before cooking.

Ciabatta with egg salad and country bread with turkey and egg

Dessert omelet

Raw eggs can be frozen. Crack the egg and whisk it lightly together or freeze yolk and white separately. Whisk the yolks lightly first. Do not freeze boiled eggs.

If you have extra egg yolks, use them in custard or in ice cream.

If you have extra egg whites, use them in almond ring cakes, meringues or angel food cake.

If you find eggs with two yolks, there is a natural explanation. Young hens often lay eggs with two yolks in their "trial and error" phase.

Cooking time for eggs
Soft-boiled 3-6 minutes
Semi-soft 6-8 minutes
Hard-boiled 8-10 minutes

Egg dishes

Basic omelet
2 eggs
2 tablespoons water
salt
butter

Beat the eggs with water and salt. Heat butter in a small skillet until bubbly. Add the eggs. Push cooked egg toward the center, to let raw egg run out. Place filling on half the egg. Fold the other half of the omelet over the filling. Turn out onto a plate so that the underside ends up on top.

Note!
This goes quickly! The egg shouldn't burn.

Ideas for fillings
Grated cheese, buttered leeks or spring onions, smoked fish, smoked turkey, bacon, herbs

Dessert omelet
2 eggs
2 tablespoons any kind of cream
sugar
unsalted butter

Make according to previous recipe. Serve with fresh or frozen berries.

Cheese omelet *in bread*
A French cheese omelet is a lovely lunch dish, especially when served with a slice or two of salami on country bread.

2 servings

6 eggs
6 tablespoons milk
100 g (1 cup) grated cheese such as Jarlsberg
salt and freshly ground pepper
butter
2 spring onions, chopped

Beat eggs and milk with half the cheese, a little salt and pepper. Heat some butter in a small pan, add the eggs and cook over low heat. When golden and set, sprinkle with spring onion and the remaining cheese.

Helpful hint
This omelet can be made in advance, cut into 4 wedges and packed in plastic.

Butter 8 slices of bread and pack in parchment paper. When it's time for lunch, place an omelet wedge between 2 slices of bread, adding a little lettuce and tomato, if desired.

Cheese omelet sandwich

Baked eggs

Baked eggs

10 servings

This is great hiking food – bread and filling all in one.

5 dl (2 cups) fine whole wheat flour
5 dl (2 cups) flour
1 teaspoon salt
50 g (1 ³/₄ oz) yeast
3 dl (1 ¹/₄ cups) warm milk
2 tablespoons butter, melted
10 eggs

Combine flour and salt. Dissolve the yeast in the milk and stir in the butter. Mix together, kneading until smooth and elastic. Cover and let rise until double. Boil the eggs for 5-7 minutes. Let cool and remove the shells. Divide the dough into 10 pieces of equal size and roll flat. Place an egg on each and enclose with the dough. Place on a baking sheet, seam down. Let rise for 30 minutes more. Preheat the oven to 250°C (475°F). Bake on the lowest rill for around 15 minutes. Halve the rolls and serve with anchovies, bacon or caviar.

Farmer omelet

Farmer omelet

4 servings

6-8 boiled potatoes
1 onion
1 leek
oil
3 smoked turkey sausages
8 eggs
1 teaspoon salt
¹/₂ teaspoon pepper
few slices salami, shredded

Preheat the oven to 200°C (400°F). Dice the potatoes and spread them over the bottom a greased ovenproof dish. Cut the onion into thin wedges. Wash and slice the leek. Sauté both in oil until soft, then place on the potatoes. Dice the sausages and brown without adding fat. Sprinkle over the potatoes. Beat the eggs, salt and pepper together and pour over the potatoes. Sprinkle with salami. Bake for around 20 minutes, until set. Serve with crusty bread.

Onion quiche

4-6 servings

Pie shell
125 g (4 ¹/₂ oz) butter
200 g (1 ¹/₃ cups) flour
2 tablespoons water

Filling
2-3 onions
butter
5 eggs
2 dl (³/₄ cup) milk
1 dl (¹/₂ cup) light cream
¹/₂ teaspoon salt
¹/₄ teaspoon pepper
100 g (1 cup) grated Jarlsberg cheese mixed with Parmesan
50 g (2 oz) spicy turkey sausage, chopped

Crumble butter and flour, add cold water and mix lightly together or pulse together in a food processor. Gather into a ball, wrap in plastic and refrigerate for around 30 minutes. Preheat the oven to 200°C (400°F). Press the dough over the

Onion quiche

Cheese soufflé

bottom and up the sides of a pie pan and prick with a fork. Bake for around 10 minutes, until it starts to turn golden.

Lower the temperature to 180°C (350°F). Slice the onion. Sauté in butter until barely tender. Arrange over the pie shell. Beat eggs, milk, cream, salt and pepper together and pour over the onion. Sprinkle with grated cheese and sausage. Bake for 25 minutes more, until set. Let rest for around 5 minutes before slicing. Serve warm with a green salad.

Cheese soufflé
4 servings

3 tablespoons butter
3 tablespoons flour
3 dl (1 ¼ cups) milk
½ teaspoon salt
5 eggs
300 g (10 oz/3 cups) grated Jarlsberg cheese

Preheat the oven to 180°C (350°F). Melt butter and stir in flour. Gradually whisk in the milk, whisking until thickened. Add salt. Let sauce cool slightly. Separate eggs. Stir yolks and cheese into the sauce. Stiffly beat the egg whites and fold into the soufflé mixture. Pour into a greased 1 ¼ liter (5 cup) soufflé dish and bake for 1 hour.

71

Milk

– a valuable cultural treasure

Earlier generations used milk in many ways. It was food, drink, winter provisions, and something to sell or barter. There are many traditional Norwegian milk dishes that should not be forgotten. Dishes with such strange names as *dravle*, *kjelost*, *mysla*, *prim* and *gomme* are all part of the Norwegian identity. Preparing them required knowledge, understanding and patience.

The recipes were handed down from mother to daughter over generations. Today, very few milk products are made in the home. The old dishes are just too time-consuming. Norwegian dairies have taken over that job and make many traditional specialties that are still modern, nourishing and appropriate food and drink for modern consumers.

Milk producers today have modern barns with milking machines and special tanks. At the farm, milk is channeled directly from machine to tank in a closed system of pipes. In the tank, it is rapidly chilled down to a maximum of 4°C (39°F), before it is picked-up and delivered to the dairy. Once there, the milk is pumped into huge storage vats. The temperature of 4°C (39°F) remains constant. Around half of all milk is used in "wet" milk products. The rest is made into butter, cheese, desserts and dry milk.

The milk is first separated into cream and skim milk in a centrifuge. The cream, the lightest part of the milk, is drained off, leaving skim milk, with only .1% fat.

Milk is homogenized to prevent the cream from rising to the top. The fat globules are split into smaller particles that are distributed throughout the milk. This does not affect the nutritional value of the milk.

According to law, all milk has to be pasteurized, heat-treated, at the dairy. This kills off any bacteria that can cause illness or spoil the milk. The nutritional value of the milk is almost identical before and after pasteurization.

From market to table
Milk is a very perishable foodstuff, very sensitive to temperature changes. It is important to maintain as stable a temperature as possible at all times. As an example, it takes around 20 hours for milk to reach its optimal storage temperature of 4°C (39°F), if it has been allowed to sit for two hours at cool room temperature (around 18°C (65°F). The longer milk is not properly refrigerated, the faster it spoils. That's why it is so difficult to know exactly how long it will keep. When in doubt, smell or taste the milk. It may still be fresh, even after the "use by" date stamped on the carton. If you are still uncertain, use the milk (or cream) in recipes that require cooking. You can always use the milk in pancakes or waffles.

Thank you cow! Norwegians are big milk consumers. They start young.

Freezing

If you have extra milk or cream and plan to be away from home for a while, you can store it in the freezer. It will not improve in quality, but it's better than throwing it away. Both milk and cream will often change texture after freezing – milk becomes watery, and cream can get grainy. But that doesn't matter if they are used in hot dishes. It might be a good idea to keep a little milk or cream in the freezer. Freeze cream in ice cube trays so that you can add a cube or two to a sauce or soup for a little extra richness.

Soured milk

Cultured milk, often called cultured buttermilk, is made of skim milk. In Norway, there are also cultured milk products with 1.5 % and 3.9% fat, Cultura and Kefir. Both are highly pasteurized and homogenized under high pressure for optimal quality. After pasteurization, the milk is lowered to 20-22°C (68-72°F), lactic acid is added, and after around 20 hours, the milk becomes thick and acidic in flavor. For Kefir, special granules that contain yeast are also added to the milk. Cultura is cultured at 37°C (98°F) with bacteria that is beneficial to the digestive system.

In certain ecological farms in the Trøndelag area, "thick milk" is made in the traditional manner, using a special kind of grass.

Cream and sour cream

Cream has always been the most prized component of milk, and cream plays a much larger role in Norwegian cuisine than in almost any other kitchen. There are many varieties of cream and products made with cream, all preserving its exquisite flavor, color and consistency.

Yoghurt

Cream desserts are still all-time favorites, and soups and sauces alwaysl taste better with that splash of cream. Sour cream is no longer exclusively summer food. It's as wonderful in a Christmas salad as it is alongside summer mackerel.

Norwegian whipping cream contains 35% fat. It's pasteurized but not homogenized, because that would make it difficult to whip. Always chill the cream thoroughly before whipping.

Norwegian light cream contains 22% fat and is good in all kinds of soups and sauces. It is excellent in puddings and cream fillings that do not require whipping capability.

Coffee cream, sometimes called half-and-half, contains 10% fat. It is used for coffee and in cooked dishes.

Powdered cream can be found in some shops. It is not made in Norway. It should not be confused with "coffee whiteners" that are made of soy protein and vegetable fat.

Soured heavy cream contains 35% fat. It is pasteurized, but only slightly homogenized, so that the fat leaches out when cooked, important when making *rømmegrøt*, traditional Norwegian sour cream porridge.

Soured light cream contains 20% fat. It is pasteurized and homogenized for a thick, smooth texture. It is good in cold sauces, salad dressings and desserts. It can separate when heated.

Crème frâiche is pasteurized, homogenized, lightly soured cream with 35% fat. It is especially good in hot dishes, soups, sauces, creamed dishes, stews, etc., because it doesn't separate when heated. It is also good cold, with fruit, berries, cakes and other desserts.

Rømmekolle is soured cream with 10% fat. It is pasteurized and homogenized and makes a lovely little dessert with crushed zwieback and sugar.

Melkering, another specifically Norwegian product, is low-fat milk that is pasteurized and homogenized first. Cream is then added and the mixture is soured. Because of that, there is a layer of cream on top, and the fat content is 3.9%. It is eaten like *rømmekolle*.

Kesam is a low-fat fresh cheese available in two varieties, Kesam Original with 8% fat and Kesam Mager (low-fat), with only 1% fat.

Yogurt – food of the gods

Soured milk has been used for eons. In warm air, lactic acid bacteria that occur naturally in milk break down milk sugar (lactose) and form lactic acid. This acid hinders growth of other bacteria, thus sour milk keeps better than fresh milk. In addition, sour milk has always been considered easier to digest than sweet milk.

In India, soured milk is known as the food of the gods. In ancient Persia, women used sour milk both as food and as anti-wrinkle cream.

People living in the steppes of Asia and in the Balkans have long been known both for their longevity and for their high consumption of soured milk. Nature and a good climate play a role, but diet and physical activity are also important factors. In Abkasia in Georgia, a place known for its active seniors, the diet is based on lots of fresh fruit and vegetables, very little meat, and lots of yogurt. A consumption of 1 liter (4 cups) per day is not unusual. According to the inhabitants, yogurt is the cream of nature's gifts. Eating it is like taking an internal bath - every day.

What is the secret?

Around 1900, the Russian microbiologist and later Nobel Prize winner, Ilia Metnikov began working at the Pasteur Institute in Paris. He regarded Bulgarian sour milk as "man's ally against aging". Eventually he discovered the lactic acid bacteria in this type of sour milk, lactobacillus bulgaricus and streptococcus thermophilus. Milk cultured with these bacteria did not just turn sour, it also acquired a very special fresh flavor. Metnikov called this milk "yogurt", the Turkish word for sour milk. A Russian in Paris gave Bulgarian sour milk a Turkish name! Eventually the name became international. Yogurt reached Norway in the middle of the 1950s and is produced in many varieties today.

The basis for yogurt is milk with the addition of 2.5% dried skim milk, making its nutritional content higher than that of regular milk. The milk is heated to 85°C (185°F) for around 30 minutes and then homogenized. A special lactic acid or yogurt culture is added.

Souring takes place at 42°C (110°F) for 3-4 hours, either in large tanks or after the milk has been tapped into containers. If the souring process takes place in tanks, the yogurt has to be stirred before it is tapped into containers. Then it's called "stirred yogurt" and is thinner in consistency than yogurt soured in containers.

Butter

Butter was both sold and bartered until well into the last century. Several hundred years ago, butter was money! After the tax reform of 1617, taxes could be paid in butter. Although butter is no longer negotiable currency, it's still the fine product it always has been, exquisite and aromatic and part of our culture worth preserving.

Milk production is the basis for farming in Norway.

The basis for all butter is fresh milk that is separated into skim milk and cream. The cream, which contains 35-42% fat, is churned into butter. It takes 20 liters (5 gallons) of full-fat milk to make 1 kilo (2 ¼ lb) butter.

Cream for butter production is subjected to rigorous heat treatment. The temperature reaches 98°C (208°F) for a few seconds, to kill off any harmful microorganisms. High pasteurization is important to prevent butter from spoiling easily.

After pasteurization, the cream is pumped into tanks and a culture made of different types of lactic acid bacteria is added. The technology

behind this is a science in itself. Butter production involves enhancing natural flavors and aroma. This occurs when certain types of lactic acid bacteria transform the lactose in cream and release the lovely flavor we associate with butter.

While in the tank, the cream also is heat-treated to create a good environment for the lactic acid bacteria and to obtain the desired consistency in the finished product.

There are several special local types of butter, made with soured cream and extra salt.

Cheese

– delicious natural products

The basis for all cheese production is milk, which is composed of close to 90% water. Cheese contains from 18 to 70% water, according to the type of cheese. The curds, or casein, contain most of the milk protein. Butterfat is added to cheese in varying amounts according to the desired fat content for the finished cheese. Cheese is a concentrated form of milk's most valuable components.

While milk stays fresh for only a matter of days, and butter for several weeks, most cheeses stay fresh for many months. Most cheeses need a relatively long time to mature and develop flavor, and there are cheeses, such as Edam, that should be aged for a year or two to develop their characteristic flavor.

Many of the cheeses that we enjoy today have been around for a long time. Norwegian oak barrels were exported to Holland, and we received Edam and Leyden cheese in return. It did not take long before both cheeses were made in Norway - as Norwegian *Edamer* and *Nøkkelost* (key cheese) – the latter because Leyden cheese was decorated with a crossed key motif.

The longer cheese is aged, the sharper it tastes. Piquant cheeses require only a minimum of accompaniments.

Specialists from Switzerland taught the people of the Østerdal valley to make Swiss cheese, and the idea to make blue mold cheese came from French Roquefort, Italian Gorgonzola and English Stilton. Norwegians learned to make cheddar in England and were inspired by the French to make Port Salut, Saint Paulin, brie and camembert. Jarlsberg and Ridder cheese are Norwegian inventions.

Today´s *Jarlsberg* was developed at the college of Agriculture in the late 1950s. A new technique and a new bacteria culture were used. The result was a cheese now known the world over.

Eventually, dairies were established, and they took over churning and cheese production. And new cheeses, methods and techniques were developed. In the past, small dairies churned butter, produced cheese and sold milk, but today, cheese production is specialized, so that

one dairy seldom produces more than one kind of cheese.

Norway is the only country in the world in which the production and sales of brown whey cheese really counts. Around 30% of all cheese consumed in Norway is brown cheese. More than any other Norwegian cheese, brown cheese derives from the mountain dairies in the countryside. The birthplace of brown cheese, a must on every Norwegian breakfast table, was the Gudbrandsdal valley. It was not unusual to boil down whey, but adding cream was something new. That idea probably came from Anne Haav from North Fron in the Gudbrandsdal valley.

Today, whey, milk and cream are mixed together and concentrated first to 50-60 degree dry solids. They are boiled in the final stage of cooking, and the cheese is transferred to machines for stirring and packing. The whey used in making brown cheese comes from standard white (really yellow) cheese production or from casein. Casein is made from skim milk and is therefore non-fat. Because the whey from casein is not soured, it is especially suitable for brown cheese. The whey left after curds are formed in standard cheese production is slightly acidic, but it still can be made into brown cheese.

The color and texture of brown cheese have always been a topic for discussion. Some like hard, dark cheese, while others prefer it light, mild and soft. This is a regional preference. In North Norway, the cheese is supposed to be almost as light as Swiss cheese, while in West Norway, it is supposed to be dark, golden brown. East Norwegians like something in between. The dairies now try to satisfy all three preferences by making light, medium and dark brown cheese.

The different types of cheese derive from different kinds of milk with different fat contents. *Ekte geitost* (Real goat cheese) is made from 100% goat milk, while *fløtemysost* (cream whey cheese) is made from cow milk, cream and whey. *Gudbrandsdalsost* (called Ski Queen when exported) is a mixture of both cow and goat milk. One kilo (2 1/4 lb) cheese is supposed to contain at least 1 liter (quart) goat milk. Full-fat brown cheeses contain 27% fat, half-fat 16%, while low fat whey cheese contains only 7% fat.

Prim is a sweetened brown cheese spread made of concentrated whey with some cream. The manufacturing process is the same as for brown cheese, but it is not reduced to the same degree. Sugar is added during the last phase of cooking. The low-fat variety has added caramel flavoring.

Quality

Brown cheese has a smooth, creamy texture with no sugar crystals, and it can be sliced when cold. It should be a light golden brown and taste clean and sweet. Real goat cheese has a pronounced goat milk flavor, while *Gudbrandsdalsost* is full-flavored but not so strong.

Prim has a smooth texture and can be spread while cold. It is an even light brown color and has a sweet, clean flavor. Low-fat *Prim* has a pronounced caramel aroma.

All brown cheeses are subjected to stringent quality control, both during production and of the end product.

Cheese does not improve with freezing, but if you are left with cheese after a party or you plan to be away for a while, it's better to freeze it than let it get moldy. Frozen cheese will often be crumbly and difficult to slice. It's better to use it in cooked dishes, such as pizza, soups, sauces, soufflés, gratins and baked goods. An exception to this rule is *gamalost*. It can be frozen without any change in texture. In this way, you can control its pungency.

Storing and aging

Depending on the variety, it can take from 1 to 15 months before the cheese is ready to sell. Cheese with a high dry solid content (low water content), such as Parmesan, is the best-suited for aging. Norwegian cheeses that age well include Edam, Norvegia, Swiss and cheddar, and under optimal conditions, they can be stored for many years.

Super-aged *Norvegia* is aged for a minimum of 15 months and has a completely different flavor and consistency from regular Norvegia, which is aged for 2-3 months. *Gamalost* (old cheese) actually has one of the shortest aging periods before it is sent to market – 3-4 weeks. Brie has a hard center when immature, but it softens, from outer edge in toward the center, as it ages.

With respect to aging, Edam is in a class of its own. Why not specialize in vintage Edams? Buy several cheeses before Christmas and store each one in its own airy wooden box. Mark it with the year of production and store it for 4-5 years in a cold cellar or refrigerator.

It's fun to build up a supply of vintage Edams. Then you make your own interesting Christmas gifts.

Edam cheese is packed in a tight red plastic covering. As the cheese matures, whey drains off and forms a layer between the plastic and the cheese. The cheese itself dries as it ages, and eventually the texture becomes similar to that of Parmesan cheese. It can't be sliced with a cheese plane, but you can cut it into chunks and enjoy it with a glass of good wine, preferably a sweet white wine, or you can use it in recipes calling for Parmesan.

Different varieties of cheeses

Firm white cheeses

Lactic acid bacteria are responsible to a great degree for the flavor, texture and kinds of holes in cheese. Some bacteria can produce carbon dioxide gas, which forms the holes. Propion acid culture is added to Jarlsberg cheese to give it its characteristic flavor and large round holes.

Norvegia – creamy and easy to slice with a cheese plane. The flavor is mild, aromatic and slightly acidic.

Variations: Low-fat, aged, well-aged and super-aged Norvegia and Ecological Norvegia.

Jarlsberg – with a slightly sweet and nutty flavor thanks to a special acid culture. Jarlsberg has large round holes and is sold with and without rind. For a couple of generations, Jarlsberg has been a very successful export to the US, Canada, Australia, Japan, and other countries in Europe.

Variations: Low-fat, and lightly-smoked Jarlsberg. The latter has been dipped in smoky brine that tints the rind brown and gives the cheese a piquant flavor.

Nøkkelost – a Norvegia type of cheese with added cloves and caraway seed.

Edam – a smooth, easy to slice cheese with a clean, aromatic, acidic flavor.

TINE Gräddost (creamy cheese) – a soft mild yellow cheese that can be cut with a knife.

Balsfjordost – a white goat cheese, rich and mild in flavor with a texture similar to *gräddost*.

Surface-ripened cheeses

During ripening, these cheeses are spread with a layer of bloom that gives them a special flavor. The intensity of flavor varies according to the degree of aging and whether the bloom layer is retained or washed off.

Port Salut – a soft cheese with a sharp, aromatic flavor that can be cut with a knife.

Ridder – smooth and easy to cut with a knife. Aromatic and piquant in flavor, it can be rather sharp. Ridder is sold both with the orange bloom and vacuum-packed without.

Moldy cheeses

All mold cheeses are matured with the help of specific mold cultures, which give them their characteristic flavors

White mold cheeses

Brie – a soft French cheese with a white rind. Norwegian Brie is stabilized, so that it has the right texture from the first day it is sold. It never becomes runny in the center. It has a creamy texture and a fresh, acidic flavor.

Camembert – a soft French cheese with a white rind. Norwegian Camembert is stabilized, so that it has the right texture from the first day it is sold. It never becomes runny in the center. It has a creamy texture and a mild, rich flavor.

Norwegian chèvre from Haukeli – a 100% goat milk cheese

Variations: With white mold and plain.

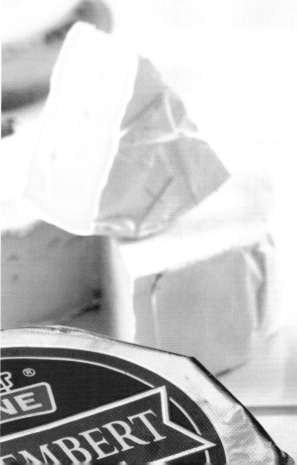

Reinheim – a rich, mature soft white mold cheese with whole green peppercorns.

Snøhetta – a rich, mature soft white mold cheese made of half goat and half cow milk.

Blue mold cheeses
Holes are poked into these cheeses to create favorable conditions for growth of mold inside. The mold is part of the maturation process and contributes to the richness and aroma of the cheeses.

Normanna – an aromatic semi-soft blue cheese that can be sliced with a cheese plane, yet is still spreadable.

Norzola – a blue cheese that can be cut with a knife.

Royal Blue – covered with white mold, veined with blue mold inside. It has a rich, aromatic flavor, a creamy texture and can be cut with a knife.

Gamalost
Made from soured skim milk, extra low-fat and low-salt. Matured with the help of mucor mucedo mold, related to penicillin.

Pultost
A curd cheese made from soured skim milk with added caraway.

Cream cheeses/fresh cheeses
These are immature cheeses and can be used in cheesecakes and frostings.

TINE Cream cheese – a soft, spreadable fresh cheese, available both plain and flavored.

Snøfrisk – a soft, fresh white cream cheese made of 80% goat milk and 20% cream from cow milk with a fresh, acidic flavor.

Fresh cheese – such as cottage cheese, which is fresh curds from sweet milk. There is also an old-fashioned variety of cottage cheese made from soured milk.

Invite your friends for cheese
A cheese table is a good alternative to a cold buffet. You can serve either cold platters or a mix of cold and hot dishes. The cheese platters should feature several families of cheeses – some mild, some sharp, some spicy, some firm and some soft varieties. The larger the table, the more variety. A cheese table can be a journey in flavors.

Don't cut up too much cheese. Place a couple of knives on each platter and let your guests take as much as they want.

Count on 250 g (8 oz) cheese per person for a meal.

Purchase the cheese right before serving, and store each cheese separately in its packaging in the refrigerator or other cold place. Do not allow the cheese to come into contact with raw vegetables or other strong-flavored foodstuffs. For the most flavor, cheese should be served at room temperature. Take it out of the refrigerator at least one hour before serving.

Add lots of exciting accompaniments. Cheese tastes wonderful with sweet fruit and berries. Nuts of all kinds are also good. Today you can buy many different dried fruits – these are delicious with cheese, especially if you have marinated them in a little port wine or aquavit first.

Whether you serve red or white wine with cheese is a matter of taste. White wine often goes extra well with cheese – serve both dry and sweet wines, so the guests can make their own combinations of wine and cheese.

Fruit juices and tea are also good with cheese.

Good advice

- Do not purchase too large chunks of cheese at once, even though it keeps well.
- Pack each chunk of cheese tightly in plastic wrap before storing, and change it frequently. Do not store cheese in a humid place.
- Store cheese in a clean refrigerator. It keeps better that way.
- Cheese tastes best when close to the "use by" date.
- The flavor and aroma of cheese are best at room temperature. Cheese for lunch-time sandwiches is good right from the refrigerator, but for extra special flavor sensations, take the cheese out of the refrigerator at least 30 minutes before serving.
- Freezing affects the texture of cheese, though the flavor is still good. It's a good idea to grate hard cheeses before freezing. Use the frozen grated cheese for cooking. Do not store cheese in the freezer for longer than 3 months.
- *Gamalost* (old cheese) is an exception to that rule and becomes creamier after freezing. Buy a whole *gamalost* and freeze it in chunks when the flavor is just the way you like it. Pack each piece separately in plastic or foil and you have good *gamalost* available whenever you want it. It can be defrosted and refrozen two or three times without deteriorating. This means that you can freeze a whole cheese for a party. Afterward, you can just put the rest back in the freezer.
- Mold cheeses can also be frozen, but they should be defrosted in the refrigerator and used as soon as possible.
- Cream cheeses do not freeze well. They become granular.
- When cooking with cheese, do not allow it to boil, because it forms threads. That's why it's best to add cheese toward the end of the cooking time.
- Count on 250 g (8 oz) per person for a cheese meal, 150 g (5 oz) as a snack, 50 g (2 oz) for a starter, and 75 g (2 1/2 oz) for dessert.
- When making a cheese platter, choose a variety of cheeses from mild to slightly sharp to very sharp.
- Do not serve too many different kinds of cheeses together at once. It's better to serve a generous amount of just a few varieties.

A cheese platter is simple and quick to prepare, and it tastes good, too. Mild cheeses are good with hearty breads.

Porridge

– bring out the porridge pots!

Porridge deserves a central place in our diet. Porridge is cheap and easy to make, and it adds variety to our daily diet. The combination of flour, grain and milk products is very nourishing.

Porridge for breakfast is easy and good. Make a big pot of porridge once a week. It keeps well in the refrigerator – for at least a week. You can reheat it one portion at a time, either in the microwave oven or on top of the stove.

Whole-wheat porridge
4 servings

1 liter (quart) low-fat milk
2 ½ dl (1 cup) coarse whole-wheat flour
1 teaspoon salt

Stir milk and flour together in a saucepan. Heat to boiling. Let simmer until thickened. Season with salt. Serve with butter, sugar, cinnamon and cold milk.

Good morning porridge.
4 servings

10 dried apricots
1 liter (4 cups) water
3 dl (1 ¼ cups) rolled oats
1 dl (½ cup) wheat bran
1 dl (⅓ cup) sunflower seeds
3 tablespoons hazelnuts
½ teaspoon salt

Cut the apricots into small pieces with a scissors and let simmer in the water for 10 minutes. Add all ingredients except salt and cook for 5 minutes. Season with salt. Serve with sweet or cultured milk or yogurt.

Oatmeal *with honey and fruit*
4 servings

3 dl (1 ¼ cups) rolled oats
1 dl (½ cup) bran
1 liter (4 cups) milk
1 dl (⅓ cup) honey
1 dl (½ cup) chopped hazelnuts
1 dl (⅓ cup) sunflower seeds
1 teaspoon salt
1 apple

Combine oats, bran and milk in a saucepan. Heat to boiling and let simmer for 5 minutes.

Add honey, nuts and seeds. Season with salt. Cut the apple into chunks and add to the porridge. Serve with cold milk or juice.

Oat gruel
4 servings

2 ½ dl (1 cup) water
2 dl (¾ cup) rolled oats
1 liter (4 cups) milk
½ teaspoon salt

Combine water, oats and milk in a saucepan. Heat to boiling, stirring constantly. Let simmer for around 10 minutes, stirring often. Season with salt and serve with sugar and cinnamon. Gruel is a wonderful sleeping agent or a great breakfast on a cold winter morning.

Helpful hint
Substitute ¾ dl (⅓ cup) rice, semolina or tapioca for oats for different flavor and texture.

Different kinds of porridge

Sunflower seed porridge
4 servings

1 liter (4 cups) water
2 ½ dl (1 cup) rolled oats
2 tablespoons sunflower seeds
1 teaspoon salt
1 dl (⅓ cup) sour cream
1 dl (½ cup) cultured buttermilk

Heat water to boiling, sprinkle with oats and sunflower seeds. Lower heat and let simmer until the oats are cooked. Season with salt. Heat the sour cream and buttermilk, but do not allow to boil or the mixture will curdle. Pour over the porridge and serve with sugar.

Rye porridge
4 servings

2 ½ dl (1 cup) coarse whole-rye flour
5 dl (2 cups) cultured buttermilk
5 dl (2 cups) full-fat milk
1 teaspoon salt

Whisk flour and buttermilk together in a saucepan. Heat carefully to boiling. Gradually whisk in the milk. Let simmer for around 10 minutes. Add salt. Serve with applesauce and buttermilk or regular milk.

Sports porridge
4 servings

1 liter (quart) milk
2 ½ dl (1 cup) coarse whole-wheat flour
1 teaspoon salt
1 dl (½ cup) raisins
4 tablespoons (¼ cup) crushed pineapple

Heat milk to boiling and gradually whisk in the flour. There should not be any lumps. Let simmer for 8-10 minutes. Season with salt. Add raisins and pineapple or your choice of fruit. Serve with sugar. Cultured buttermilk can be substituted for some of the milk.

Telemark porridge
4 servings

2 ½ dl (1 cup) water
60 g (2 oz) butter
5 dl (2 cups) whipping cream
2 ½ dl (1 cup) cultured buttermilk
1 egg
around 125 g (1 scant cup) flour
1 teaspoon salt

This porridge is easier to make than *rømmegrøt*. In the past, this porridge was often cooked with a little barley flour. That made it darker and more intensely flavored.

Heat water and butter to boiling. Whisk cream, cultured milk and egg together, then whisk into the hot water. Let simmer for 15 minutes. Serve with cured meats, flatbread and lefse. For a more filling meal, serve *gamalost*, *pultost* and real *geitost* on buttered lefse alongside.

Sour cream porridge
6-8 servings

1 liter (4 cups) natural sour cream (do not use light sour cream or any sour cream with stabilizers, starches or gelatin added)
3 ½ dl (1 ½ cups) flour
1 liter (4 cups) milk
2 teaspoons salt

Heat sour cream to boiling, cover and let simmer for 2 minutes. Stir in half the flour. Stir vigorously until the butterfat begins to leach out. Skim off the butter and stir in the remaining flour. Add the milk and stir until smooth. No lumps should remain. Let simmer for 3 minutes. Season with salt. Serve with your choice of the following: grated brown cheese, lightly sweetened strawberries, raisins, chopped nuts, sugar and cinnamon. For a bigger meal, serve a platter of cured meats alongside the porridge.

Helpful hint
This porridge also can be prepared with equal parts regular and cultured milk. That gives it a fresh, slightly sour flavor.

Prize-winning *rømmegrøt*

from West Norway
4 servings

6 dl (2 ½ cups) whipping cream
1 egg
3 dl (1 ¼ cups) flour
6 dl (2 ½ cups) cultured buttermilk
1-2 teaspoons salt

Whisk cream and egg in a saucepan. Sprinkle over half the flour. Heat to boiling and let simmer without stirring until the butterfat begins to leach out. Skim off the butter and stir in the remaining flour. Add the milk and stir until smooth. Let simmer for around 5 minutes, stirring often. Season with salt and serve with the butter, sugar, cinnamon and red berry juice.

Rice porridge

4 servings

1 ½ dl (⅔ cup) rice
4 dl (1 ⅔ cups) water
1 liter (quart) milk
1 teaspoon salt

Cook rice in water, add milk and simmer until the rice is tender and the porridge is thickened. Serve with butter, sugar and cinnamon. Red berry juice tastes good alongside.

Semolina porridge

4 servings

1 liter (quart) milk
1 ¼ dl (½ cup) semolina
2 tablespoons butter
2-3 tablespoons sugar
2-3 drops almond extract

Heat milk to boiling. Whisk in the semolina and reheat to boiling. Cover and let simmer for 15-20 minutes, stirring occasionally. Add butter and sugar. Serve hot or cold – with red berry juice or berries or red fruit sauce alongside.

Rice-semolina porridge

4 servings

2 dl (1 cup) porridge rice
½ dl (¼ cup) semolina
14 dl (5 ½ cups) milk
½ - 1 teaspoon salt

Combine rice, semolina and milk in a saucepan and heat to boiling, stirring often. Let simmer for around 20 minutes, stirring occasionally. Season with salt and serve with butter, sugar and cinnamon.

Minute pudding

4 servings

5 dl (2 cups) cold milk
1 tablespoon flour
1½-2 tablespoons potato starch
1 egg
1 tablespoon sugar
1 tablespoon butter
2 tablespoons chopped almonds (optional) or 3 drops almond extract (optional)

Combine milk and both flours in a saucepan and heat to boiling, stirring often. Let simmer for around 1 minute. Whisk together egg and sugar. Remove from the heat and whisk in the egg. Stir in the butter and almonds or extract. Serve porridge hot or cold with red berry sauce.

Rømmegrøt

Pancakes and waffles

– old favorites served in new ways

Waffles, pancakes, coin pankakes and lefse. Young and old alike have enjoyed these every-day favorites for generations. Local specialities like *dravle*, *søst* and egg cheese are delicions alongside.

Coin pancakes – *basic recipe*
Around 30 pancakes

3 tablespoons butter
4 dl (1 ²/₃ cups) flour
3 dl (1 ¼ cups) milk
5 eggs
3 ½ tablespoons sugar
½ teaspoon salt
1 teaspoon baking powder
butter

Melt the butter and pour into a food processor with the remaining ingredients. Process until smooth. Let batter rest for around 15 minutes. Fry in a little butter in a hot non-stick pan. Flip when the batter begins to dry on the surface. Eat warm with jam or berry compote.

Rice pancakes
Around 20 pancakes

3 dl (1 ¼ cups) cold rice porridge
3 eggs
3 ½ tablespoons flour
3 ½ tablespoons sugar
½ teaspoon baking powder
½ teaspoon vanilla sugar
½ teaspoon salt
butter

Place all ingredients in a food processor and process until smooth. Let batter rest for around 15 minutes. Fry in a little butter in a hot non-stick pan. Flip when the batter begins to dry on the surface. Serve warm, preferably with lingon-berries and sour cream.

French toast
2 servings

2 eggs
2 tablespoons sugar
2 ½ dl (1 cup) milk
½ teaspoon cardamom
¼ teaspoon cinnamon
4 slices white bread
butter

Lightly beat eggs with sugar, milk and spices. Soak the bread in this mixture until thoroughly moistened. Fry in butter in a non-stick pan over medium heat until golden on both sides. Serve piping hot with jam.

Tips
French toast was originally served with red berry sauce, and it's really delicious.

Waffles
Around 10

100 g (3 ½ oz) butter
4 eggs
4-5 tablespoons sugar
½ teaspoon cardamom
5 dl (2 cups) flour
½ teaspoon baking powder
5 dl (2 cups) milk

Melt the butter. Combine in a bowl with the remaining ingredients and beat until smooth. Let the batter rest for around 15 minutes. It should be the texture of a thick sauce. If too stiff, add a little cold water. Bake on a greased hot waffle iron. Freshly baked, lukewarm waffles are delicious with sour cream and jam, and cold waffles are good with butter and brown goat cheese.

French toast

Helpful hint
Leftover buttermilk, cream or sour cream? Use it as part of the milk in the above recipe. You can also substitute whole grain flower or rolled oats for part of the flour.

Sour cream waffles
12 waffles

4 dl (1 ⅔ cups) whipping cream
1 dl (scant ½ cup) sour cream
3 ½ dl (1 ½ cups) flour
4 tablespoons (¼ cup) water

Whip cream and sour cream. Sift the flour, add the water and some of the whipped cream. Stir until smooth. Carefully stir in the remaining cream and let the batter rest for 10 minutes.

Heat the waffle iron and grease it before baking the waffles to a golden brown color. Place the finished waffles on a rack to keep them crisp. Serve with butter, jam or brown cheese.

Waffles

Pancakes – basic recipe
15-20 pancakes

3 dl (1 ¼ cups) sifted flour
½ teaspoon salt
5 dl (2 cups) milk
4 eggs
butter

Combine flour and salt. Whisk in half the milk. Stir until thick and lump-free. Add the remaining milk and whisk in the eggs. Let the batter rest for around 15 minutes. Fry thin pancakes in butter in a non-stick pan over relatively high heat. Flip when the batter begins to dry on the surface and the bottom is golden. Serve with blueberry jam.

For heartier pancakes, use 1 ½ dl (⅔ cup) whole wheat flour for half the flour.

Oven pancake
15-20 pancakes

200 g (8 oz) bacon
basic recipe for pancakes (see above)
2-3 tablespoons chopped parsley

Preheat the oven to 220°C (400°F). Cut bacon into chunks or shreds. Pour pancake batter into a small ovenproof dish. Sprinkle with bacon. Bake for around 15 minutes, until cooked through and light golden brown. Serve with salad and crusty bread.

Crêpes Suzette

Crêpes Suzette
10 crêpes

Suzette sauce
2 tablespoons butter
2 egg yolks
1 dl (scant ½ cup) confectioner's sugar
grated zest and juice of 1 orange and ½ lemon
2 tablespoons cognac
2 tablespoons orange liqueur

Melt the butter in a pan. Whisk together egg yolks, sugar and citrus juice. Pour into the pan. Add the pancakes and heat lightly. Pour over the cognac and liqueur and ignite. When the flames have died down on their own, the pancakes are ready to serve. Garnish with orange and lemon peel and serve with ice cream or whipped cream.

Raised pancakes

4 eggs
6 tablespoons sugar
450-500 g (3-3 ½ cups) flour
1 tablespoon baking soda
½ teaspoon hornsalt (or 1 ½ teaspoon baking powder)
1 liter (quart) cultured buttermilk
2 tablespoons melted butter

Beat eggs and sugar until light and lemon-colored. Combine dry ingredients and add alternately with buttermilk. Stir in melted butter. Let the batter rest for around 30 minutes. Bake on a griddle. Let cool. Spread the cold pancakes with butter and sprinkle with sugar. Fold over. These pancakes also taste good with butter and brown cheese.

Raised pancake

Thick lefse

1 kg (2 ¼ lb) flour
2 tablespoons baking powder
120 g (4 oz) butter
4 tablespoons (¼ cup) sugar
2 eggs
5 dl (2 cups) milk

Combine flour and baking powder and cut in the butter. Whisk sugar and eggs together, then whisk in the milk. Stir into the flour mixture. Work quickly to make a stiff dough. Divide into small pieces and roll into thin sheets. Bake on a griddle until golden. Serve with butter and sugar or with egg cheese.

Søst

3 dl (1 ¼ cups) sugar
1 liter (quart) cultured buttermilk
1 liter (quart) full-fat milk
4 dl (1 ⅔ cups) raisins
300 g (10 oz) low-fat *prim* or grated brown cheese
2 ½ dl (1 cup) semolina

Caramelize the sugar in a heavy pot. Gradually add the milk and the remaining ingredients. Heat to boiling, stirring constantly. Lower the heat and let simmer for 15 minutes, stirring constantly. Let cool. *Søst* tastes good with waffles, lefse and whole grain bread.

Ryfylke *dravle*

2 liter (½ gallon) milk
2 dl (1 cup) whipping cream
2 cinnamon sticks
6 dl (2 ½ cups) cultured buttermilk
1 dl (½ cup) sugar
5 eggs

Heat milk, cream and cinnamon to boiling. Whisk together remaining ingredients and whisk into the hot milk. Reheat to boiling. The mixture should curdle. Remove around 1/3 of the whey that is left after the curds form. Stir the remaining mixture in the pot and let simmer for around 1 ½ hours. Eat with a spoon when serving with waffles, lefse or alongside cured meats.

Red *dravle* *from Voss*

6 liter (1 ½ gallons) milk
1 ½ teaspoons rennet

Heat the milk to 32°C (90°F) in a large pot. Add rennet and set the pot of milk in a warm place to set. Return the pot to the stove and cut through the milk a few times. Heat to boiling and let the milk simmer over very low heat for 2-3 hours until golden brown. This is festive food when served with cured meats and lefse.

Songraut *from Oppdal*

10 liter (2 ½ gallons) milk
1 teaspoon rennet
2 dl (1 cup) rice
2 dl (1 cup) raisins
sugar
cinnamon

Heat the milk to 32°C (90°F) in a large pot. Remove 8 liters and add rennet. Heat the remaining milk (2 liter/ ½ gallon) to boiling. After around ½ hour, the rennet-milk should have set. Ladle large chunks of set milk into the boiling milk. Let simmer for 5-6 hours, until light brown. Add rice and raisins and let simmer for 45 minutes. Add sugar to taste. Serve in large soup bowls with sugar and cinnamon, or let cool and serve with waffles.

Grandma's good *gomme*

1 ½ liter (6 cups) milk
2 dl (1 cup) cultured buttermilk
3 dl (1 ¼ cups) raisins
4-5 tablespoons flour
2-4 tablespoons sugar
2 tablespoons cardamom
cinnamon

Heat milk to boiling. Remove from heat and add buttermilk. Whisk until the mixture begins to curdle (there should not be any large lumps). Stir in raisins. Partially cover and let simmer over low heat for 4 hours. Stir in flour, sugar and cardamom. Sprinkle with cinnamon just before serving.

Egg cheese

Søst

Egg cheese *from Flekkefjord*

1 liter (quart) milk
4 dl (1⅔ cups) cultured buttermilk
2-5 eggs
2 tablespoons sugar
sugar and cinnamon

Heat milk to boiling. Whisk together butter, eggs and sugar and whisk into the milk. Low heat and reheat slowly to boiling, until curds rise to the top with clear whey underneath. Remove from heat and let cool. Spoon curds into a sieve or colander lined with cheesecloth and let drain. Place the egg cheese in a pretty bowl and sprinkle with sugar and cinnamon. Serve with waffles or lefse. Freeze the whey and use in baking bread.

Pizza
– Norwegian style

Norwegians consume more frozen pizza per inhabitant than those of any other country! Hard to believe when you consider that it is a relative newcomer to the dinner table.

Tomato sauce *for pizza*
Enough for one pizza

1 large onion
1 tablespoon oil
5 ripe tomatoes
3 tablespoons tomato paste
2 teaspoons pizza herbs
1 tablespoon sugar
1 teaspoon salt

Peel and chop onion. Fry in oil until soft. Chop tomatoes and add. Heat to boiling. Add remaining ingredients and let simmer, uncovered, for 10 minutes, or until thick.

Pizza crust
1 crust

25 g (1 oz) fresh yeast
1 $^1/_2$ dl ($^2/_3$ cup) lukewarm water
$^1/_2$ teaspoon salt
2 tablespoons melted butter or oil
4 $^1/_2$ dl (1 $^3/_4$ cups) flour

Dissolve yeast in water and stir in salt and butter. Add flour and knead until smooth and elastic.

Cover and let rise in a warm place to double. Roll into a 30 cm circle. Place on a greased oven tray and spread with sauce.

Here are some suggestions for filling:

Filling 1
Pizza sauce
Shrimp
Mussels
Sliced artichoke bottoms
Chopped herbs
200 g (2 cups) grated cheese

Filling 2
Pizza sauce
Onion rings
Sliced mushrooms
Sliced zucchini
Sun-dried tomatoes, chopped
Olives
Oregano
200 g (2 cups) grated cheese

Filling 3
Pizza sauce
Pepperoni or salami
Sliced tomato

Sliced bell pepper
Sliced onion
Oregano
200 g (2 cups) grated cheese

Filling 4
Pizza sauce
Thinly sliced eggplant
Sliced zucchini
Chopped onion
Sliced tomato
Sliced red and green bell pepper
Oregano
Salt and pepper
150 g (1 $^1/_2$ cups) grated cheese

Filling 5
Pizza sauce
Sliced sausage
Chicken or turkey ham
Grilled chicken
Cured turkey sausage
Sliced tomato, pineapple, onion, mushrooms, bell pepper
Grated cheese

Filling 6

Pizza sauce

400-500 g (1 lb) fried fish, in chunks

1 dl (½ cup) grated cheese

1 teaspoon pizza herbs

3 tablespoons shredded basil leaves

2 tablespoons chopped chives

Helpful hint

Vary with smoked mackerel, lightly salted cod or dried fish and vegetables and fruit according to taste. Let the fish simmer in the pizza sauce until done. Spread over the crust and sprinkle with cheese and herbs. Black or green olives are also good on cod pizza.

Mini pizzas
12 pizzas

2 cans tuna in water
1 dl (½ cup) corn
2 dl (¾ cup) thick tomato sauce
1 tablespoon dried oregano
½ teaspoon salt
pepper
1 yellow paprika
15 cherry tomatoes
12 pita bread (12 cm/5") in diameter
150 g (1 ½ cups) grated cheese

Preheat the oven to 200°C (400°F). Drain tuna and corn well. Combine tomato sauce, oregano, salt and pepper. Mash tuna with a fork and stir into tomato sauce. Chop the bell pepper, quarter the tomatoes. Arrange the pita on 2 oven sheets lined with baking parchment. Spread with tomato mixture. Top with corn, pepper and tomato. Bake in the center of the oven for 10 minutes. Sprinkle with cheese and bake 8 minutes more, until cheese is melted and golden. Cool on a rack. Halve each pizza. These freeze well, but separate each pizza with parchment paper.

Pizza pinwheels
20 pinwheels

50 g (1 ¾ oz) fresh yeast
2 tablespoons butter
3 dl (1 ¼ cups) skim milk
1 teaspoon salt
500 g (3 ¾ - 4 cups) flour

Filling
1 small can (around 70 g/2 ½ oz) tomato paste
½ teaspoon salt
freshly ground pepper
100 g (4 oz) boiled ham, chopped
2 red bell peppers, diced
½ onion, minced
100 g (1 cup) grated cheese

Preheat the oven to 200°C (400°F). Crumble the yeast in a large bowl. Melt the butter, add the milk and heat to lukewarm. Pour over yeast and stir until dissolved. Add salt and enough flour to form a stiff dough. Knead until smooth and elastic. Roll into a 25x40 cm (14x16) rectangle. Spread with tomato paste and sprinkle with salt and pepper. Sprinkle remaining ingredients over the dough. Roll up, starting at one long side. Cut into 20 slices. Place on an oven sheet lined with baking parchment. Cover with plastic and let rise in a warm place for 20 minutes. Bake for around 20 minutes. Cool on a rack. These freeze well, but separate each roll with parchment paper.

Pizza pinwheels

Vegetables

fruit and berries – a colorful combo

Vegetables are interesting, and there are hundreds of them from all over the world. This food group is becoming a greater part of our diet with every passing day. In 1934, Norwegians ate 19 kg (about 42 lb) of vegetables (excluding potatoes) per person per year. By 1980, consumption had increased to 49 kg (107 lb) and in 2000, it was around 60 kg (132 lb) per person per year. In other words, Norwegians have changed their diet considerably. We are now a salad-eating nation. We can thank celery cabbage for that!

In the past, vegetables were considered side dishes. Today, they can stand on their own and they form the basis for a wealth of different, exciting dishes.

Eat more fruit and vegetables

The Norwegian Council for Nutrition and Physical activity recommends two servings of fruit and three servings of vegetables per day –"5 a day". According to the council, if these guidelines are followed, 20% or more of the most common forms of cancer can be prevented.

This recommendation means close to doubling our daily consumption of fruit and vegetables. A high intake of fruit and vegetables is seen as very beneficial against cancer, heart disease, high blood pressure, overweight, diabetes and digestive problems. Fruit and vegetables are important parts of the daily diet because they contain valuable vitamins, minerals and fiber, and at the same time very little fat and few calories. In other words, we get all the useful nutrients without unnecessary calories. Fruit and vegetables are our only source of Vitamin C, and they contribute approximately 30% of our total Vitamin A intake, 70% of Vitamin B6, 25% of folates, 16% of iron, 8% of calcium and 47% of total fiber on a daily basis.

Storage

Most traditional Norwegian vegetables should be stored at 0-5°C (32-40°F) with 85-100% humidity. It is easiest to maintain this degree of humidity by packing or covering them in plastic.

Vegetables and lettuce that will be stored for a short time in the refrigerator are best wrapped in plastic or in a container with a tight-fitting lid. Onion and garlic should be stored in a cool, dry place.

Long-term home storage is not recommended, as most homes do not maintain optimal conditions for that kind of storage. In addition, we have access to fresh products year-round, so this should not be necessary.

Tomatoes and cucumbers should not be stored at such low temperatures. They are best at a temperature of 10-14°C (50-60°F). Since these are products are used quickly, just leave them on the kitchen countertop. They keep well and taste better that way.

and "carve" out what you need and return the rest to the freezer immediately. Do not defrost before using or they become slimy and bitter.

Fruit and berries

Today fruit comes from close by and very far away almost year-round. Apples are the most popular fruit, and most of our apple consumption is from domestic orchards. We eat around 20 kilos (44 lb) of apples per person per year. After Sweden, we are world leaders in banana consumption, at 12 kilos (26 lb) per person per year. We consume around 15 kilos (33 lb) of oranges and tangerines per person per year.

And we love our strawberries. Norwegian strawberries mean that summer is here in all its glory. We eat them mostly on their own, as a dessert with cream, ice cream or vanilla sauce, and in whipped cream cakes.

Storage

Most fruit and berries should be stored at 0-5°C (32-40°F) and at high humidity. The best temperature for apples is 2-4°C (36-40°F). Bananas should not be refrigerated. They are best stored at 14-16°C (58-63°F). Grapefruit and mango are best at 12-14°C (54-58°F). Watermelon is increasing in popularity and should be stored at 7-10°C (44-51°F).

Most of us don't store anything other than apples in our own cellar or cold storage room. Even that is difficult in newer houses. It is important to keep an eye on the apples throughout the fall, so that rotten apples can be removed before they spoil the rest.

Freezing

Fruit can be frozen, but that takes up a lot of space. It can be frozen raw or after a quick boil in sugar syrup (8 dl/3 1/3 cups sugar per liter/quart water). Apples, pears and plums have to be cut into chunks or wedges before being frozen either raw or cooked. If you choose to give the fruit a quick boil, which gives the best result, you just add the cut fruit to the boiling syrup. Let it simmer for a few minutes until the fruit just begins to soften. Remove from the

syrup, let cool, then freeze in the cool syrup. Many like to freeze berries. Although strawberries change radically after freezing, we freeze them more than we do any other fruit. The simplest is to freeze the cleaned berries in layers with a sprinkling of sugar. They should be defrosted slowly, preferably in the refrigerator. Berries for garnish should be frozen singly – place pretty berries on a tray and place in the freezer. When they are frozen, pack individually and return to the freezer. In this way, they do not freeze together. Just select the number you need.

Raw frozen jam is also good. Crush the berries or stir them with sugar and freeze. Count on 1-2 dl (1/2- 3/4 cup) sugar per liter/quart berries. For thicker jam, add pectin for freezing. Raw frozen jam does not keep well after defrosting, so freeze in small quantities.

It is also practical to freeze applesauce, apple preserves and apple juice, as these do not store well in the cellar. Use plastic freezer containers. Glass can shatter in the freezer.

Making preserves

Many people still like to make fruit preserves – either to add their own personal touch, to reduce the amount of sugar or to preserve the resources of their own garden or walks in the forest. You can use one or many kinds of fruit, and a combination of fruit and berries is lovely – apples and lingonberries are a good combination.

Quick preserves are easy and the result is always good. It's important that all berries be cooked for the shortest possible time, so it's a good idea to make small batches. Sort out bad berries. Place in a pot, cover and heat to boiling, stirring occasionally. After 8-10 minutes, the berries are usually cooked and you can add sugar. Count on 400 g (2 cups) per kilo (2 1/4 lb) berries. Heat to boiling, stirring well until sugar is dissolved. Quickly pour into clean jars. Wipe the edge. Close the jars immediately and let cool. Store jam in a cold, dark place.

Freezing

Freezing is still a popular way to store vegetables, but frozen vegetables do not have the freshness, texture and crispness of fresh. Most need to be parboiled before freezing. They should be cleaned, washed and cut into bite-size pieces and given a quick boil in unsalted water. Cooking time varies according to the vegetable and the size of the pieces. Average time is 3-4 minutes. Snow peas need only around 1 minute, whole beans 2 minutes and corn on the cob 6-8 minutes. Plunge the vegetables in ice water immediately after cooking. Then drain thoroughly, pack well and freeze.

Note: All frozen vegetables should be taken right out of the freezer and placed in boiling water when used. If defrosted at room temperature, they become limp.

You don't have to parboil herbs such as parsley and chives. Just cut into lengths and pack in airtight containers. Take right from the freezer and add to the dish you are making. Just use a fork

Making juice

Many people also like to make juice. One or more kinds of berries and even fruit can be pressed into juice. Making juice with steam is the easiest and most popular method. It results in strained juice that can be tapped right into clean bottles.

You need a juice kit for this. Fill the pot with water to around 3 cm (1 ¼") from the edge. Place the hopper on top. Add berries and even fruit layered with sugar. Sugar increases the amount of juice and adds flavor. Tightly screw on the lid. The water should just simmer. The berries and fruit should be steamed until they have released juice and turned color. Average recommended steaming time is 1 ½ hours. The amount of sugar is a matter of taste, but the recommended amount is 100-150g (½- ¾ cup) per kilo (2 ¼ lb) berries.

Pour the juice into clean bottles immediately. Seal and let cool. Store in a cold, dark place.

Potatoes

The potato is one of the most important products in the Norwegian kitchen. It is a fact that the potato and the herring rescued our people through both war and bad times.

Today, the potato is the fourth most important agricultural product in the world after wheat, rice and corn, with a total production of 300 million tons. Our potato consumption has gone down over the last 50 years. That's no surprise, as the amount of other food available has increased. But potato consumption is still high at 36 kg (79 lb) per person per year. In addition, we consume around 33 kg (72 lb) industrially processed potatoes per person per year.

Potatoes are an exciting food. Traditionally, we have used potatoes in many variations as the

Pressing juice concentrate from berries, making jam, and pickling vegetables is a lot of work, but it's a good feeling to preserve summer flavors for winter. Homemade is always best!

natural accompaniment to both meat and fish. Potatoes feature in their own separate dishes, too, such as dumplings, salads and soups. Potatoes are also used in bread, lefse, lompe (two traditional tortilla-like breads), flatbread and in cakes.

Potato varieties

There are many different varieties of potato, but a much smaller number is produced commercially. Older varieties are now being grown and new ones developed. We can choose potatoes with different flavors, shapes and colors. We can buy potatoes for specific dishes according to flavor and other criteria.

Some potatoes are associated with particular dishes. Norwegians like *Ringerik* potatoes with *lutefisk*, almond potatoes with fermented fish and *Kerrs pink* with lamb and cabbage stew, and many many more.

Beate is our most popular potato. New varieties, such as *Asterix* and *Blue Congo* are becoming popular. Asterix is red-purple, while Blue Congo is deep purple. Both taste good and add color to a salad bowl. *Ottar* and *Gullauge* grow well in North Norway. Gullauge is a very old North Norwegian variety, but it is also sold in other parts of the country. *Rutt* is the most popular early harvest potato. *Laila* and *Ostara* are the

most important middle harvest potatoes. Newer varieties are *Brage, Grom, King Edward, Peik, Troll, Rosewald, Folva, Fjellmandel from Vågå* and *Snåsamande. Pimpernell* is one of our most popular winter potatoes.

Potatoes should be stored at 4-6°C (42-46°F). Potatoes keep best when they are stored un-washed in a cool, dark place.

Root vegetables

Carrot, parsley root, parsnip, celeriac, black salsi-fy, rutabaga and Jerusalem artichoke are begin-ning to stage a comeback. These are old root vegetables with long traditions in the Norwegian kitchen. They are good in soups, sauces and mashed, and they can be served boiled, fried and grated raw.

The carrot is originally from the Middle East and Central Asia, where it has been cultivated for at least 2000 years. The Arabs brought it to Spain around 1000 years ago, and from there, it spread throughout Europe. The carrot thrives in both warm and cool climates and is grown in great parts of the world. There are many types. It is the most popular vegetable in Norway, eaten both raw and cooked. For many, a raw carrot is a good between-meal snack or a good finale to a packed lunch. Grated raw carrot is delicious with fried fish, while boiled carrots are excellent with most fish and meat dishes. It's also good in soups and stews, stir-fries, in pickles, as jam and in cakes.

The parsley root is from the inner part of the Mediterranean, where it still grows wild. It origi-nated thousands of years ago and is a variety of curly parsley. Parsley root has a milder flavor than celeriac and is good boiled or fried, with meat and fish dishes, and in soups and stews. Grated raw parsley root is good in slaws and salads.

The parsnip is another very old vegetable, well known even in Roman times. Before the potato came to Norway, the parsnip was the most important source of starch in the Norwegian diet. It can be grated raw for slaw and salads and is good in stir-fries. Serve boiled with meat

and fish dishes, or serve it creamed and baked in the oven.

Celeriac comes from the Mediterranean area and is cultivated all over Europe. It has been grown in Norway for a long time and used mostly as a soup vegetable in which both root and plant are utilized. Fried or boiled celeriac can be served with meat and fish dishes, and it is also good in stir-fries. Grated raw celeriac, as well as the leaves, can be used in slaw and salads.

Black salsify is an old root vegetable originally from Spain. It can grow to a length of 20-30 cm (8-12"). The peel is dark brown or black. Under the peel, the vegetable is pure white and emits yellow-white milky juice when peeled. It has a mild flavor slightly reminiscent of asparagus. It can be used like other root vegetables, in soups and stews or gratinéed. It is not eaten raw. Peel and cook for 15-20 minutes. Add a little lemon, milk or vinegar to prevent it from darkening.

The rutabaga has been cultivated in Norway since the mid-1600s. It is a good source of Vitamin C, and for that reason, it has been called "the orange of the North". Boiled rutabaga is good with meat and fish dishes. The Norwegian kitchen features rutabaga in many soups and stews, as well as mashed rutabaga as a tradi-tional side dish. It can be grated raw for slaws and salads and is good in stir-fries. Rutabaga (and carrot) sticks are good served as snacks with dip.

Jerusalem artichoke is a special vegetable origi-nally from North America. It came to Europe in the 1600s and eventually spread over great parts of the continent, including Scandinavia. Before the potato became widespread, the Jerusalem artichoke was a popular vegetable in Norway. It is a small root that thrives even in harsh conditi-ons. Its crispy, juicy meat is white or light yellow with a sweet, delicate flavor. It can be used raw grated in slaws and salads. It should be dipped in lemon juice to prevent darkening. It is good pureed, gratinéed, boiled with chicken and alongside meat. Do not peel until after it is cooked.

Herbs

Herbs are among the oldest beneficial plants. Herbs have been used for medicinal purposes for eons. For many generations, they have been used in cooking and cosmetics. Monks were the first to bring herbs and knowledge of their uses to Norway. It was common for herbs to be grown in monastery gardens. We can still find wild thyme and rosemary that probably derive from monastery gardens.

Fresh herbs have become more and more popular in cooking. During the past 20 years, a revolution has taken place in the production, access to and use of fresh herbs in Norway. We can buy herbs in pots and leaves and stalks in bags. The selection is large, aromatic and appealing!

Storage

Many feel that it is difficult to keep herbs in their pots. They can't be kept in a warm place, such as over the radiator, nor do they like sunny windowsills, and they don't like it cold either. They are best on the kitchen countertop. They like light and normal heat. Under 16°C (60°F) they wither. Water them in their dish, not directly in the pot. Pluck out the stalks, and use them often in hot and cold dishes.

Areas of use

Fresh herbs are good with most things, in meat and fish dishes, with all kinds of white meat, in omelets, in soups, sauces and dressings, in fruit and berry desserts, and in yeast baking. As a rule, you need twice as much fresh herbs as dried.

Here are some suggestions for using fresh herbs:

Basil is good with fish and meat, in tomato sauce, dressings, in butter and in desserts and breads.

Thyme is lovely with pea soup, in fish and meat dishes, on pizza, in marinades, in soups and sauces and breads.

Rosemary is a must with lamb dishes, but it is also good with pork, chicken, in marinades, in potato dishes and breads.

Tarragon is delicious in egg dishes, with chicken, fish, in béarnaise and other sauces and dressings and in salads.

Oregano is great in ground meat dishes, in sauces, in tomato dishes, on pizza and in breads.

Mint is lovely in fruit desserts, in sauces and salads, in ice cream and tea.

Dill – the thin, threadlike leaves are used to flavor and garnish new potatoes, marinated, boiled and fried fish, and herb butter. The flower of the plant is used in brine for pickles and to season vinegar.

Chervil is used finely chopped, either alone or with other herbs in salads, green sauces and in soup. It is good with chicken and veal. It tastes like parsley and smells like anise.

Coriander is good with chicken and pork. In Asia, coriander is just as popular as parsley is here. It is good in Chinese, Thai and Indian dishes.

Parsley in Norway is mostly curly, good with fish, sauces, vegetable dishes, soups, stews, finely cut over new potatoes and as garnish. It is indispensable in the Norwegian kitchen.

Sage is used together with other herbs in fish and meat dishes, in forcemeats and in stuffing for chicken and turkey. Also used in herb tea.

Lemon verbena adds a lemony flavor and is good in fruit salads, vegetable salads, fish dishes, sauces and sweet desserts, and also as a garnish on cakes and desserts.

Breakfast salad

4 servings

6 hard cooked eggs
2 apples
1 dl (½ cup) shredded leek
2 ½ dl (1 cup) sour cream
salt

Cut eggs lengthwise and crosswise with an egg slicer. Grate the apples. Combine all ingredients. Season with salt if necessary.

Ham salad

4 servings

1 small iceberg lettuce
2 celery stalks
100 g (4 oz) mushrooms
200 g (8 oz) boiled ham
10 prunes
1 apple

Dressing
2 dl (1 cup) plain yogurt
1 teaspoon prepared mustard
½ bunch parsley

Shred the lettuce and thinly slice the celery and mushrooms. Cut the ham and prunes into thin strips. Cube the apple. Combine ingredients in dressing. Layer the salad ingredients with the dressing. Serve with bread.

Ham salad

Summer salad

4 servings

12 green asparagus
1 fennel, sliced
3 tiny turnips, in thin wedges
300 g (10 oz) snow peas
½ summer cabbage, shredded
1 bunch radishes
200 g (8 oz) smoked salmon, in strips
100 g (4 oz) cooked mussels

Dressing
4 tablespoons (¼ cup) olive oil
2 tablespoons white wine vinegar
salt and freshly ground pepper

Blanch asparagus, fennel and turnips in lightly salted water for 3 minutes. Immediately plunge into ice water. Blanch snow peas and cabbage for 30 seconds. Immediately plunge into ice

Breakfast salad

water. Drain well. Arrange on a platter. Shred the radishes and arrange with the salmon and mussels on the greens. Combine dressing and pour over the salad. Serve with bread.

Salade Niçoise

4 servings

4 hard cooked eggs
1 can tuna
1 small iceberg lettuce
4 tomatoes
1 green bell pepper
½ red onion
8 radishes
8 anchovy fillets
8 black olives

Dressing
6 tablespoons olive oil
2 tablespoons red wine vinegar
sea salt and freshly ground pepper

Cut the eggs into wedges. Drain the tuna and separate into chunks. Shred the lettuce. Cut the tomato into wedges, the pepper into cubes, the onion into paper-thin rings, and the radishes into thin slices. Layer all ingredients in a bowl or on a platter. Arrange anchovies and olives on top. Combine dressing and pour over the salad. Serve with bread.

Potato salad

4 servings

1 kilo (2 ¼ lb) boiled potatoes
1 shallot
1 garlic clove
3 scallions
1 large apple
fresh mint

Dressing
4 tablespoons (¼ cup) olive oil
2 tablespoons fresh lemon juice
2 tablespoons white wine vinegar
2 teaspoons prepared mustard

Peel and slice the potatoes. Peel and mince the shallot and garlic. Chop the scallions and dice the apple. Shred the mint. Combine in a bowl. Combine dressing and pour over the salad. Garnish with mint. Serve on its own or alongside meat or fish.

Salade Nicoise

Potato salad with onion, apple and mint

Waldorf rolls

Furuly salad

4 servings

125 g (4 oz) cabbage
125 g (4 oz) carrots
2 apples
50 g (2 oz) prunes
50 g (1/2 cup) chopped hazelnuts

Dressing
juice of 1/2 lemon
1 tablespoon sugar
minced parsley

Shred the cabbage, grate the carrots and dice the apples. Shred the prunes. Combine all ingredients in a bowl. Combine lemon juice and sugar and pour over the salad. Sprinkle with parsley. Serve on its own or alongside fish or meat.

Warm vegetable salad

4 servings

3 leeks
1 celeriac
3 carrots
2 tablespoons butter
1/2 teaspoon salt
1/2 teaspoon freshly ground pepper
1 tablespoon vinegar
1/2 tablespoon sugar
minced parsley

Clean and slice the leeks into thin rings. Dice the celeriac and carrots. Melt the butter and add the vegetables. Cook, stirring frequently, over low heat until tender. Season with salt, pepper, vinegar and sugar. Just before serving, stir in minced parsley. Serve with meat or fish dishes, but it also tastes good on its own with fresh bread.

Warm vegetable salad

Waldorf rolls

4 servings

1/2 iceberg lettuce
1 red apple
2 celery stalks
50 g (2 oz) blue grape
10 walnut halves
10-12 slices boiled ham

Dressing
1 dl (1/2 cup) sour cream
1/2 dl (1/4 cup) low-fat mayonnaise
fresh lemon juice
salt and freshly ground pepper

2 tomatoes, in wedges

Shred the lettuce. Dice the apple and thinly slice the celery. Halve the grapes and chop the nuts. Combine the dressing. Stir the apple, celery, grapes and walnuts into the dressing. Arrange the salad on the ham and roll up. Arrange shredded lettuce on a platter. Arrange the ham rolls on the lettuce. Garnish with tomato. Serve with bread.

Furuly salad

Broccoli with cheese sauce

Broccoli *with cheese sauce*
4 servings

1 kg (2 ¼ lb) broccoli
1 dl (½ cup) water
1 ½ teaspoons salt
1 tablespoon butter

Sauce
1 ½ tablespoons butter
1 tablespoon flour
2 dl (1 scant cup) milk
50 g (½ cup) shredded cheese
salt
200 g (8 oz) bacon

Clean and cut the broccoli into florets. Cook until barely tender in the water. Melt the butter, stir in the flour and gradually whisk in the milk. Heat to boiling. Add cheese and season with salt. Cut the bacon into thin strips and fry until crisp. Arrange the broccoli on a serving platter. Pour over the sauce and garnish with bacon.

Potato dumplings
4 servings

lightly salted stock or bouillon
6 raw potatoes
2 cold boiled potatoes
2 dl (1 cup) barley flour
½ dl (¼ cup) flour
1 teaspoon salt
½ teaspoon pepper

Heat stock in a large pot to boiling. Peel and grate the raw potatoes. Grate the boiled potatoes and combine with the remaining ingredients, mixing well. Make small balls. Let them simmer in hot stock for 25-30 minutes. Do not allow the stock to boil. These are usually served with salt mutton, Voss sausages, fried bacon and mashed rutabagas. The best potatoes for dumplings are Beate, Laila, Pimpernell and Troll.

These dumplings are usually called *raspeball* in Norwegian, but they have many regional names such as *klubb, krumme, kumpe, kumla, raspeka-ko,* and *potetball.*

Potato dumplings

Stuffed potato dumplings
4 servings

1 kilo (2 ¼ lb) raw potatoes
1 dl (½ cup) rye or whole barley flour
2 dl (1 cup) flour
2 teaspoons salt
200 g (8 oz) salt pork, in large cubes
lightly salted stock or bouillon

Peel and grate the potatoes. Press out as much water as possible with the help of a kitchen towel or sieve. Knead in the flour and salt. Form large balls. Make a hole in each and press in a piece or two of pork. Press the ball back together. Let the balls simmer in the stock for around 1 hour. Serve with salt meat, fried pork belly, boiled rutabagas and carrots or mashed rutabagas and/or carrots.

Midnight snack
2 servings

1 leek
1 tomato
2 boiled potatoes
½ cauliflower, cooked
1 carrot, cooked
2 tablespoons butter
2 eggs
minced parsley

Slice the leek and cut the tomato into wedges. Cube the potatoes, cauliflower and carrot. Quickly sauté the leek and tomato butter. Add the remaining vegetables and fry until lightly colored. Break the eggs over and cook until just done. Sprinkle with parsley.

This is a typical leftover dish. Instead of breaking the eggs over the vegetables, you can fry them separately and place one on top of each serving.

Cauliflower

with green cheese sauce and cured ham
4 servings

1 cauliflower
4 slices (not too thin) cured ham

Sauce
2 tablespoons butter
2 tablespoons flour
4 dl (1 2/3 cups) milk
½ teaspoon salt
½ teaspoon white pepper
2 dl (1 cup) grated cheese
2 tablespoons chopped parsley
2 tablespoons chopped chives

Cook the cauliflower in lightly salted water until barely tender. Shred the ham. Melt the butter, stir in the flour and whisk in the milk. Heat to boiling and season with salt and pepper. Stir in cheese and herbs. Arrange the cauliflower on a platter. Pour over the sauce and sprinkle with ham and chopped parsley. Garnish, if desired with lettuce and tomato wedges.

Bacon can be used instead of ham.

Midnight snack

Cauliflower with green cheese sauce and cured ham

Stuffed zucchini au gratin

Stuffed zucchini au gratin
4 servings

200 g (8 oz) ground beef
2 garlic cloves, minced
1 onion, minced
100 g (4 oz) fresh mushrooms, chopped
1 can chopped tomatoes
1 teaspoon thyme
1 tablespoon fresh oregano (or 1 teaspoon dried)
4 zucchini
100 g (1 cup) shredded cheese

Preheat the oven to 200°C (400°F). Sauté beef, garlic, onion and mushrooms until soft. Add tomatoes and herbs and let simmer until thickened. Halve the zucchini and place in an oven-proof dish. Remove the seeds and chop. Stir into the sauce. Spoon sauce into the zucchini and sprinkle with cheese. Bake for 15-20 minutes. Serve hot with bread.

You can also stuff mushrooms and peppers in the same way. Reduce baking time to 10 minutes.

Zucchini pancakes

4 servings

500 g (1 lb) zucchini
salt
4 eggs
1 ¹/₂ dl (²/₃ cup) flour
2 tablespoons chopped dill
2 tablespoons chopped parsley
2 tablespoons chopped fresh tarragon
(or 2 teaspoons dried)
¹/₂ teaspoon salt and ¹/₂ teaspoon pepper
70 g (²/₃ cup) grated cheese
olive oil

Zucchini pancakes

Grate the zucchini and place in a colander. Sprinkle with salt and let drain for 30 minutes. Press out as much liquid as possible from the zucchini with towels. Beat eggs and flour to-gether. Add the remaining ingredients and let rest for a little while. Fry small pancakes in olive oil. These are good with chicken and grilled foods.

Bruschetta

An Italian appetizer served before a meal. It's also good as a snack.

3 servings

6 tomatoes
4 garlic cloves
shredded basil
2 tablespoons olive oil
salt and pepper
6 slices day-old white bread

Peel, seed and chop the tomatoes. Mince the garlic and add with basil and oil. Season with salt and pepper. Toast the bread and halve each slice. Spoon the tomato mix onto the bread and serve immediately, before the bread gets cold and soggy.

Bruschetta

Soups

Onion soup
4 servings

6 onions
2 garlic cloves
2 tablespoons butter
1 ¾ liter (7 cups) stock or bouillon
2 teaspoons strong mustard
1 bay leaf
salt and pepper

Clean, peel and thinly slice the onion. Mince the garlic. Cook in butter over low heat until soft. Pour over stock and add mustard and bay leaf. Let simmer for around 45 minutes. Season with salt and pepper.

Serve piping hot with bread or top each soup bowl with slices of bread with melted cheese on top.

Onion soup

Creamy potato soup
4 servings

500 g (1 ¼ lb) potatoes
1 leek
1 onion
1 carrot
1 ½ liter (6 cups) water
1 bouillon cube
2 tablespoons butter
1 teaspoon salt
½ teaspoon pepper
1 egg yolk
1 dl (½ cup) whipping cream
chopped parsley

Peel and dice the potato. Slice the leek, onion and carrot. Heat the water to boiling. Add bouillon cube, butter, salt, pepper and vegetables. Cook until tender. Remove from the heat. Whisk egg yolk and cream together and pour into the soup, stirring gently. Sprinkle with parsley. Do not allow the soup to boil.

A soup with egg should not boil or the egg will scramble.

Creamy potato soup

Cauliflower soup

4 servings

1 cauliflower
1 large carrot
1 leek
2 celery stalks
4 parsley sprigs
1 liter (4 cups) meat stock or bouillon (preferably vegetable)
salt and pepper
3 tablespoons butter

2 ½ tablespoons flour
2 egg yolks
1 ½ dl (⅔ cup) light cream
crisp bacon cubes

Clean the cauliflower and divide into small florets. Clean the vegetables and peel the carrot. Cut all into small chunks and add to a pot with the stock. Heat to boiling and let simmer for around 15 minutes. Season with salt and pepper. Strain, reserving the cauliflower florets. Melt the butter, stir in the flour and whisk in the stock.

Add the cauliflower and keep the soup warm. Whisk egg yolks and cream together and add a little soup. Return the mixture to the pot and stir until it thickens. Do not allow to boil after the egg yolks are added or the eggs will scramble. Heat to just below the boiling point. Serve with a sprinkling of crisp bacon cubes.

Cauliflower soup

Cauliflower cheese soup

4 servings

1/2 onion, minced
2 tablespoons butter
4 tablespoons (1/4 cup) flour
1 1/2 liter (6 cups) bouillon
1 cauliflower, in florets (use the stalk, too)
1 dl (1/2 cup) whipping cream
2 dl (1 cup) grated cheese
1/2 bunch radishes, sliced
salt

Sauté onion in butter. Sprinkle with flour and whisk in the bouillon. Add the cauliflower and let simmer for 10 minutes. Combine cream and cheese and whisk into the soup. Stir in the radishes and season with salt.

Tomato soup

4 servings

12 tomatoes
2 onions
2 tablespoons olive oil
1 liter (4 cups) vegetable or beef stock
salt and pepper
2-3 tablespoons shredded basil

Peel, seed and chop the tomatoes. Clean and mince the onions. Sauté the onion in oil. Add the tomato and stock and heat to boiling. The soup can be pureed, if desired. Season with salt and pepper. Serve piping hot with a sprinkling of basil. The soup can also be served with wedges of cooked egg, macaroni or tiny meatballs.

Broccoli soup

4 servings

250 g (8 oz) fresh broccoli
3 potatoes
1 onion
8 dl (3 1/3 cups) chicken stock
2 dl (1 cup) milk
salt and pepper
2 hard-cooked eggs

Clean the broccoli, peel the potatoes and onion. Coarsely chop, using the stalk of the broccoli as well. Cook until barely tender in stock and milk. Reserve some of the florets. Puree the soup with an immersion blender or in a food processor. Reheat to boiling. Add more stock if the soup is too thick. Add the broccoli florets. Place half a cooked egg in each soup bowl. Pour over hot soup.

Gazpacho

3 servings

2 onions
2 cucumbers
5 tomatoes, peeled
1 red bell pepper
1 garlic clove

Gazpacho

1 dl (1/3 cup) cold vegetable stock
salt and pepper
lemon juice
3 slices white bread
2 tablespoons butter

Chop the vegetables and place in a food processor with the cold stock. Puree until smooth. Season with salt, pepper and lemon juice. Refrigerate for 1 hour. Remove the crusts and cube the bread. Brown in butter and let cool. Serve the soup with the croutons and garnish with chopped parsley, cucumber and bell pepper. Drizzle with olive oil, if desired.

Minestrone – *Italian winter soup*

This is a pure vegetable soup. If you want a little meat, you can dice 150 g (5 oz) bacon or salt pork and fry it before adding the vegetables to the pot.

3 potatoes
3 carrots
1 zucchini
1 small wedge cabbage,
2 tomatoes
1/2 red chili
1 garlic clove
4 tablespoons (1/4 cup) olive oil
6 dl (2 1/2 cups) stock or bouillon
1/2 can chopped tomatoes
1 cup cooked macaroni
1 can large white beans, drained
fresh rosemary
salt and pepper
sugar

Cube the potatoes. Slice the carrots and zucchini. Shred the cabbage. Peel the tomatoes and cut into wedges. Remove the ribs from the chili and mince. Mince the garlic and sauté in oil until soft. Add the vegetables and stir-fry for 4-5 minutes, stirring often. Add stock and tomatoes and let simmer for 10-15 minutes, until vegetables are tender. Add pasta, beans and rosemary and heat to boiling. Season with salt, pepper and a little sugar. Serve the soup piping hot with a sprinkle with parsley, grated cheese and fresh bread.

Minestrone – Italian winter soup

Fish and shellfish

– gifts from the sea

Fish and shellfish make up a category with a wide range of uses. Along the Norwegian coast, around 45 different species of fish are found in quantities large enough for commercial fishing. Otherwise, the total is close to 200 different species, plus a few that appear periodically.

In addition to all the wild fish and shellfish in the sea, we have developed the ability to farm certain species under controlled conditions. The most popular farmed fish are salmon and trout, and they have been farmed in Norway for decades. During recent years, the selection has been expanded to include halibut, Arctic char, cod, wolffish and mussels. Because of this, fish markets now get regular deliveries of these species year-round.

We can't forget the frozen food counter. Fish that's caught and frozen at sea is of excellent quality. The selection of wild fish is seasonal and varies according to the time of year. Modern freezing techniques have extended the season for most of these varieties.

What are the nutritional components of fish?

The main components in fish flesh are protein, water and fat. Most fish are 80% fat and water. That means that fatty fish have a lower water content. The protein content is relatively stable at 16-20%. The fat content varies with the species, the season and the availability of food. Different species store fat in different ways – in the liver, in the muscles, under the skin, around the bases of the fins, or as "suet" around the intestines. Fatty fish, such as salmon, herring and mackerel, can contain up to 30% fat at certain times of year. Some kinds of fish, especially herring, mackerel and pollock, store fat in the dark muscle flesh. That part of the fish contains fatty acids with a stronger flavor. Those acids are perishable and the dark flesh gets stale faster than white or light muscle flesh. Members of the cod family store fat in the liver, and the flesh usually contains less than 1% fat. Fish that store fat in this way are considered lean.

Medium-fat fish store fat in both muscle and liver, and that gives them other qualities as food. Fat within the muscles often makes the fish more flavorful and helps to keep it juicy after cooking.

Fat fish store all fat in the muscle, and at certain times of the year, the fat content is very high. Herring and mackerel are fatty fish. A lot of fat in the muscle often makes the fillet crack or pull apart – that is not a sign of poor quality in mackerel.

Fish flesh contains many kinds of protein, and they all react differently to heat. This has to be

Excellent ingredients from fresh, unpolluted water. The total value of ocean fishing is over 6 billion kroner, while coastal fishing is worth 4 billion kroner (1999).

considered when cooking fish. Two main proteins make fish firm at 30-50°C (86-122°F) and hard and fibrous at 65-73°C (149-165°). For good eating, fish should not be cooked beyond 60°C (140°F).

In addition to protein, water and fat, all seafood contains traces of most important vitamins and minerals. Fat content varies the most with fish. Fish fat is very healthy because it is unsaturated and contains essential fatty acids and vitamins

Handling and storage
of fish and shellfish

Fresh fish and lightly salted fish should be stored on ice at around 0-1°C (32°F). Smoked fish should be stored cold and well ventilated at 2-4°C (35-38°F). Lightly salted fish should be stored in brine at around 0-1°C (32°F). Cooked fresh crab, lobster, ocean crayfish and shrimp should be stored under 2°C (35°F). Crab and lobster should be stored "belly up" to hinder juices from running off and drying out the meat. Live mussels, oysters and other mollusks should be stored in damp seaweed or wet newspaper. The temperature should be between 5 and 10°C (41 and 50°F), depending upon the type.

The refrigerator does not always maintain the correct temperature for fish and shellfish. If you plan to refrigerate raw fish and shellfish for a couple of days, you should place a bag or two of ice with the fish. The ice serves as an additional cooling element. Place a bag of ice in the bottom of a plastic container and place the fish on top, preferably with another bag of ice on top. Never store fish uncovered in the refrigerator, as it absorbs odors from other foodstuffs.

Freezing
If you live along the coast or fish for a hobby, you may need to freeze some of your catch – that way, you will always have fresh fish in the house. Freeze only fish that is very fresh and at the peak of condition. The fish must be cleaned, washed and dried. It's best to make it as ready to cook as possible, and that saves time later.

It is important to freeze seafood at low temperatures, preferably as low as -25°C (-13°F). Do not attempt to freeze too much at once, or the temperature inside the freezer will rise. It's a good idea to lower the temperature in the freezer on the day before you plan to freeze the fish.

Defrosting
Defrost frozen fish in the refrigerator. That minimizes loss of liquid, and the fish stays juicy. Partially defrosted fish can be used in some cooked and baked dishes, but for best results, the fish should be completely defrosted and at room temperature. This is especially important if the fish is going to be fried.

Portion estimates
Average amount per serving (as a main course)

Fish: headless, gutted or sliced	300-400 g (10-14 oz) per serving
Fish fillet	200-250 g (7-9 oz) per serving
Lutefisk	500-1000 g (1-2 1/3 lb) per serving
Shrimp in the shell	400-500 g (14-18 oz) per serving
Crab or lobster	1, around 500 g (18 oz) per serving
Crayfish	8-10 per person
Mollusks	500-600 g (18-22 oz) per person

For lightly salted and smoked fish, as well as fatty fish such as salmon, halibut, herring and mackerel, count on somewhat less per serving.

Recommended storage time in the freezer

Lean fish	6 months
Fatty and medium-fat fish	3 months
Fish cakes, fish pudding and fish quenelles	6 months
Smoked and salted fish	3-4 months
Shrimp, crab, crayfish and lobster	6 months
Shellfish/mollusks	6 months

Packages must be water, air and odor tight. Aluminum foil, freezer foil and plastic are all suitable for packing fish. Then wrap in paper and write the date, weight and kind of fish.

Preparation of fish

Fish can be used in different dishes and in many combinations. Lean fish need careful handling so they don't fall apart during cooking. Fatty fish have firmer flesh and retain their shape better. The temperature is the most important factor in cooking fish, both in poaching and in frying. Fish flesh is "cooked" at 60°C (140°F). Controlling the temperature is very important when preparing fish dishes. Fish is sensitive to overheating. The most common mistake in preparing fish and seafood is too high heat over too long time. The fish becomes dry and tasteless. If you use lean fish in a soup or stew, it should simmer until just done. No energetic stirring, just careful movement of the pieces of fish, so they retain their shape until the dish is served.

Helpful hint

The best results are achieved with fish that has been allowed to reach room temperature before poaching or frying. Ice cold fish releases a lot of water during poaching and frying.

Poaching

Heat the water with salt and other flavorings to the boiling point. Use ½ dl (3 ½ tablespoons) salt per liter/quart water, somewhat less if you plan to use the cooking water in a sauce. Remove the pot from the heat, add the fish/seafood and reheat to boiling. Remove the pot from the heat and let the fish/seafood simmer until done. Thick pieces of fish, large quantities or very cold fish may have to be heated to boiling one more time. Lightly salted and smoked fish should simmer in water without added salt. Fatty fish need longer cooking time than lean fish. Slices or fillets that are around 2-3 cm (1") thick cook in 5-8 minutes if lean, 10-12 minutes if fatty. If cooking a whole fish, count on 50 minutes for a fatty fish weighing 2 kilos (4 ½ lb), around 15 minutes less for a lean fish.

One herring and one more herring… Norway exports herring valued at more than 1 billion kroner.

Frying

Frying on both sides
Brown the butter in the pan. Dry the fish fillets, place them in the pan and fry over medium heat. Fry the fish until completely done on one side before turning over. Be patient! Count on 3-4 minutes per side for 2-3 cm (1") thick pieces, less time for lean fish and thinner slices. Season after frying.

Frying on one side
Fillets with skin can be fried on only one side. Wash or scrub the skin side thoroughly. Dry the fish and cut into serving pieces. Brown the butter in the pan. Sprinkle a little salt and spices on the fish flesh and place in the pan, skin side down. Remove the pan from the heat when the fish skin begins to brown. Keep alternating on and off the heat until the fish is cooked. It takes a little time and patience, but the result is worth it – a juicy fish fillet with crispy skin. And remember to eat the skin. You might want to cover the pan when the fish is off the heat.

Butter, magarine or oil
You don't need to use any particular kind of fat when frying seafood. Use butter, margarine, oil or a mixture of butter and olive oil. Do not use virgin olive oil or diet margarine.

Breading

Breading adds a crunchy surface texture, and it adds flavor to the fish. Dip the fish in seasoned flour or in breadcrumbs, salt and seasonings before frying. You can also dip the fish in flour, then in beaten egg and finally in breadcrumbs. Cornmeal, sesame seeds, chopped almonds or cornstarch can be substituted for breadcrumbs. There are many other possibilities, too.

Is the fish ready yet?

Cooking times in recipes are always approximate. The time will vary according to the equipment, the stove, the size and the temperature of the fish.

Look! When the fish is cooked, it loses its translucency. The flesh becomes firm and matte in color. The layers of muscle become more visible and the fish flakes easily.

Feel! A firm texture and muscle layers that flake and separate under light pressure are all signs that the fish is done.

Take the back fin test! When the back fin loosens and the skin is easy to remove on a whole fish or fish with bones, it is thoroughly cooked. When a whole trout is cooked, the eyes turn white. But that applies only to trout, not to salmon.

Preparation in a microwave oven

Quick and easy for small servings. Fish is always good when cooked in a microwave, because it cooks in its own juices. Preparation is quick, so keep track of time. The power of the microwave determines cooking time. If in doubt, use less time than you think. You can always cook it a little longer, but there is no way back if the food is overcooked.

Remember! Read the instructions for your microwave thoroughly. Always add a tablespoon of water to compensate for evaporation. Always cover the food with a lid or another dish, and let the food rest for a couple of minutes. Use less salt and seasoning than usual. The flavors of the ingredients are better preserved when cooked in a microwave oven. A microwave is suitable for cooking from 1 to 4 servings of fish.

Baking

Baking is an easy way to prepare fish. It is cooked or baked in the oven in a minimum of added liquid and retains its flavor very well. The oven temperature should be 170-200°C (350-400°F). The cooking time depends upon the amount and thickness, kind of fish and its temperature when placed in the oven – from 10 to 30 minutes. A full dish with room-temperature fish in a single layer cooks in around 20 minutes. It's a good idea to use a thermometer on whole fish or large pieces of fish. When the internal temperature reaches 60°C (140°F), the fish is done. When fish is packed in aluminum foil, the oven temperature can be increased to 200°C (400°F).

Baked fish

Preheat the oven. Grease an ovenproof dish and arrange the fish in the bottom. Sprinkle with salt and seasonings. Add vegetables, if desired, and pour over liquid or sauce. Bake.

The Norwegian Arctic cod is a fantastic ingredient and the most important commercial species in Norwegian ocean fishing.

Stir-frying

The idea behind stir-frying is quick frying at high temperature. All ingredients should be cleaned and cut up beforehand. Everything happens quickly at high heat, and the food fries as it is stirred. This method lends itself especially well to seafood.

Grilling

Clean the grill. Preheat the grill. Grease the rack with oil. The fish should be room temperature. Leave the skin on, but scrape well. Brush with oil, clarified butter or an oil-based marinade. Sprinkle with salt right before grilling or afterward. Do not grill the fish for too long or it will dry out. Turn with a wooden spatula or tongs. Do not pierce the fish. A double rack is good for grilling fish, as it makes it easier to turn. Serve the fish as soon as it is cooked.

Fish prepared raw, marinated or cured

It's a widespread assumption that we don't use raw fish in Norway, but that is incorrect. We have been salting, marinating, curing and smoking fish for centuries. We marinate salmon, trout, char, herring and mackerel. We use salted herring, cured herring and smoked salmon. All of these products are raw fish, even though they have been treated in such a way that they no longer are quite so raw. Today, we use nearly raw fish in Norway. We make carpaccio and ceviche, and even sushi and sashimi have won an audience in Norway. These are methods of preparation that have been brought back from abroad. For these dishes, you need the best quality fish. All wild fish to be eaten raw should be frozen to at least –20°C (-5°F) for at least 24 hours before being eaten. This is not necessary with farmed fish such as salmon, trout, halibut and any other farmed fish.

Side dishes

All kinds of side dishes and vegetables can be served with fish and seafood. Use what you like. Try some untraditional combinations, and use what you gather from nature or what you grow in your kitchen garden. Use wild mushrooms picked in the forest instead of cultivated mushrooms. The recipes include suggestions for side dishes.

Freshly-caught fish prepared by the water tastes especially delicious.

Flavorings and seasonings

Most kinds of fish are neutral and mild in flavor, which allows for unlimited variation in use of seasonings and side dishes. There are many tips in the recipes. You don't need to follow the recipes exactly. Vary as you like. Seasoning is a personal matter.

There are many traditional and typically Norwegian ways to prepare fish. But we can also prepare fish and seafood in a more international way. Fish and other seafood have been exported from Norway for centuries. Dried fish is Norway's oldest export article, and dried salt fish is almost as old, followed by fresh fish. Today, farmed salmon and trout top the export statistics. Dried fish dishes from Italy, as well as dried salted fish dishes from Spain, Portugal and Brazil, all found their way to Norway. They were first prepared by fish traders and their families, and eventually the recipes spread throughout the country, at least along the coast. It works like that today, too. We export Norwegian seafood all over the world and eventually import those dishes that feature Norwegian fish. Such dishes gain widespread acceptance more rapidly than before, because Norwegians travel extensively abroad and bring back ideas, and because Norwegian chefs study the international kitchen. The media help a lot too. And, we import other foodstuffs in great quantities - both seasonings and other international foods are available in Norway.

Baked whole trout

Whole fish

We don't often prepare whole fish, at least not ones of any great size. But whole boneless fillets of salmon or trout or a whole halibut of moderate size are all easy to make when many gather for a meal. Whole fish is also perfect for buffets. Small whole fish in individual serving sizes are good for dinner, at least for grown-ups. The younger generation prefer boneless fish. Whole small fish are perfect for grilling in the summer. Whole fish must be cleaned and rinsed well, both inside and out. The head and tail can be removed or left on, but remember to remove the gills. Use your choice of seasonings and side dishes, or try those recommended in recipes. Whole fish can be stuffed with fresh herbs, even several at a time. Be careful with strong flavors, and choose side dishes according to season, occasion and type of fish. As a rule, fatty and

medium-fat fish are best with fresh, somewhat acidic accompaniments.

Baked whole trout
4-6 servings

1 whole trout, 1-1 ¹/₂ kg (2-3 ¹/₄ lb)
salt and pepper
juice of ¹/₂ lemon
¹/₂ fennel, finely chopped
2 celery stalks, finely chopped
¹/₂ red bell pepper
¹/₂ leek
2 tablespoons minced parsley
1 tablespoon chopped dill
1 teaspoon minced tarragon leaves

Sauce
Cooking juices from the fish
3 dl (1 ¹/₂ cups) whipping cream
2 dl (1 cup) dry white wine
fish stock
lemon juice
2 egg yolks
1 teaspoon minced parsley
1 teaspoon chopped dill

Preheat the oven to 200°C (400°F). Clean the fish well, remove the head and tail. If you want to leave the head on, just remove the gills. Sprinkle inside with salt, pepper and lemon juice and stuff with vegetables and herbs. Place the fish on a greased doubled sheet of aluminum foil. Pack the foil tightly around the fish and place in an oven tray, seam side up. Bake for 30-50 minutes. Thick fish and very cold fish need the longer cooking time. Check after 30 minutes. A basic rule: When the back fin loosens, the fish is done. Stick a hole in the foil and let the juices run out into the pan. Transfer the package to a platter and keep warm. Strain the cooking juices into a saucepan, add the cream (remove a couple of tablespoons to mix with the egg yolks) and white wine and let boil uncovered for 5 minutes. Season with fish bouillon powder, lemon juice, salt and pepper. Remove from the heat. Stir the egg yolks into the remaining cream and whisk into the sauce. Heat until thickened, whisking constantly, but do not allow to boil. Stir in the herbs. Unwrap the fish. Remove the skin and serve with boiled potatoes, asparagus, lemon wedges and fresh herbs.

Fried mackerel
4 servings

4 small mackerel, around 200 g (7 oz) each
2-3 tomatoes, sliced
butter
1 tablespoon flour
1 tablespoons breadcrumbs
1 teaspoon salt
1½ teaspoons pepper
2 tablespoons capers

Clean, rinse and dry the fish. Remove the head and tail and make a couple of slits in the skin on each side. Fry the tomatoes lightly on each side in butter. Transfer to a warm platter. Combine flour, crumbs, salt and pepper. Dip the mackerel in the flour mixture and fry until golden on both sides. Arrange the fish on the tomatoes. Add the capers to the pan and heat lightly. Pour over the fish. Serve with boiled potatoes.

Fried Arctic char
4 servings

4 Arctic char
salt and pepper
4 tablespoons (¼ cup) minced fresh herbs, such as basil, parsley and rosemary
2 tablespoons olive oil
2 tablespoons butter

Potato purée
1 kg (2 ¼ lb) potatoes
2 dl (¾ cup) 2% milk
1 dl (½ cup) light cream

Tomato-fennel sauce
4 plum tomatoes, peeled and coarsely chopped
1 fennel, finely chopped
½ shallot, minced
2 tablespoons tomato paste
2 tablespoons olive oil

Remove the gills and season the fish with salt and pepper. Stuff the fish with vegetables and herbs. You can use one or more types of herbs, as desired. Use less if using only rosemary. Heat the olive oil in a frying pan, then add the butter. Fry the fish for 3-4 minutes per side. Whole char is also good grilled. Brush with olive oil or melted butter and grill in a double rack.

Cook the potatoes, drain and mash. Heat milk, cream and butter and gradually mix into the potatoes until light and fluffy. You may not need to use all the liquid. Season with salt and pepper.

Fried Arctic char

Fried Arctic char can be served with a variety of side dishes. Boiled potatoes and a mixed salad with sour cream dressing are a good alternative. Or make a sour cream sauce by adding 2 dl (1 cup) sour cream or crème fraiche to the pan after the fish is cooked. Heat to boiling and serve alongside the fish with potatoes and marinated cucumbers.

Fried mackerel

Slices or steaks

Slices or steaks are cut from fish that have been gutted and cleaned inside, and the largest fins have been removed. Salmon, trout and cod are sold this way. Monkfish can also be marketed like this, but monkfish steaks are skinless.

Fish slices or steaks can be fried, grilled or poached. Since the skin and bones have to be removed before eating, fish steaks are best in dishes with accompaniments and sauce served alongside. Seasonings and side dishes recommended in the following dishes also go well with other kinds of fish.

Poached trout
4 servings

800 g (1 ¾ lb) trout, in slices or fillets
2 tablespoons salt per liter water
1 teaspoon peppercorns

Aioli
100 g (½ cup) mayonnaise
1-2 garlic cloves, minced
3 tablespoons minced fresh parsley
salt and pepper
lemon juice

Clean and trim the fish. Heat water, salt and peppercorns to boiling in a pot large enough to hold the fish in one layer. Remove from the heat and add the fish. Reheat to boiling and let the fish simmer for around 15 minutes. The water should not boil. Combine mayonnaise, garlic and parsley. Season with salt, pepper and lemon juice. Arrange the fish on a hot platter and serve boiled potatoes, broccoli and the aioli alongside.

Poached trout is also good with other vegetables, baked potatoes and Sandefjord butter.

Helpful hint
Poached trout is also delicious when served cold and is a popular buffet dish in Norway. Add 1 bay leaf and 1 teaspoon vinegar to the poaching water, and let the fish cool in the water.

Fried salmon
4 servings

800 g (1 ¾ lb) salmon, in slices or fillets
2 tablespoons flour
1 teaspoon salt
½ teaspoon pepper
½ teaspoon dried thyme
butter and/or oil

Wash and dry the fish. Combine flour, salt and herbs. Coat the fish on both sides with the seasoned flour and fry in butter or a mixture of butter and oil in a hot pan until golden. Arrange the fish on a hot platter and serve with boiled potatoes, sour cream and cucumber salad.

Cucumber salad
1 seedless cucumber
2 dl (¾ cup) water
3 tablespoons clear vinegar
3 tablespoons sugar
2 tablespoons finely diced bell pepper

Slice the cucumber with a cheese plane and place in a bowl. Combine water, vinegar, sugar and a little pepper and pour over the cucumber slices. Refrigerate until serving. Just before serving, sprinkle with bell pepper.

Poached trout

Fried salmon

water for extra flavor. If the roe is to be fried later, let it cool in the cooking liquid.

Cooking the fish

Heat 1 liter (quart) water with ½ dl (3 ½ table-spoons) salt to boiling. Remove the pot from the heat and add the fish. Reheat to boiling, set the pot off to one side and let the fish simmer for around 4 minutes.

Serve the cod on heated plates with slices of cod roe, liver and boiled potatoes.

Kams

500 g (1 lb) cod liver
1 teaspoon salt
1 teaspoon light syrup
1-2 tablespoons cultured buttermilk
3 tablespoons coarsely ground whole wheat flour
125-150 g (1 – 1¼ cups) barley flour
½ - 1 tablespoon caraway seed

Remove any membrane and large veins from the liver. Mash with a fork. Stir in the remaining ingredients. Form into flattened patties and simmer in fish stock or lightly salted water for 15-20 minutes. Do not allow the water to boil. Serve with poached cod.

Norwegian-style cod
4 servings

300 g (10 oz) cod liver
salt
1 teaspoon vinegar
5-6 peppercorns
500 g (1 lb) cod roe
fresh dill (optional)
1 ½ kg (3 lb) fresh cod, in slices

Preparing the liver

Remove any membrane and large veins from the liver, rinse and dry well. Heat 2 dl (1 cup) water with 2 teaspoons salt, vinegar and peppercorns to boiling. Add the liver, lower the heat and let simmer for 20 minutes. Some of the liver fat

melts into the cooking liquid, and together with the pepper and vinegar, it makes a good sauce for the fish.

Or

Cut the cleaned liver into small chunks and place in a saucepan. When the cod slices are cooked, spoon some of the cooking liquid over the liver. Heat carefully to boiling, lower the heat and let simmer for 2-3 minutes. Many feel that cod liver is best when prepared in this way.

Preparing cod roe

Heat 5 dl (2 cup) water with 1 ½ teaspoons salt to boiling. Wash the roe and wrap in parchment paper or plastic foil to keep whole. Let simmer for 20-40 minutes. Add fresh dill to the cooking

Norwegian-style cod

Making a fish "butterfly"

This way of dividing a fish fillet is used primarily for salmon and trout. Start with a boneless fillet with the skin on. Scale and scrub the skin thoroughly. Cut the fillet into 3 cm (1 ¼") thick slices. Cut each in half down to the skin, but do not cut through. Fold out the two sections like a butterfly, so that the skin sides touch underneath.

See illustration.

Salmon butterfly
with mushrooms and nut jus
4 servings

800 g (1 ¾ lb) salmon butterflies
2 tablespoons butter
3 tablespoons olive oil
1 teaspoon salt
½ teaspoon coarsely ground pepper mix

Nut jus
500 g (1 lb) mixed mushrooms, cultivated or wild
4 potatoes, peeled and cubed
1 dl (⅓ cup) walnut oil
2 tablespoons coarsely chopped walnuts
2 dl (¾ cup) fish stock
2 tablespoons butter
salt and pepper
2 teaspoons chopped fresh thyme

Making a fish "butterfly"

Make the nut jus first. Clean the mushrooms and cut into bite-size pieces. Sauté the potatoes and mushrooms in walnut oil. Add the nuts and stock. Simmer until the potatoes are tender. Stir in the butter and season with salt, pepper and thyme. Sauté the salmon in butter and oil until golden on both sides. Season with salt and pepper. Serve with a fresh green salad with lemon or vinaigrette dressing.

Butterflied salmon is also good with mashed potatoes and mustard sauce. Use a sauce for *gravlaks* and serve with coleslaw.

Sautéed halibut
4 servings

800 g (1 ¾ lb) halibut, in slices or fillets
1 dl (scant ½ cup) salt
1 liter (quart) water
2 tablespoons butter
3 tablespoons olive oil
1 teaspoon crushed rosé pepper

Hollandaise sauce
3 egg yolks
150 g (5 oz) butter, melted
salt and white pepper
lemon juice

Halibut is extra juicy if soaked in brine before cooking. Clean and rinse the fish. Dissolve the salt in the water and add the fish. Let soak for 10 minutes. Remove and dry thoroughly. Fry in a mixture of butter and olive oil for 2-3 minutes per side. Sprinkle with crushed pepper. For the sauce, beat the egg yolks in a double boiler until frothy. Beat in the butter by the tablespoon. Season with salt, pepper and lemon juice. If the sauce is too thick, add a little fish stock. Serve the fish with boiled potatoes, green beans and hollandaise sauce.

For a change of pace, try horseradish cream with fried halibut

Horseradish cream

2 dl (1 cup) whipping cream
2 tablespoons freshly grated horseradish
½ teaspoon sugar
½ teaspoon salt
vinegar

Whip the cream and stir in the horseradish. Season with sugar, salt and a little vinegar.

Salmon butterfly with mushrooms and nut jus

Sautéed halibut

Tropical salsa

1. Begin at the backbone and cut from the nape toward the tail, with a cut above and below the dorsal fins. At the level of the anus, slice through from backbone to belly.

2. Then let the knife follow the backbone back toward the tailfin. Now the fillet is loose from the anus.

3. Grasp the ear-like bone with the left hand, press the knife against it through the bone. Draw the knife toward the anus, letting it follow the bones all the time. Do not use force. The knife should almost work on its own. Cut out the fillet. Remove the black membrane. Just pull it from the gut toward the head with wet fingers. Cut out the remaining fins and other bones.

4. Remove the skin with a flaying knife or another broad, flat knife. Start at the base of the tail, grasp the skin tightly and pull, while at the same time allowing the knife to work forward.

Tropical salsa

Tropical salsa is a fresh accompaniment to all kinds of fried or grilled fish, and it's especially good with trout and salmon

4 servings

1-2 red chilis, minced
300 g (10 oz) chopped mango, papaya or pineapple, or a mixture
1 spring onion, chopped
juice of 2 limes

Combine all ingredients and refrigerate for a couple of hours before serving.

Both steaks and butterflied slices of salmon and trout are good on the grill. And they are extra good when marinated.

Marinade *for grilled fish*

4 servings

1 dl (½ cup) olive oil
4 tablespoons (¼ cup) lemon juice
4 tablespoons (¼ cup) lime juice

Flavorings

2 teaspoons grated fresh ginger
2 tablespoons sugar
1 sprig fresh thyme
grated zest of 1 lime

Combine ingredients for marinade. Add flavorings of choice. Place the fish in a glass dish and pour over the marinade. Let marinate for around 30 minutes. Brush the fish with marinade or oil and place in a double grill rack or directly on the grill. Grill until golden on each side. Add seasonings after the fish is cooked.

Dividing the fillet into different parts for different uses

A skinless, boneless fish fillet can be cut into pieces. But from the neck to the tail, a fish fillet varies both in thickness and in quality. Keeping this in mind, we can divide the fillet as illustrated here.

The finest part of the fillet is called the loin. In large fish, it can be cut into two or three pieces or into individual portions. The back part is the

tail. The thinnest part of the fillet, the belly, is often too thin for frying and poaching, but it can be cut into small pieces for soups or stews or used in fish cakes. In large fish, this piece is, of course, thicker and in some markets abroad, salmon belly is a delicacy. The fillet should be boned, and in most cases, skinned before cooking. Fried and grilled fish can be skin-on, but remember to scale the fish ahead of time.

Marinated summer mackerel
4 servings

6 dl (2 ½ cups) water
1 bay leaf
1 onion, thinly sliced
2 tablespoons vinegar
salt and pepper
fresh dill
1 carrot
1-2 cucumber
600-700 g 1 ½ lb) summer mackerel fillets

Combine the first 6 ingredients and heat to boiling. Let cool. Cut the carrot and cucumber into thin strips and place on the mackerel fillets. Roll up from tail to head and fasten with wooden picks. Place the mackerel rolls in the marinade and heat carefully to the boiling point. Remove from the heat and cool the fish in the cooking liquid. Serve with boiled potatoes, rye bread, dill and pickles.

Marinated summer mackerel

Almond-crusted Arctic char
with potato gratin
4 servings

800 g (1 ³/₄ lb) boneless fillet of Arctic char
100 g (²/₃ cup) flour
1 teaspoon salt
1 tablespoon pepper
1-2 eggs
1 ¹/₂ dl (²/₃ cup) flaked almonds
2 tablespoons butter
2 tablespoons oil

Potato gratin
1 kg (2 ¹/₄ lb) potatoes
2 shallots, minced
1 garlic clove, minced
1 tablespoon butter

Almond-crusted Arctic char with potato gratin

5 dl (2 cups) light cream
2 tablespoons grated horseradish
2 tablespoons Dijon mustard
1 teaspoon salt
¹/₂ teaspoon pepper

Make the potatoes first. Preheat the oven to 200°C (400°F). Peel and slice the potatoes, and mince the shallots and garlic. Sauté shallots and garlic in butter until soft and shiny. Add the cream and heat to boiling. Add the potatoes and simmer for a few minutes, stirring carefully until thickened. Add the remaining ingredients. Pour into an ovenproof dish and bake until potatoes are tender, around 30 minutes. Let the gratin rest for a few minutes before serving.

Scale the fish. Dip the skin side in a mixture of flour, salt and pepper, then in beaten egg, and finally in flaked almonds. Heat butter and oil in a large skillet. Brown the fish, skin side down. Fry until the nuts are golden, around 1 minute. Turn and fry on the meaty side for 1 minute. Serve on heated plates with the potato gratin and finely shredded iceberg lettuce with a dressing of 1 ¹/₂ dl (2/3 cup) natural yogurt, 1 tablespoon 7% vinegar, 1 tablespoon sugar and 1 tablespoon lemon juice. Pour over the salad just before serving or serve alongside.

Fried herring
with several accompaniments
4 servings

8 herring fillets, skinless and boneless
1 dl (¹/₂ cup) flour
1 teaspoon salt
¹/₂ teaspoon pepper
butter

Dressing
1 dl (¹/₂ cup) mayonnaise
1 dl (¹/₂ cup) yogurt
1 tablespoon capers
1 tablespoon chopped pickle
¹/₂ teaspoon minced red chili pepper

Fried herring in tortilla wrap

Accompaniments

shredded iceberg lettuce
8 tortilla wraps
10 radishes, in sticks
$1/2$ cucumber, in sticks
1 red bell pepper, in strips
2 tomatoes, sliced
1 red onion, thinly sliced
parsley

Dry the herring well. Dip in a mixture of flour, salt and pepper and fry in butter on both sides until golden. Combine all ingredients for dressing. Place lettuce on a tortilla and top with a herring fillet. Add vegetables and spoon over dressing. Roll up and enjoy!

Alternative

Serve the fried herring with potatoes instead of tortillas. Toss lettuce and vegetables and serve the dressing on the side.

Warm tomato salad for fried herring

6 tomatoes
1 onion
olive oil
2 tablespoons shredded basil
salt and pepper
2 tablespoons minced parsley

Slice tomatoes and onion. Sauté the onion in oil, add basil and season with salt and pepper. Add the tomato slices to the onion mixture and heat. Place tomato slices on the fried herring fillets. Drizzle over a little onion-oil mixture and sprinkle with parsley.

Fried plaice or flounder

with tomato sauce
4 servings

800 g (1 $3/4$ lb) plaice or flounder fillets
2-3 tablespoons flour
1 teaspoon salt
$1/2$ teaspoon freshly ground pepper
2 tablespoons butter
3 tablespoons olive oil

Fried plaice or flounder with tomato sauce

Tomato sauce

1 garlic clove, minced
$1/2$ dl (3 $1/2$ tablespoons) olive oil
1 can (14 oz) chopped tomatoes (or 6 fresh, peeled, seeded and chopped)
4 tablespoons ($1/4$ cup) white wine
4 tablespoons ($1/4$ cup) shredded fresh basil
salt and pepper
sugar
8-10 black olives

Dip the fish in a mixture of flour, salt and pepper and fry in butter and olive oil until golden on both sides. Sauté the garlic in oil for a few minutes. Add tomatoes and heat to boiling. Add wine and basil and simmer for a few minutes. Season with salt, pepper and a little sugar, if desired. Serve the fried flounder with cooked pasta and tomato sauce. Garnish with olives.

Try fried flounder with onion compote, steamed spinach and boiled potatoes

Onion compote

4 servings

8-10 shallots
1 garlic clove
3 tablespoons butter
2 tablespoons water
1 tablespoon chopped fresh thyme or
1 teaspoon dried
3 springs fresh rosemary
juice of 1 lime
$1/2$ teaspoon salt
$1/2$ teaspoon freshly ground pepper

Mince shallots and garlic. Sauté in butter and water until the water has evaporated. Add the herbs and lime juice. Season with salt and pepper

Grilled plaice or flounder in pita

Grilled plaice or flounder
4 servings

800 g (1 ³/₄ lb) plaice or flounder fillets
3 tablespoons melted butter or olive oil
¹/₂ teaspoon freshly ground pepper
1 teaspoon salt

Brush the fish with melted butter or oil and
sprinkle with pepper. Grill in a double rack.
Sprinkle with salt after cooking. Serve with
potato salad and fresh vegetables, or stuff pita
bread with fish and top with lettuce and
dressing.

The following dishes are all baked in the oven.
This is an easy way to prepare fish and there are
endless variations. Fish in a packet can also be
changed in many ways. Just make your own
combination of fish and vegetables and pack in

foil or parchment paper. When made with foil,
it's perfect for hiking. Just place the packet on
hot coals or on a grill. All recipes can be used
with any fish and just about any vegetable.

Fish *in a packet*
4 servings

600-800 g (1 1/3- 1 ³/₄ lb) boneless, skinless
salmon fillet
400 g (14 oz) mixed frozen vegetables
1 teaspoon salt
¹/₂ teaspoon pepper
1 sprig fresh thyme or 1 teaspoon dried
juice and grated zest of 1 orange

Preheat the oven to 200°C (400°F). Cut the fish
into 4 pieces of equal size. Divide the vegetables
among 4 sheets of aluminum foil (50 cm (20″)
wide) or arrange in a greased ovenproof dish.
Top with the fish. Sprinkle with salt, pepper,
thyme, orange zest and juice. Pack foil tightly
around each package or cover the ovenproof
dish with foil. Bake for 10-15 minutes (the longer time when prepared in the ovenproof dish).
Serve in the packets with baked potato wedges.

Alternative
Use fresh vegetables instead of frozen. Try a
combination of diced carrot, sliced leek and
broccoli florets. Blanch for 1 minute before
placing in packets.

Baked potato wedges
6-8 potatoes
2 tablespoons olive oil
1 teaspoon chopped fresh thyme
salt and pepper

Preheat the oven to 200°C (400°F). Scrub the
potatoes well and cut into wedges. Place on a
greased baking sheet. Drizzle with oil and
sprinkle with thyme, salt and pepper. Bake for
around 40 minutes.

Fish in a packet

Baked trout
4 servings

2 scallions
2 celery stalks
1 carrot
6 mushrooms
2 tablespoons butter
600-800 g (1 $^1/_3$-1 $^3/_4$ lb) boneless, skinless trout
fillet
1 dl ($^1/_2$ cup) white wine
1 dl ($^1/_2$ cup) vermouth
2 dl (1 cup) crème fraiche (or dairy sour cream)

Preheat the oven to 175°C (350°F). Slice the
vegetables and sauté in butter until almost tender. Arrange in an ovenproof dish. Cut the fish
into serving pieces and place on the vegetables.
Season with salt and pepper. Add wine and vermouth, cover with aluminum foil and bake for
around 15 minutes. When the fish is cooked,
pour off the juices and strain into a saucepan.
Stir in the crème fraiche and heat to boiling. (If
using sour cream, heat through but do not boil.)
Season with salt and pepper. Pour over fish and
vegetables and serve with rice.

Trout with bell pepper sauce

Baked trout

Trout *with bell pepper sauce*
4 servings

600-800g (1 $^1/_2$ lb-1 $^3/_4$ lb) boneless, skinless trout
fillet
1 teaspoon salt
$^1/_2$ teaspoon white pepper
1 teaspoon crushed rose pepper
2 teaspoons butter

Bell pepper sauce
1 red bell pepper
1 green bell pepper
1 tablespoon olive oil
3 tablespoons shredded fresh basil
$^1/_2$ teaspoon rose pepper

4 dl (1 $^2/_3$ cups) fish stock
1 teaspoons cornstarch
1 dl ($^1/_2$ cup) light cream
salt

Preheat the oven to 175°C (350°F). Cut the fish
into serving pieces and placed in a greased ovenproof dish. Sprinkle with salt, and both peppers.
Dot with butter. Bake for 10-15 minutes. Make
the sauce while the fish is cooking. Dice the peppers and sauté in oil. Add basil, pepper and
stock and reduce over high heat until around $^1/_3$
of the original amount remains. Stir the cornstarch into the cream and whisk into the pepper
mixture. Heat to boiling. Adjust the seasoning.
Serve the fish with sauce, potatoes and broccoli.

Mexican fish packet

4 servings

600-800 g (1 1/3-1 ¾ lb) boneless, skinless cod or haddock
1 small can (200 g/7 oz) corn
1 red or green bell pepper, chopped
1 ½ dl (⅔ cup) prepared salsa or taco sauce
1 dl (⅓ cup) chopped fresh coriander or parsley

Preparation in a microwave oven

Cut the fish into 4 pieces of equal size. Place on 4 sheets baking parchment. Top with corn, peppers and salsa. Leaving a bit of air space, make a double fold of paper in each direction over the fish to seal. Place on a dish and cook in the microwave oven for 4-6 minutes at 600 watts. Let rest for 1-2 minutes before serving. Open the packets and pass around the chopped coriander. Serve with rice.

To bake in a regular oven

Preheat the oven to 200°C (400°F). Brush aluminum foil with oil and make the packets as described above. Place on a baking sheet and bake for around 15 minutes.

Mexican fish packet

Fried pollock with onions

Fried pollock *with onions*
4 servings

800 g (1 ¹/₃-1 ³/₄ lb) boneless, skinless pollock
fillet
1 teaspoon salt
¹/₂ teaspoon pepper
3 tablespoons flour
2 tablespoons butter
1-2 red onions, in slices or wedges

1-2 onions, in slices or wedges
2 garlic cloves, minced
1 dl (¹/₃ cup) chopped chives

Cut the fish into serving pieces and sprinkle with salt and pepper. Dip in flour. Melt the butter and heat until golden. Fry the fish on both sides. Fry onion and garlic in the remaining butter until soft. Sprinkle with salt, pepper and chives. Serve with boiled potatoes, grated carrots and crème fraiche.

Fried pollock is also good with warm tortillas, taco sauce, sour cream and tomato, bell pepper and cucumber slices.

Baked pollock with tomatoes, bell peppers and red onions

Stir-fried pollock
4 servings

800 g (1 ¹/₃-1 ³/₄ lb) boneless, skinless pollock
fillet
1 dl (¹/₃ cup) corn oil
1 teaspoon salt
¹/₂ teaspoon freshly ground pepper
1 red onion, in thin wedges
1 carrot, in strips
150 g (5 oz) broccoli, in small florets
1 dl (1/2 cup) bean sprouts
100 g (4 oz) fresh spinach, shredded
2 tablespoons sweet chili sauce
3 tablespoons soy sauce
3 tablespoons fish sauce
a few drops sesame oil
¹/₂ dl (¹/₄ cup) fresh chopped coriander

Cut the fish into 2-3 cm (1") cubes. Heat the oil in a wok and stir fry the fish on all sides. Sprinkle with salt and pepper and remove from the pan. Stir-fry the vegetables in order. Add the sauces, sesame oil and fish and let simmer for 1 minute. Serve over egg noodles and garnish with coriander.

Helpful hint

This dish is also good over rice. Vary the vegetables by using shredded Chinese cabbage instead of spinach.

Baked pollock
with tomatoes, bell peppers and red onions
4 servings

800 g (1 1/3-1 ³/₄ lb) boneless, skinless pollock
fillet
salt and pepper
olive oil
2 red onions, sliced
1 red bell pepper, sliced
1 yellow pepper, sliced
1 garlic clove, minced
6 tomatoes (peeled and seeded) in 1 cm (¹/₂")
strips
3 tablespoons minced parsley
3 tablespoons shredded fresh basil
juice of 1 lemon

Stir-fried pollock

Preheat the oven to 200°C (400°F). Cut the fish into serving pieces and sprinkle with salt and pepper. Place in a greased ovenproof dish. Brush the fish with oil. Bake for around 15 minutes. Sauté the onion in olive oil until soft. Add the peppers and sauté for around 5 minutes. Add the garlic and tomatoes, cover and let simmer for around 5 minutes. Stir in the parsley and basil and adjust the seasonings. Drizzle lemon juice over the fish and serve with the vegetables, boiled potatoes or rice.

Fish and chips

4 servings

Batter

4 tablespoons (¼ cup) flour
1 teaspoon salt
1 teaspoon oil
1 ½ dl (⅔ cup) water
2 egg whites

Tartar sauce

1 ½ teaspoons English mustard
1 ½ dl (⅔ cup) mayonnaise
1 teaspoon minced green olive
½ teaspoon minced capers
1 teaspoon minced chives
1 teaspoon minced parsley
½ teaspoon minced sour pickle
oil
4 cod fillets of equal size, around 175 (6 oz) each

Whisk together flour, salt, oil and half the water for the batter. Whisk in the remaining water. Let the batter rest for a while. Combine all ingredients in the tartar sauce and refrigerate. Heat the oil until it bubbles around a wooden spoon handle. Dip the fish in the batter, letting any excess batter run off. Fry in the hot oil until golden and crispy. Drain on paper towels and sprinkle with salt. Serve with fried potatoes and tartar sauce.

Fish and chips

Fish for a prince
A traditional fish dish

This is a very special dish from Bergen that was composed in honor of a visiting Swedish prince over 100 years ago. The prince wanted cod for dinner, and the recipe was invented to avoid having to make poached cod for so many guests. The dish is not as simple as it sounds.

Fish for a prince is composed of cod fillets that are poached in lightly salted water until barely done. They are then placed on a hot platter, covered with béchamel sauce and garnished with asparagus, lobster and puff pastry triangles.

There are many variations of this dish. The fish is prepared in the same way, but the side dishes are different.

4 servings

800 g (1 ¹/₃-1 ³/₄ lb) boneless, skinless cod fillet
5 dl (2 cups) water
1 teaspoon salt

Sauce
2 tablespoons butter
2 ¹/₂ tablespoons flour
3 dl (1 ¹/₄ cups) fish stock
2 dl (1 cup) light cream
2 egg yolks
1 tablespoon lemon juice

Poach the fish, preferably in one layer, in water with salt, until just barely done, around 5 minutes. Arrange the fish overlapping on a heated platter. Melt the butter and stir in the flour. Let cook slightly. Whisk in the stock and cream, and let simmer for around 5 minutes. Remove from the heat, whisk in the egg yolks, and cook until thickened. Season to taste with lemon juice. Pour over the fish. Garnish with shrimp, asparagus spears and chopped parsley. Serve with boiled potatoes and mixed vegetables.

Cod *with sweet and sour sauce*
4 servings

600-800 g (1 ¹/₃-1 ³/₄ lb) boneless, skinless cod or haddock fillets
2 teaspoons mustard
3 tablespoons flour
1 teaspoon salt
¹/₂ teaspoon pepper
butter and/or oil

Sweet and sour sauce
1 small onion
¹/₂ green bell pepper
¹/₂ small carrot
1 tablespoon oil
1 teaspoon tomato paste
2 tablespoons ketchup
2 pineapple rings, in chunks
2 tablespoons vinegar
2 tablespoons sugar
1 tablespoon soy sauce
2 dl (1 cup) vegetable stock
2 teaspoons cornstarch
¹/₂ dl (¹/₄ cup) pineapple juice
shredded parsley

Cut the fish into serving pieces and spread with mustard. Combine flour, salt and pepper. Dip the fish in the mixture and fry in oil until golden on both sides. Chop the onion, cut the pepper into strips and the carrot into slices. Sauté in oil for 3 minutes. Stir in the tomato paste and ketchup. Add pineapple, vinegar, sugar soy sauce and stock and heat to boiling. Stir the cornstarch into the pineapple juice and whisk into the sauce. Simmer, stirring often, until the sauce is shiny and thick. Garnish with parsley. Serve over rice.

Fish for a prince

Cod with sweet and sour sauce

Fried cod tongues
4 servings

1 kg (2 ¼ lb) cod tongues
3 tablespoons flour
2 teaspoons salt
1 teaspoon pepper
butter

Wash and trim the tongues. Dry well. Combine flour, salt and pepper. Dip the tongues in the mixture and fry in butter over medium heat until golden. Garnish with lemon slices and serve with brown butter spiked with a little fish stock and wine, boiled potatoes and grated root vegetables.

Fried cod tongues

Whale meat

Whale *with mushrooms and berries*
4 servings

600 g (1 ⅓ lb) whale meat, partially frozen
butter
8 fresh mushrooms
3 ½ tablespoons water
2 dl (1 cup) crème fraiche
1 teaspoon crushed juniper berries
salt and pepper
2 tablespoons fresh blueberries
2 tablespoons fresh lingonberries
2 tablespoons fresh cloudberries

Cut the meat into thin slices while still partially frozen. Sauté quickly in butter in a hot skillet. Slice the mushrooms and add. Fry for a few minutes. Add the water, crème fraiche and juniper berries and heat to boiling. Season with salt and pepper. Carefully stir in the berries. Serve with mashed potatoes.

Whale with mushrooms and berries

Whale as beef

Whale *as beef*
4 servings

800 g (1 ¾ lb) whale meat
1 red onion
100 g (4 oz) zucchini
1 yellow bell pepper
butter
salt and pepper

Cut the meat into 4 pieces of equal size. Slice the onion and zucchini. Cut the pepper into strips. Sauté in butter until soft but not brown. Remove from the pan and keep warm. Sprinkle with salt and pepper. Fry the meat in browned butter for around 3 minutes per side. Season to taste. Arrange the meat on a bed of the vegetable mixture and serve with baked potatoes.

Basic recipe

Around 2 kg (4 ½ lb) fish trimmings, heads,
backbones or small fish
green part of a leek
½ onion
chunk celeriac
1 teaspoon peppercorns
1 bay leaf
1 ½ liter (6 cups) water
2 tablespoons salt

Wash the trimmings and fish well. Remove all
blood and gills. Clean and cut the vegetables
into large chunks. Place everything in a pot and
add cold water to just cover. Heat to boiling and
let cook at a rolling boil for 1 minute. Skim well.
Lower the heat and let simmer for 20 minutes.
Skim frequently. When the stock is finished,
strain through a fine sieve or through a clean
kitchen towel. For a stronger flavor or a more
concentrated stock that takes up less room in
the freezer, reduce by half.

Classic basic sauces

White wine sauce
4 servings

3 shallots
1 tablespoon butter
2 dl (1 cup) white wine
5 dl (2 cups) fish stock
3 dl (1 ¼ cups) whipping cream
salt and pepper

Mince the shallots and sauté in butter until shiny.
Add the wine and stock and reduce by half. Add
cream and reduce until thickened. Strain and
season with salt and pepper. If desired, add fresh
herbs right before serving. Use the same herbs
as in the fish dish.

Fish stew

Light fish sauce
4 servings

2 tablespoons butter
3-4 tablespoons flour
4 dl (1 ⅔ cups) fish stock
1 teaspoon salt
½ teaspoon white pepper
chopped herbs (optional)

Melt butter and stir in flour. Let cook for a minute or two. Gradually whisk in the stock. Let
simmer until thickened. Season with salt and
pepper. Milk or light cream can be used in place
of some of the stock. Add herbs as desired.
Remember to add fresh herbs right at the end,
while dried herbs should be added at the beginning, to develop flavor and aroma. Curry powder
and tomato paste should be sautéed with the
onion for best flavor development.

Bechamel sauce (white sauce)
4 servings

2 tablespoons butter
3 tablespoons flour
4 dl (1 ⅔ cups) milk
½ teaspoon salt
½ teaspoon nutmeg

Melt butter and stir in flour. Let cook for a minute or two. Gradually whisk in the milk. Let
simmer until thickened. Season with salt and
nutmeg.

Fish stew

300 g (10 oz) rutabaga
300 g (10 oz) carrots
600 g (1 ⅓ lb) potatoes
2 liters (8 ¼ cups) water
2 teaspoons salt
1 kg (2 ¼ lb) boneless, skinless fish fillet
1 teaspoon sugar
1 teaspoon 7% vinegar
chopped parsley

Clean rutabaga and carrots and cut into 1x3 cm
sticks. Peel and rinse potatoes and cut into
chunks. Heat water and salt to boiling. Cook
potatoes for around 5 minutes, then add the
other vegetables and cook until almost tender.
Cut the fish into chunks and add. Let simmer for
2-3 minutes. Season with salt, sugar and vinegar.
Just before serving, sprinkle with parsley.

Monkfish and halibut are good in this dish, but
cod and pollock also work well.

Easy everyday soup

2 tablespoons chopped parsley
salt and pepper

Cut the fish into large chunks. Shell the shrimp. Make stock with the shrimp shells and fish trimmings. Steam the mussels and remove the meat. Reserve the stock and add to the fish and shrimp stock. Coarsely chop the onions, peel and cube the potatoes, and mince the garlic. Sauté vegetables in oil until the onions are shiny. Add fennel, thyme, stock and wine. Heat to boiling and let boil for 15 minutes. Add the fish and let simmer until fish is cooked through. Add shrimp, mussels and parsley. Season with salt and pepper.

Easy everyday soup
1 packet dehydrated fish soup
1 onion, coarsely chopped
1 carrot, diced
1/2 leek, thinly sliced
1 dl (1/2 cup) light cream

100 g (4 oz) fish pudding or fish meatballs
50 g (2 oz) peeled shrimp (optional)

Follow the directions on the soup packet, but use 1 dl (1/2 cup) less liquid. Add the vegetables and cook for the required time. Add cream and heat to boiling. Add the fish pudding and let simmer until heated through. Add shrimp. Readjust the seasoning.

Bouillabaisse means a stock that has been reduced. Bouillabaisse originated in southern France. The dish is called a soup, but it is often so rich and full of ingredients that it can be called a stew. It is based on local ingredients and comes in many different versions. This recipe is adapted to include Norwegian ingredients – shall we call it à la norvegienne?

Clear fish and shellfish soup
4 servings

500 g (1 lb) boneless, skinless fillets from white fish
300 g (10 oz) shrimp in shells
300 g (10 oz) mussels in shells
2 onions
4 potatoes
2 garlic cloves
1 tablespoon vegetable oil
1 teaspoon fennel seed
1 teaspoon dried thyme
8 dl (3 1/3 cups) fish stock
2 dl (1 cup) dry white wine

Clear fish and shellfish soup

Bouillabaisse *à la norvegienne*
4-6 servings

200 g (7 oz) boneless, skinless halibut fillet
200 g (7 oz) boneless, skinless wolffish fillet
200 g (7 oz) boneless, skinless trout or salmon
fillet
300 g (10 oz) cooked shrimp, lobster or crab
claws
1 onion
3 tomatoes
2 garlic cloves
3 ½ tablespoons oil
1 ⅓ liter (6 ¼ cups) fish stock
1 herb bouquet (parsley, thyme, bay leaf, leek,
celery stalk)
grated zest of ½ orange
pinch saffron
salt and pepper
2 tablespoons minced parsley

A soup is only as good as the stock that goes
into it, so be sure to have good fish stock on
hand. Cut the fish into chunks and shell most of
the shrimp. Cut onion and tomatoes into thin
wedges and mince the garlic. Sauté onion,
tomatoes and garlic in oil. Add stock, fish, herbs
and zest, and simmer until the fish is cooked
through. Add saffron, salt and pepper. Add the
shrimp and heat through. Sprinkle with parsley.
For an elegant touch, garnish with lobster or
crab claws. Serve with garlic bread.

Bouillabaisse à la norvegienne

Norwegian fish soup
4 servings

1-2 carrots, diced
1 small onion, coarsely chopped
1 small leek, sliced
1 liter (4 cups) fish stock
4 tablespoons (¼ cup) butter
4 tablespoons (¼ cup) flour
2 dl (1 cup) milk
400 g (14 oz) boneless, skinless fish fillets
½ dl (¼ cup) dairy sour cream
1 tablespoon chopped chives

Cook the vegetables in fish stock until almost
tender. Melt the butter, then add the flour. Cook
for a couple of minutes. Whisk in the milk, then
whisk in the vegetable stock. Return the vegetables to the pot. Cut the fish into chunks and
add. Let simmer until cooked through. Whisk in
the sour cream and heat through. Do not allow
to boil. Garnish with chopped chives.

Norwegian fish soup

Ground fish products

While foreigners may not be familiar with products made from ground fish, these are as popular in Norway as those made with ground meat are abroad. Fish can be ground coarsely enough so that the structure of the fish is visible. Salmon, trout, pollock, mackerel and herring are often coarsely ground. Freshness is important. Fish that has been frozen does not bind well, and the ground fish will be loose. That is not so important in making coarse fish patties. When grinding fish that has been frozen, it's a good idea to increase the amount of potato starch by 30% and add 1-2 eggs per kilo (2 ¼ lb) fish.

Finely ground fish, also called fish forcemeat, is best made from white fish. Salt is added to increase the binding ability of the fish, so that more liquid can be absorbed. This mixture is white and smooth and can be used for fish patties, fish pudding or quenelles. A meat grinder or a food processor are best for grinding fish. Coarsely ground fish can also be made in a food processor. There are a few important things to remember when making ground fish.

1. Raw materials should be ice cold and of good quality. Try to maintain as low a temperature as possible during preparation.
2. Work the salt well into the mixture, so that it becomes finely textured and elastic before adding liquid.
3. Fry a trial patty, then add more salt, seasonings or potato starch, as necessary.

Coarsely ground fish
4 servings

500 g (1 1b) pollock, salmon, herring or mackerel fillet
1 teaspoon salt
1 – 1 ½ dl (½-⅔ cup) milk

Pollock is excellent for ground fish products.

1 tablespoon potato starch
½ teaspoon pepper
seasonings

This mixture can be made in a food processor and used for burgers.

Cut the fish into chunks and place in a food processor with the salt. Pulse until evenly chopped. This takes seconds. Add ⅓ of the milk at a time, processing between each addition until the mixture is smooth. Add potato starch and seasonings at the end. Fry a trial patty and season to taste.

Seasoning suggestions
Minced parsley, chives, thyme, basil, tarragon, grated fresh ginger, one or a blend of two or more. Or minced onion, leek, bell pepper, chili or other vegetables, preferably with one or two herbs. Do not combine too many flavors at once.

Finely ground fish
1 kg (2 ¼ lb) boneless, skinless fillets of haddock, cod, whiting or other white fish
25 g (1 ¼ tablespoons) salt
7 dl (scant 3 cups) ice-cold milk
25 g (2 tablespoons) potato starch
¼ teaspoon grated nutmeg

This smooth white forcemeat can be made into fish patties, quenelles or fish pudding. Cut the fish into strips and place in a food processor with the salt. Pulse for a few seconds until elastic. Gradually add milk, then starch and nutmeg. Make and fry a trial cake. Adjust the seasoning, if necessary.

For quenelles, heat 1 liter (4 cups) water and 2 teaspoons salt to a boil, or use fish stock. Form small dumplings with a spoon and carefully place in the water. Let simmer for 6 minutes, until the quenelles float. Remove with a slotted spoon. The remaining cooking water can be used in sauce.

Fine fish pudding

4 servings

500 g (1 lb) haddock, pike, wolffish or other firm
white fish
1 ½ teaspoons salt
1 tablespoon potato starch
¼ teaspoon mace
3-4 dl (1-1 ⅓ cups) milk

Preheat the oven to 120°C (250°F). All ingredients should be as cold as possible. Cut the fish into chunks and place with salt, starch and mace in a food processor and puree until thick and relatively smooth. With the motor running, add the milk in a thin stream. All the milk should be incorporated into the fish mixture. Pour into a greased loaf pan, pressing the mixture down into the corners. Smooth the surface and wipe the edges. Bake for approximately one hour. The pudding is done when it resists light pressure in the middle. Chopped vegetables, herbs and other seasonings can be added to the fish pudding for more flavor.

Fish quenelles in curry sauce

Extra fine fish forcemeat

Cream can be substituted for some or all of the milk. Eggs (3-4 eggs per kilo (2 ¼ lb) fish fillets) can be used instead of potato starch. A fish pudding made with this mixture is sensitive and should be heated carefully. It is best cooked in a water bath. If the mixture contains a high proportion of egg, it can become grainy if cooked at too high a temperature. Follow the same directions for cooking as above, but place the pan in a water bath.

In the following recipes, you can use fish quenelles, fish pudding, fish cakes or fish burgers made from one of the above recipes. Canned fish quenelles or balls in broth are available in shops that sell Scandinavian imports.

Fish quenelles *in curry sauce*

4 servings

2 onions, minced
1 garlic clove, minced
1 tablespoon butter
2 teaspoons curry powder
1 tablespoon flour
3 dl (1 ¼ cups) milk
1 dl (⅓ cup) fish stock or liquid from canned fish
quenelles
500 g (1 lb) fish quenelles
salt and pepper

Sauté onion and garlic in butter until shiny. Stir in the curry and let cook for a few minutes. Stir in the flour. Whisk in the milk and stock and heat to boiling, whisking constantly. Let simmer for a couple of minutes. Add the quenelles and heat through. Season to taste. Serve with rice and broccoli.

Oriental fish quenelles

4 servings

1 tablespoon butter
2 teaspoons curry powder
1 tablespoon flour
3 dl (1 ¼ cups) milk
1 dl (⅓ cup) fish stock or liquid from canned fish
quenelles
2-3 celery stalks, in 2 ½ cm (1") chunks
1 small can pineapple chunks
500 g (1 lb) fish quenelles
1 dl (⅓ cup) raisins
½ dl (3 tablespoons) unsalted peanuts

Melt the butter, stir in the curry and let cook for a couple of minutes. Stir in the flour. Whisk in the milk and stock and heat to boiling, whisking constantly. Let simmer for a couple of minutes. Add celery and pineapple and return to boiling. Add the quenelles and heat through. Stir in raisins and peanuts just before serving. Serve with rice and broccoli.

Juicy salmon burgers

Pollock patties

with dill-mustard sauce
4 servings

600 g (1 ⅓ lb) pollock fillet
1 ½ teaspoons salt
1 ½ dl (⅔ cup) milk
1 tablespoon potato starch
1 small onion, minced
2 tablespoons chopped chives
½ teaspoon pepper
butter

Dill-mustard sauce

2 tablespoons butter
3-4 tablespoons flour
5 dl (2 cups) 2% milk
1 tablespoon whole grain mustard
2 tablespoons finely chopped dill
salt and pepper

Prepare coarsely ground fish according to the recipe on page 140. Add onion, chives and pepper. Form into 4 or 8 flat patties and fry in butter over medium heat until golden brown. For the sauce, melt the butter and stir in the flour. Whisk in the milk and let simmer for 2-3 minutes. Add mustard and dill and season with salt and pepper. Serve with vegetables and potatoes.

Mackerel patties

with mushroom-tomato compote
4 servings

600 g (1 ⅓ lb) mackerel fillets

Mushroom-tomato compote

1 onion, minced
50 g (2 oz) bacon, finely diced
2 tablespoons butter
8 fresh mushrooms, thinly sliced
3 tomatoes, peeled, seeded and chopped
1 tablespoon minced chives
salt and pepper

Prepare coarsely ground fish according to the recipe on page 000 and fry in butter. Fry onion and bacon in butter over low heat for 2-3 minutes. Add the mushrooms and sauté until shiny. Add tomato and chives and season with salt and pepper. Serve with the fish patties with sour cream on the side.

Juicy salmon burgers

4 servings

600 g (1 ⅓ lb) boneless, skinless salmon fillet
100 g (4 oz) smoked salmon
1 tablespoon potato starch
1 egg
½ teaspoon salt
½ teaspoon ground pepper
2 teaspoons minced fresh thyme or basil
3 ½ tablespoons sliced scallions
butter

Cut fresh and smoked salmon into chunks. Place in a food processor with the starch, egg, salt and pepper. Process until smooth. Stir in remaining ingredients. Let rest for a while in the refrigerator. Form into flat patties and fry in butter over medium heat until golden and cooked through. Serve on a bun with lettuce and dressing or with boiled potatoes and vegetables.

Pollock patties with dill-mustard sauce   Right: Mackerel patties with mushroom-tomato compote

Herring patties

Herring patties

4 servings

750 g (1 2/3 lb) fresh herring fillets
2 teaspoons salt
1 ½ dl (2/3 cup) milk
2 tablespoons potato starch
1 onion, chopped
3 tablespoons minced parsley
½ teaspoon pepper

Prepare coarsely ground fish according to the recipe on page 000. Add onion, parsley and pepper. Form into 4 or 8 flat patties and fry in butter over medium heat until golden brown. Serve the patties on whole grain bread or in pita or hamburger buns with dressing and lettuce.

Herring patties can also be served with fried onions, boiled potatoes, sour cream, pickled beats and grated carrots and apples

Hitraball

Blandabaill

6 servings

1 kg (2 ¼ lb) boneless, skinless fresh haddock fillet
2 onions, in wedges
1 liter (4 cups) peeled potato chunks
2 tablespoons salt
1 dl (⅓ cup) milk
3 tablespoons potato starch
1 tablespoon flour
150 g (5 oz) bacon, diced

Grind the fish once with onion, potatoes and salt. Gradually stir in the milk. Add the starch and flour, mixing well. Make large balls and put a piece of bacon in each ball. Simmer in salted water (½ teaspoon salt per liter/quart) until cooked through, around 20 minutes. Serve with boiled carrots, fried bacon cubes and potatoes.

Hitraball

4 servings

500 g (1 lb) boneless, skinless haddock fillet
1 teaspoon salt
3-5 dl (1 ¼-2 cups) 2% milk
1 ½ tablespoons potato starch
½ onion, minced
75 g (3 oz) suet, diced
5-8 dl (2-3 cups) fish stock

Blandabaill

Prepare finely ground fish according to the recipe on page 140. Add onions and form into large balls. Place a suet cube in each ball. Let simmer in good fish stock for 15-20 minutes. Serve with boiled potatoes, fried bacon and rutabagas.

Preserved products

Dried salted fish

Norwegian klippfish is cod (or other members of the cod family) that has been salted and dried in a special process. Treated in this way, the fish retains its flavor and nutrients – only the water is removed. It is healthy, tasty and it keeps well – a truly natural product. It is sold in many grocery stores and specialty shops, either whole or in pieces, loose or prepackaged. In Norway, some stores sell it pre-soaked and cleaned, frozen or refrigerated.

Cleaning and soaking

Cut the fish into smaller pieces. Remove the skin, which is easy with dried fish, so soaking doesn't take so long. Soak the fish in lots of cold water for 24-72 hours, changing water once a day. The larger and thicker the fish, the longer it needs to soak. If the fish is thick (5-6 cm/2-2 ¼ "), it should be soaked for 72 hours. Fish that will be fried needs to be soaked longer than fish that will be poached. If you are uncertain, you can taste a little piece from the thickest part of the fish. Cook a piece for 5 minutes. It should have a mildly salty flavor. Salt fish that has been soaked can be frozen for later use. It's a good idea to soak a large amount and freeze it down. Then if you get the urge for bacalao, it's easy to prepare.

Estimating portions

1 kg (2 ¼ lb) dried salted fish corresponds to 1 ½ kg (3 lb) soaked. After cleaning, there should be around 1 kg (2 ¼ lb) ready to cook fish. When buying klippfish, count on 100-150 g (3 ½ - 5 oz) dried salted fish per person.

Bacalao à la viscaina

4 servings

700 g (1 ½ lb) soaked and cleaned klippfish
1 dl (1/3 cup) olive oil
4 onions, sliced or diced
2 tablespoons tomato paste
6 tomatoes, sliced (or same amount canned)
6 potatoes, sliced
2 red or green bell peppers, sliced
½ red or green chili, minced (or ½ teaspoon cayenne pepper)

Cut the fish into 4 cm (1 ½") pieces. Heat the oil in a heavy pot. Sauté the onion until shiny and stir in the tomato puree. Layer all ingredients in the sauce. Heat to boiling, lower the heat, and let simmer over low heat until all ingredient are cooked, around one hour.

Klippfish storehouse special

4 servings

1 large onion, coarsely chopped
2 garlic cloves, minced
1 dl (⅓ cup) olive oil
2 tablespoons diced red bell pepper
1 teaspoon tomato paste
1 tablespoon minced red chili
1 can (24 oz) chopped tomatoes
¼ teaspoon sugar or honey
salt, pepper and hot pepper sauce
1 liter (4 cups) fish stock
500 g (1 lb) soaked and cleaned klippfish

Sauté onion and garlic in olive oil until soft. Add pepper, tomato paste and chili and sauté for a couple of minutes. Add tomatoes and let cook for a couple of minutes more. Season with sugar, salt, pepper and hot pepper sauce. Divide the fish into serving pieces. Heat the stock and add the fish. Let simmer for around 10 minutes, until fish is flaky and cooked through. Serve the fish with the tomato sauce and boiled almond potatoes. Sprinkle with raw onion rings and olive slices.

Bacalao à la vizcaina

Klippfish storehouse special

Salt fish

Lightly salted redfish
4 servings

¾-1 kg (1 ¾ - 2 ¼ lb) lightly salted redfish

Cut the fish into serving pieces. Heat the water to boiling and add the fish. Let simmer for 8-10 minutes, until the fish separates from the bone. Serve with boiled potatoes and creamed carrots. Cooked vegetables and béchamel sauce or egg butter with chopped parsley is also good with lightly salted redfish.

Red pollock

Lightly salted redfish

Red pollock
4 servings

600 g (1 ⅓ lb) red pollock

Soak the fish in cold water for 4-5 hours. Clean and cut into serving pieces. Place in a pot with water to cover. Heat to boiling. Drain. Heat new water to boiling, add the fish and let simmer for around 10 minutes. Serve with boiled potatoes and mashed root vegetables. Creamed peas, fried bacon, boiled potatoes and flatbread are traditional side dishes.

Smoked haddock
4 servings

1 kg (2 ¼ lb) whole smoked haddock (less if using fillets)
4 dl (1 ⅔ cups) water or fish stock

Cut the fish into serving pieces. Heat water to boiling and add the fish. Let simmer for 10-12 minutes, depending upon the size. Serve with boiled potatoes

Salt herring *and new potatoes*
4 servings

4-6 salt herring fillets
8-12 new potatoes, cooked
1 onion, thinly sliced
1 dl (½ cup) diced pickled beets

Cut the herring fillets into wide strips on the diagonal. Cut the potatoes into thick slices. Arrange herring, onion, potatoes and beets on a platter and serve with flatbread and dairy sour cream.

Salt herring and new potatoes

Smoked haddock

Boknafisk

Boknafisk or *hjellosing* is cod that has hung on drying racks for 12-14 days or up to 3 weeks, according to the size of the fish. Bokna fish, which is really half-dried fish, has a rather acidic flavor and aroma, and many prefer this variation to standard dried fish. If the fish seems hard in the thinner sections, you can soak it for a few hours, preferably overnight, before cooking.

250-300 g (9-11 oz) fish per person

Cut the fish into 2 cm (¾") slices. Heat a large pot of water to boiling and add 2 tablespoons salt per liter (quart) water. Add the fish and let it simmer for around 20 minutes, until it begins to separate from the bone. Serve with boiled carrots and browned butter. Many like to add bacon cubes to the browned butter.

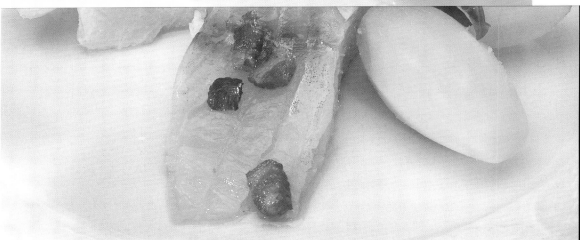

Lutefisk

Dried fish Mediterranean style

Dried fish

Dried fish has to be soaked before cooking. During the drying process, around 70% of the water is removed. Some of that has to be replaced before cooking. Soak the fish in lots of cold water. It is important to keep the fish cold, 4°C (40°F) or colder. Split or filleted dried fish needs only half the soaking time of whole fish. Remove skin and bones after soaking but before cooking. For a casual dinner, leave the skin and bones on and let everyone clean their chunks of fish at the table.

Dried fish fricassee

500 g (1 lb) soaked and cleaned dried fish
3 tablespoons salt
1 liter (quart) water
2-3 carrots, in chunks
1 leek, rutabaga or other vegetables, in chunks
1 tablespoon butter
1 tablespoon flour
3 dl (1 ¼ cups) milk and vegetable stock
½ teaspoon salt
white pepper

Gradually whisk in the milk and stock and heat to boiling, whisking constantly until thickened. Season with salt and pepper. Arrange the fish on a platter with the vegetables alongside. Pour over sauce.

Dried fish *Mediterranean style*

600 g (1 ⅓ lb) soaked and cleaned dried fish
4 potatoes, peeled and cut into wedges
1-2 tomatoes, peeled, seeded and diced
1 dl (⅓ cup) olive oil
juice of 2 oranges
1 teaspoon salt
½ teaspoon pepper
chopped parsley

Cut the fish into 5 cm (2") pieces and let simmer, covered, for 10 minutes. Add the potatoes, cover and cook for 15 minutes more. Add the remaining ingredients, cover and shake a few times. Garnish with chopped parsley.

Lutefisk
4 servings

3 kg (6 ½ lb) lutefisk
2-3 tablespoons salt
coarsely ground pepper

Lutefisk is best cooked without adding water in the oven. Preheat the oven to 200°C (400°F). Place the fish, skin down, in an ovenproof dish. Sprinkle with salt and pepper. Cover with aluminum foil and bake in the middle of the oven for around 40 minutes. Check for doneness after 30 minutes. A smaller amount of fish should cook in less time. Count on 15 minutes per kilo (2 ¼ lb) fish. Remember that the temperature of the fish when it is placed in the oven determines the cooking time. Large cold pieces take longer to cook than small pieces at room temperature. Serve lutefisk piping hot on heated plates with creamed peas, boiled potatoes and crisp diced bacon with bacon fat. Place coarse salt, a pepper mill, lefse and mustard on the table. According to tradition, cold beer and aquavit are the best accompaniments. Other alternatives are light beer or lemonade.

Gravlaks

Marinated fish

Fatty fish are best in marinated dishes. Salmon, trout and char are usually prepared in this way, but mackerel, herring, whitefish and halibut also lend themselves to marinating. Lean fish like pollock and cod can be marinated, but they become firmer in the process. Wild fish may be infested with a small roundworm, the anisakis larva. It dies when cooked, fried, heavily salted or frozen to -24°C (-11°F) for at least 24 hours. For that reason, you should freeze fish that you plan to marinate for at least 24 hours. It doesn't matter if the fish is frozen before or after, but it is most practical to do this ahead of time. Marinated fish can be frozen. Norwegian farmed fish does not contain parasites, so salmon, trout and char can be marinated without freezing first. Marinated

Gravlaks *(marinated salmon)*

1 kg (2 ¼ lb) boneless salmon fillet (2 small fillets)
fresh dill
3 tablespoons salt
3 tablespoons sugar
1 teaspoon coarsely ground white pepper

Pluck out any small bones in the fish. Dry thoroughly. Arrange a bed of dill in the bottom of a glass dish large enough to just hold the fish. Combine salt and sugar and rub into the flesh side of both fillets. Place one in the dish skin side down. Sprinkle with chopped dill and pepper. Top with the other fillet, skin side up. Sprinkle with dill. Cover with plastic wrap and place under light pressure (a cutting board with

and cut into thin slices on the diagonal. This dish keeps in the refrigerator for 4-5 days. It can be frozen.

Alternative
For a different flavor, sprinkle 1 dl (⅓ cup) crushed juniper berries and 2-3 tablespoons aquavit over the flesh of the fillets. Otherwise, the same amount of salt, sugar and pepper as before. Serve sour cream and hearty bread alongside.

Mustard sauce *for gravlaks*
4 servings

½ dl (¼ cup) mustard (do not use hotdog mustard)
1-2 tablespoons white wine vinegar
1 tablespoon sugar
⅛ teaspoon ground pepper
1 dl (½ cup) oil (at room temperature)
½ dl (¼ cup) chopped dill
salt
Whisk together mustard, vinegar, sugar and pepper. Whisk in the oil in droplets. Stir in the dill and let steep at room temperature. Adjust the seasoning.

Alternative

For a milder sauce, add sour cream instead of oil. Start with equal amounts of mustard and sour cream.

Aquavit-marinated salmon

This recipe gives a slightly different flavor to the fish. The proportion of salt and sugar to fish is low, so be sure to follow the recipe carefully, practice good hygiene and store at the recommended temperature.

1 kg (2 ¼ lb) boneless salmon or trout fillet (2 small fillets)
2 tablespoons salt
1 ½ tablespoons sugar
1 teaspoon coarsely crushed pepper
1 teaspoon crushed caraway seed
1 teaspoon ground anise or fennel
6 tablespoons aquavit (preferably Løiten or Lysholm)

Pluck out any small bones in the fish. Dry thoroughly. Combine salt and sugar and rub into the flesh side of both fillets. Combine spices and sprinkle half over the bottom of a dish just large enough to hold the fish. Place one fillet in the dish skin side down. Sprinkle with remaining spices and drizzle with aquavit. Top with the other fillet, skin side up. Cover with plastic wrap and place under light pressure (a cutting board with a couple of cans on top, for example).

Refrigerate for 48 hours. Ideally, the fish should be stored at 8-10°C (45-50°F). Turn the fish and spoon any brine that appears onto the fillets every 12 hours. When the fish is ready, wipe off the brine and cut into thin slices on the diagonal. This dish keeps in the refrigerator for 2-3 days. It can be frozen. Serve with mustard sauce seasoned with the same spices as the fish plus a little aquavit.

Fermented fish *from Valdres*

3 kg (6 ½ lb) fresh mountain trout of the highest quality
200 g (1 ½ dl) coarse sea salt
1 tablespoon sugar

Clean and rinse the fish in lots of cold water. Do not let it come into contact with the ground (any dirt or earth). Dry well and sprinkle a little salt in the belly of each fish. Arrange the fish, belly slightly up, on the diagonal, in a well-scrubbed, clean wooden barrel. Sprinkle salt over, under, and between the fish in the barrel. Place a weight on the fish and let it rest at room temperature for 24 hours, then move it to a cold cellar. After 2-3 days, brine will form. If the brine does not cover the fish, make some brine and add it. Cook brine with 3 liter (quarts) water, 1 dl (scant ½ cup) salt and 2 teaspoons sugar. Let the brine cool completely before adding to the

Fermented fish from Valdres

Seafood with potato waffles

fish. The fish is ready after 5-6 weeks. If mold forms, pour off all the brine and make new. Sometimes the finished fish is so ripe that it can be spread with a knife. Serve with boiled potatoes, butter and flatbread, or sour cream and red onions.

Smoked fish

Smoked salmon, trout, mackerel and herring are delicious and can be used in vegetable and pasta salads, in egg dishes, or they can be served sliced with potato salad, sour cream and cheese on the side, just to name a few combinations. Of course, smoked fish is excellent as sandwich filling. Here are a few recipes to give you an idea of how versatile smoked fish can be.

Seafood *with potato waffles*
4 servings

Waffles
2 dl (1 cup) flour
1 ½ dl (¾ cup) milk
½ teaspoon baking powder
½ teaspoon salt
300 g (11 oz) peeled, grated raw potatoes
3 tablespoons chopped chives
50 g (3 tablespoons) melted butter

Filling
100 g (4 oz) smoked salmon
100 g (4 oz) golden caviar
100 g (4 oz) salmon caviar
4-6 tablespoons crème fraiche or dairy sour cream
dill or flat leaf parsley

Combine ingredients for waffles and let rest for 30 minutes. Make waffles in a well- greased iron. Arrange two waffle hearts on a plate and top with salmon and caviar. Top with crème fraiche and dill or parsley.

Smoked salmon/trout
with apple salad
4 servings

2 sweet red apples
2 tablespoons vinaigrette
½ head oak leaf lettuce
200 g (8 oz) smoked salmon or trout

Vinaigrette
1 tablespoon wine vinegar
½ teaspoon Dijon mustard

Smoked mackerel snack

1 teaspoon clear honey
1 small garlic clove, minced
3 tablespoons olive oil
salt and pepper

Make the dressing first. Combine all ingredients in a jar with a tight-fitting lid. Shake until emulsified. Cut the apples into thin wedges. Toss apples with dressing. Divide lettuce among four plates. Top with apples. Cut fish into thin slices and arrange with the apples.

Salmon *with avocado*
4 servings

2 avocados
juice of 1 lime
coarsely ground black pepper
300 g (11 oz) smoked salmon
chervil

Halve the avocados and remove the pits. Peel and slice each half and arrange on plates. Sprinkle with lime juice and sprinkle with pepper. Cut the salmon into strips and drape over the avocado. Garnish with chervil and lime. Serve with a dressing made from sour cream and chopped chervil.

Smoked trout tartar
4 servings

300 g (11 oz) smoked trout
1 tablespoon Dijon mustard
2 tablespoons lemon juice
3 tablespoons olive oil
1 tablespoon finely chopped fresh dill
3 tablespoons minced shallots
salt and pepper
4 hard-cooked eggs
1-2 tablespoons minced red onion
1 tablespoon capers

Cut the trout into fine dice. Whisk together mustard, lemon juice and oil. Stir in dill and shallots and season with salt and pepper. Fold in the trout. Cover with plastic wrap and refrigerate. Coarsely chop the egg whites and press the yolks through a sieve. Form the trout mixture into 4 patties. Place each in the middle of a plate. Arrange egg white, egg yolk, onion and capers all around. Serve with toast.

Smoked mackerel snack
4 servings

400 g (14 oz) warm-smoked mackerel
400 g (14 oz) pepper-smoked mackerel
400 g (14 oz) cold-smoked mackerel
6 eggs
chopped scallions
butter
lettuce
bell pepper rings
celery stalks, in chunks

Clean and fillet the fish. Cut the warm and pepper-smoked mackerel into medium-thick slices. Cut the cold-smoked mackerel into very thin

Smoked herring omelet

slices. Scramble the eggs with chopped scallions in butter. Arrange fish and eggs on a platter with the fresh vegetables. Serve with whole grain bread, butter and sour cream.

Smoked herring omelet
4 servings

4 smoked herring
4 tomatoes
2 tablespoons chopped dill
4 eggs
1 dl (½ cup) milk
salt

Preheat the oven to 180°C (350°F). Remove skin and bones from the herring and arrange in a greased ovenproof dish. Slice the tomatoes and place on the fish. Sprinkle with dill Beat the eggs with milk and salt and pour over the herring. Bake for around 20 minutes. Serve hot with bread and butter.

Smoked salmon/trout with apple salad

Shellfish

Mollusks

Many kinds of shellfish are found along the Norwegian coast. With an aroma of the sea and color nuances from white to yellow to golden orange, we are tempted even before we taste. And they taste wonderful! For Norwegians, mussels are the favorite, but in other countries, oysters and scallops are the most popular.

Norwegian shellfish farming is a new industry, still in the beginning stages, but development looks promising for the future. Soon Norwegian mussels, oysters and scallops will be marketed all over the world. This development also means that Norwegian consumers will have more access to different kinds of shellfish in their own shops throughout the year. And the quality of Norwegian shellfish is excellent.

The shellfish found along the Norwegian coastline can provide many an exciting dinner. It's important to note that shellfish are best in the winter and through the spring, until they spawn. Spawning dates vary according to the air and water temperature and the particular type of shellfish.

Many Norwegians like to dig for shells on the seashore. It's important to avoid places where the water might be polluted or contain poisonous algae. Common sense tells us to stay away from areas where there might be run-off from industry or residential areas. There is a central "Mollusk telephone" (22 24 62 99) number in Norway with information about where to dig for safe shells. The Institute for Marine Research website also gives information about Norwegian mollusks. Samples of shellfish sold in retail outlets are taken regularly to insure safety.

Shellfish is good winter food, when mollusks and other shellfish are at their very best.

Preparation of live mollusks

Fresh live mollusks should close their shells when tapped. Open shells are dead and should be discarded. Remember that mollusks are live animals and should not be frozen raw. Cooked mollusk meat freezes very well. Mollusks that remain closed after cooking should also be discarded. All varieties of scallops are an exception and can be frozen once out of the shell.

Buying shellfish

Type of shellfish	Time span
Live: Mussels, horse mussels, oysters, scallops and cockles	September-April/May
Processed, frozen: Scallops in shell with topping	Year-round
Processed: Mussels in brine, semi-conserved	Year-round
Frozen: Raw queen scallops and raw scallops (cleaned), mussels in shells	Year-round
Canned: Mussels in broth	Year-round

Cleaning scallops

1. Place the scallop on a thick cloth napkin. Hold with the blunt end toward you. Place the knife between the shells. Press and cut over the closing muscle that is just a little inside the edge of the blunt end.

2. Carefully lift the upper shell. Remove the gills that lie like a brown ring around the scallop muscle and the coral.

3. The edible parts are the muscle and the coral (roe and milt).

Mollusks can be used in main dishes, salads and soups as well as in other kinds of dishes. Try them – it's a new experience.

Norwegian cultivated mussels

The basic recipe for mussels is based on the traditional dish "Moules à la mariniere" or mussels like the fisherman's wife prepares them. It can be varied with different herbs, other vegetables, cream or wine. These ingredients should be added after the shells have opened. In that way, the flavors are absorbed. Norwegian farmed mussels should not be steamed too long or they become tough and tasteless. Prepare only 1 kg (2 ¼ lb) at a time and serve immediately.

Basic recipe for mussels
1 serving

1 kg (2 ¼ lb) Norwegian farmed mussels
½ small onion, chopped
5 cm (2") leek, chopped
½ celery stalk, chopped
1 tablespoon butter or olive oil

Place all ingredients in a pot. Cover and cook at high heat for 3-4 minutes. Shake the pot several times so that the bottom shells rise to the top and the top shells fall to the bottom. Cook for 3-4 minutes more, until all the shells have opened.

Mussels in white wine

1 serving

1 kg (2 ¼ lb) mussels prepared according to basic recipe
2 dl (¾ cup) dry white wine
2 garlic cloves, minced
2 tablespoons minced parsley

Prepare according to basic recipe. When the shells have opened, add wine and garlic. Shake, reheat to boiling, sprinkle with parsley and serve immediately.

Mussels au gratin

Remove the empty half of each mussel. Place the remaining shells with the meat in a large oven-proof dish or on a baking sheet. Sprinkle with chopped chives, parsley, garlic, coarsely ground pepper and grated cheese. Bake for a few minutes in a hot oven or place under the grill for 3-4 minutes.

Pan-fried mussels

4 servings

48 mussels prepared according to basic recipe
1 lemon, in wedges
3 tablespoons flour
2 tablespoons butter
salt and pepper
1 teaspoon chopped parsley

Remove the mussel meat from the shells. Place half of the shells on a platter. Reserve a couple of lemon wedges for garnish and squeeze the juice out of the rest. Reserve. Place the flour in a plastic bag, add the mussel meat and shake to coat. Heat the butter in a frying pan until light brown. Fry the mussels for 2-3 minutes. Place each mussel in an empty shell. Stir the lemon juice and parsley into the butter in the pan. Pour over the mussels. Serve immediately with lemon wedges.

Mussels in white wine

Mussels au gratin

Pan-fried mussels

Sautéed scallops

4 servings

1 tablespoon minced shallot
1 tablespoon grated fresh ginger
3 dl (1 ¼ cups) dry white wine
1 tablespoon whipping cream
100 g (3 ½ oz) butter
salt and white pepper
juice from pickled ginger
8 scallops
butter

Cook shallot, ginger and wine until liquid is almost evaporated. Stir in cream and beat in butter in pats. Season with salt, pepper and ginger juice. Strain and keep warm, but do not allow to boil. Slice the scallops into two or three parts and sauté lightly in butter or grill in a grill pan. Make a mirror of sauce in each plate. Top with scallops. Garnish with poached leek and beet shreds and a slice of pickled ginger.

Scallops and pears

4 servings

2 pears
8 scallops
juice of 1 lime
2 tablespoons hoisin sauce
black vinegar
1 tablespoon warm sesame oil
lettuce and fresh herbs

Sautéed scallops

Peel the pears and cut into a cylinder the same diameter as the scallops. Cut into thin slices and mix with half the lime juice. Clean the scallops and cut into thin slices. Combine with remaining lime juice. Arrange pear and scallop slices alternately on a dish. Combine hoisin sauce, a little black vinegar and drizzle around. Pour sesame oil over. Garnish with lettuce and fresh herbs.

Scallops and pears

Raw oysters
4 servings (main dish)

6-12 oysters per person
2 lemons, in wedges
pepper

Use only live oysters. Wash and scrub well. Open with an oyster knife. Arrange on ice with lemon wedges. Try to place the oysters level, so that the juice does not run off. Raw oysters should be enjoyed with a few drops of lemon and perhaps a little pepper. They should not be swallowed raw, but rather they should be chewed carefully so that you taste the nutty flavor. Serve with bread and butter.

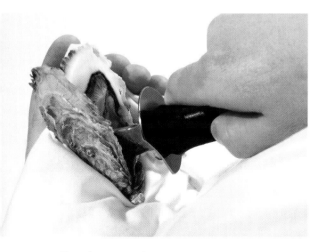

Opening an oyster

Raw oysters

Shrimp

Marinated shrimp
with couscous and grilled vegetables

1 eggplant
1 zucchini
1 red bell pepper
1 ½ dl (⅔ cup) olive oil
salt and pepper
200 g (7 oz) couscous
1 tablespoon chopped fresh mint
350 g (13 oz) shelled cooked shrimp
juice of 1 lime
juice of 3 lemons
1 tablespoon chopped coriander
1 lime, sliced

Slice the eggplant and zucchini. Cut the pepper into strips. Brush with some of the oil and grill on both sides. Cut the vegetables into 2 cm (¾″) squares and season with salt and pepper. Prepare couscous according to package directions. Stir in the mint. Combine the shrimp and remaining ingredients. Arrange couscous in the bottom of a platter. Top with grilled vegetables and marinated shrimp. Garnish with lime slices. Use the shrimp marinade as dressing for the salad.

Marinated shrimp with couscous and grilled vegetables

Shrimp salad
4 servings

½ red bell pepper
½ zucchini
2 tablespoons chopped chives
2 tablespoons chopped parsley or dill
400 g (14 oz) shelled cooked shrimp
2 tablespoons white wine vinegar
1 dl (⅓ cup) olive oil
salt and pepper
½-1 iceberg lettuce
1 dl (½ cup) chopped black olives

Dice the pepper and zucchini. Combine with herbs and shrimp. Combine vinegar and oil for dressing and season with salt and pepper. Carefully stir dressing into shrimp mixture. Serve on a bed of lettuce and garnish with olives. Serve with bread and butter.

Shrimp salad with fresh herbs

Crab salat with tropical fruits

Lobster, crab and crayfish

Preparing lobster

Heat a large pot of salted water (50 g/2 ½ tablespoons salt per liter) (or prepare a court bouillon) to boiling. Add the live lobster, a couple at a time, maximum, to the rapidly boiling water. Do not add too many at once, as the water temperature will go down too much. Cover and reheat to boiling. Lower the heat and let simmer just under the boiling point. Allow 12 minutes for the first 500 g (lb) lobster, then 8 minutes for the next 500 g (lb). It is finished cooking when the color changes from black-brown to brilliant orange-red. Remove the lobster from the water and let it cool, belly up, to prevent the juices from running off. Lobster should be eaten warm or when refrigerated for no more than 24 hours after cooking. Cooked lobster freezes well.

Court bouillon

1 liter (4 cups) water
1 carrot, sliced
1 bay leaf
1 thyme sprig
30 g (1 ½ tablespoons) salt
1 ½ dl (⅔ cup) white wine vinegar
2 parsley stalks
10 black peppercorns

Simmer all ingredients for around 30 minutes. Increase amount as needed according to the number of lobsters.

To serve the lobster

Twist off the claws at the base, Halve the lobster lengthwise, back up, with a sharp knife. Start at the head and proceed back. Turn over and halve the head lengthwise. Remove and discard the large sac behind the eyes. It should come out easily. Crack each claw joint to make removing the meat easier. A lobster fork comes in handy, too.

Lobster *as a starter*
4 servings

2 small lobsters, around 350-400 g (¾-1 lb) each, cooked
lettuce
mayonnaise
1-2 lemons
toast
butter

Halve the lobsters and arrange on lettuce leaves with mayonnaise and a couple of lemon wedges. Serve with toast and butter.

Crab salad *with tropical fruits*
4 servings

300 g (11 oz) cleaned crabmeat
2 tablespoons olive oil
2 tablespoons chopped fresh coriander
1 green chili, cleaned and minced
juice of ½ lime
salt and pepper
1 large mango, peeled and thinly sliced
1 papaya, peeled and thinly sliced
2 kiwi fruit, peeled and sliced
1 small fresh pineapple, peeled and cut into chunks

Combine crabmeat with oil, coriander, half the chili, lime juice, salt and pepper. Arrange the fruit on a platter. Top with the crab salad. Sprinkle with the remaining chili.

Preparing crab

Heat a large pot of salted water (50 g/2 ½ tablespoons salt per liter) to boiling. Add the live crabs, a couple at a time, to the rapidly boiling water. Do not add too many at once, as the water temperature will go down too much. Cover and reheat to boiling. Lower the heat and let simmer until done. Cooking time for crabs is 15 minutes for the first 500 g (1 lb) and then 10 minutes for the next 500 g (1 lb). A crab is finished cooking when the small claws can be pulled out easily. Remove from the cooking liquid and let the crabs cool belly up, to prevent the juices from running off. Boiled crabs are best eaten warm or when refrigerated for no more than 24 hours after cooking. Cooked crabs freeze well.

Crab *as a starter*
4 servings

4 crabs
French bread
butter
mayonnaise
2 lemons
vinegar
pepper

If you buy live crabs, prepare according to the directions above. The crabs can be served as they are, or you can make it easier for your guests by cleaning them before serving. Remove and discard the sac behind the eyes and the gills. Crack the claws with a nutcracker. Put the crab back together before serving. Some of the fun of eating crab is to work a little for the food. Serve with bread, butter and mayonnaise. Garnish with lemon wedges, vinegar and place the pepper grinder on the table. You can also serve it with chili sauce.

Chili sauce
4 servings

1 dl (½ cup) dairy sour cream
½ dl (¼ cup) mayonnaise
½ dl (¼ cup) tomato-based chili sauce
1 tablespoon lemon juice
½ teaspoon mustard
½ teaspoon Worcestershire sauce
sugar

Combine all ingredients and season to taste with sugar.

Crab served in its shell

White meat

– a healthy ingredient that's increasing in popularity

It's healthy and low in calories, quick and easy to prepare. These are the advantages of white meat. The selection of products made with white meat has increased with the rise in consumption. Until the late 1950s, little was available other than stewing hens, and the most common poultry dishes were chicken soup and fricassee. Today, Norwegian consumers can choose from over 100 white meat products.

Chicken

Chicken breast filets contain almost no fat, only 1%. Unlike other meat, there is no marbling of fat within the meat. It's all concentrated just under the skin. If the skin is removed, most of the fat is also removed. Chicken fat contains beneficial fatty acids, so it is only natural that chicken is an important part of the modern, varied diet.

Chicken is one of the world's most popular meats, and everyone can eat it– there are no taboos against it in any religion or culture, and it does not cause allergic reactions or intolerance. Chicken can be varied endlessly. With its mild, delicate flavor, it can be used in all kinds of dishes, whether cooked whole or in filets. All kinds of seasonings, fruit and vegetables go with chicken, and it can even be combined with other kinds of meat, fish and seafood. It can be used in exotic recipes, but it also can be the basis for traditional Norwegian dishes.

A whole Norwegian chicken usually weighs around 1 kg (2 ¼ lb), but you can find those that weigh as much as 3 ¼ kg (7 lb). The largest chickens are usually sold to gourmet restaurants, but you can also find them in specialty shops. Chicken can be roasted whole or in parts. And the carcass can be cooked for stock, a good base for sauce or soup.

Chicken with skin contains 13.6% fat, without skin, 2.1% fat. It also contains valuable proteins and B-vitamins.

Grilled chicken
Whole chickens can be purchased in almost every grocery store, both frozen and grilled. Most of these chickens weigh between 750 and 1000 g (1 ⅔ – 2 ¾ lb), but both larger and smaller can be found as well. Meat from grilled chickens can be used in salads, casseroles and pasta dishes, or it can be served "as is" with a big salad and rice alongside. Norwegian chickens, unless from a special producer, never have wings. These are removed and sold separately.

Marinated chicken
There are many varieties of marinated chicken in Norway, but the most common are marinated chicken parts in ready-to-roast aluminum foil pans. These are available frozen in most grocery stores in a variety of marinades.

Chicken filets and chicken breasts
Chicken filets are just right for quick stews or wok dishes, in soups and salads, or simply sautéed for a few minutes per side and served with good side dishes. The flavor is so mild that all sorts of herbs, spices and vegetables can be added. If there's time, you can marinate it before cooking (see page 166).

Chicken filet - 1% fat
The meat is always tender and can be served like beef. Sauté over medium heat for 3-4 minutes per side. Let the meat rest for a few minutes before serving.

Chicken breast - 4.6% fat
Chicken filet with skin and wing bone. The breast can be sautéed or baked, but the easiest and best way to prepare it is to roast it in the oven at 180°C (350°F) for around 25 minutes. Let the meat rest for a few minutes before serving. For extra flavor, sprinkle with chopped herbs, or insert between the skin and the meat before roasting.

Chicken leg with skin – 11.4% fat
Chicken legs can be divided into two parts at the joint – "drumsticks" and thighs. Drumsticks are best roasted, while thighs are good in braised dishes. Whole legs can be roasted plain or seasoned. Extra flavoring can be inserted between the skin and the meat before roasting.

Chicken wings with skin – 12.2% fat
Chicken wings are fun food. They can be purchased cooked at grocery stores or snack bars. Raw chicken wings are available fresh or frozen.

Chicken liver – 5% fat
Chicken liver is a delicacy with a light, mild flavor. It is excellent in patés, terrines and in sautés.

Prepared foods
Recently, a number of prepared foods have appeared on the market. Chicken patties, meatballs and breaded chopped formed chicken bits are a few of these products.

Storage
Frozen chicken should be used within 4-6 months. Defrosted chicken should be cooked immediately, but it can be stored for a couple of days in the refrigerator.

Chicken parts
Halving a chicken
Cut along the breastbone, flatten out, and cut along the backbone on both sides.

Quartering a chicken
First halve the chicken, then cut at the natural division between breast and leg.

Cutting a chicken into 8 parts
Halve each breast into equal parts. Divide each leg at the joint.

Preparation
For best results, chicken should be room temperature before cooking. Whole chicken should be roasted at 180-200°C (350-400°F) for 1¼ - 1½ hours, depending on the size. To check for doneness, insert a knife at the base of the thigh. If the juices are clear, the chicken is cooked. Always let the chicken rest for 10-15 minutes before carving.

Seasoning
Rosemary, basil, sage, marjoram, tarragon, ginger, garlic, curry, paprika and pepper are just a few of the seasonings that work with chicken. Mix the seasoning with butter or oil and rub into

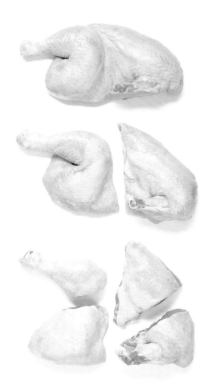

the skin before cooking. Or fill the cavity with herbs, garlic, lemon or fruit, or insert flavoring under the skin before roasting.

Marinades
Shredded meat should be marinated from 30 minutes to 3 hours. Whole pieces can be marinated overnight, covered and refrigerated. Do not add salt if the chicken is going to be marinated for a long time, as salt draws out liquid. It's better to salt the meat after cooking. Combine all marinade ingredients in a plastic bag. Add the chicken parts and knot. Turn the bag several times to redistribute the marinade.

Red wine marinade
3 dl (1 ¼ cups) red wine
3 ½ tablespoons oil
1 garlic clove, minced
½ teaspoon salt
1 tablespoon sugar
4 white peppercorns, crushed
1 teaspoon dried thyme
2 bay leaves, crumbled

Herb marinade
1½ dl (⅔ cup) oil
2 tablespoons wine vinegar
3 tablespoons chopped fresh herbs (tarragon, thyme, basil and rosemary)
1 teaspoon salt
freshly ground pepper
1 garlic clove, minced

Tandoori marinade
2 ½ dl (1 cup) natural yogurt
3 garlic cloves, minced
2 tablespoons grated fresh ginger
2 teaspoons garam masala
2 teaspoons salt
1 teaspoon chili powder
1 teaspoon ground paprika

Roast chicken with herb sauce

Chicken *with 40 cloves of garlic*
This is a classic dish. Do not be afraid of all the garlic. It becomes mild and flavorful after cooking.

4 servings

1 chicken, around 1 kg (2 ¼ lb)
40 garlic cloves, unpeeled
1 small bunch parsley (preferably flat leaf) and other herbs
olive oil
salt and freshly ground pepper
a little grated lemon zest
around 1 dl (1/2 cup) dry white wine

Preheat the oven to 200°C (400°F). Place a few garlic cloves and half the herbs inside the chicken. Truss. Brush with oil and sprinkle with salt and pepper. Place in an ovenproof dish. Sprinkle with lemon zest and arrange the rest of the garlic and herbs around the chicken. Pour the wine into the bottom of the dish and cover with aluminum foil. Bake for around 45 minutes. Remove the foil, increase the temperature to 225°C (425°F) and bake for 20-30 more minutes. Strain the pan juices. Serve with bread, salad and pan juices.

Helpful hint
Slit the garlic and press out the contents. Mash to a paste, add a little chopped herbs and season with salt and pepper. Delicious on fresh bread or toast.

Roast chicken *with herb sauce*

1 chicken, around 1 kg (2 ¼ lb)
2 tablespoons lemon juice
2 tablespoons brown sugar
1 tablespoon honey
1 garlic clove, minced
3 ½ tablespoons soy sauce

Preheat the oven to 180-200°C (350-400°F). Truss the chicken. Combine the remaining ingredients and brush onto the chicken. Roast for 1¼ hours, brushing with the mixture a couple of times during roasting. Let the chicken rest for 10-15 minutes before carving. Serve with rice and herb sauce.

Helpful hint:
Cut small slits in the skin over the breast and insert thin slices of garlic and herbs.

Green herb sauce
2 dl (1 cup) peas
4-5 dl (2 cups) fresh spinach leaves
butter
1 dl (½ cup) chicken stock
1 ½ dl (¾ cup) milk
3 tablespoons chopped fresh herbs (such as coriander or basil)
3-4 tablespoons crème fraiche (or dairy sour cream)
salt and freshly ground pepper
2 tablespoons cold butter

Sauté the peas and spinach in a little butter for a few seconds. Add stock and milk and heat to boiling. Pour into a blender, add the herbs and puree until smooth. Whisk in the crème fraiche. Return to the saucepan, reheat carefully and season with salt and pepper. Beat in cold butter at the end for a shiny, thick sauce.

Chicken with 40 cloves of garlic

Chicken *prepared like ptarmigan*
4 servings

1 chicken, around 1 kg (2 ¼ lb)
salt and pepper
butter
2 onions
250 g (9 oz) fresh mushrooms
2 dl (1 cup) chicken stock (1 cube + water)
6-8 juniper berries
1 teaspoon dried thyme
2 dl (1 cup) crème fraiche (or dairy sour cream)
1 tablespoon cornstarch stirred into 1 tablespoon water

1 dl (½ cup) lingonberries or chopped cranberries

Truss the chicken and rub with salt and pepper. Brown on all sides in butter in a cast iron pan. Set aside. Clean and chop the onion, halve or quarter the mushrooms. Brown the onions and mushrooms in the same pan. Return the chicken to the pan, breast up, add stock, juniper and thyme, cover and let simmer until tender, around 1 hour. Around 15 minutes before the chicken is finished cooking, add the crème fraiche. Stir in the cornstarch mixture and the lingonberries and let the sauce simmer for 2 minutes, until thickened. If using sour cream, add at the very end

and do not allow the sauce to boil (as it may separate). Carve the chicken and serve with sauce, mashed potatoes, Brussels sprouts or other vegetables.

Alternative:
This dish can also be made with 4 grilled chicken legs. Brown the legs rapidly in butter, then set aside. Brown onions and mushrooms, add stock and crème fraiche and let simmer for around 15 minutes. Thicken the sauce with cornstarch and add the lingonberries. Return the chicken legs to the pan and let simmer for around 15 minutes. Serve with the side dishes mentioned above.

Quick chicken and rice
3-4 servings

3 dl (1 ¼ cups) rice
2 onions, in wedges
3 tablespoons oil
7 dl (3 cups) chicken stock (1 ½ cubes + water)
1 grilled or roasted chicken
1 package frozen vegetables (or same amount fresh)
1 small can corn

Sauté rice and onion in oil in a pot. Add the stock and heat to boiling. Cover and lower heat. Cut the chicken into small pieces and place on the rice. Pour over the vegetables. Let simmer for around 15 minutes, until the rice is cooked and the chicken and vegetables are warm. Serve with crusty bread.

Quick chicken and rice

Grilled chicken *with vegetables*
4 servings

1 grilled or roasted chicken
4 bacon slices
1 package frozen wok vegetables
4 dl (1 ⅔ cups) cooked rice (cooked with ½ teaspoon tumeric for color)
4 tablespoons sweet chili sauce

Quarter the chicken and heat in the oven or in a frying pan. Fry the bacon until crisp, then remove from the pan. Sauté the vegetables in the bacon fat. Stir in the rice and chili sauce. Top with bacon. Serve with the chicken.

Grilled chicken with vegetables

Easy chicken casserole

Oven-fried chicken legs

Easy chicken casserole
3-4 servings

1 grilled or roasted chicken

Sauce:
1 packet dehydrated mushroom broccoli soup
4 dl (1 ²/₃ cups) water
2 dl (²/₃ cup) crème fraiche (or dairy sour cream)
1-2 teaspoons green curry paste or chili paste
(sambal oelek)
150 g (5 oz) fresh mushrooms
a few potato chips
chopped fresh parsley

Preheat the oven to 200°C (400°F). Cut the chicken into serving pieces and place in an oven-proof dish. Combine the soup, water, crème fraiche and curry paste in a saucepan and heat to boiling. Slice and fry the mushrooms and stir into the sauce. Pour over the chicken and bake for 20 minutes. Crush the potato chips and sprinkle with the parsley over the chicken just before serving. Serve with cooked vegetables or a salad and rice.

Oven-fried chicken legs
4-6 servings

1 egg
1 ¹/₂ tablespoons sesame seeds
2 tablespoons fine breadcrumbs
3 tablespoons grated parmesan cheese
¹/₂ teaspoon ground paprika
salt and pepper
8 chicken legs

Preheat the oven to 200°C (400°F). Beat the egg. Combine the sesame seeds, crumbs, cheese and paprika. Dip the chicken in egg, then coat with the sesame seed mixture. Arrange in a greased ovenproof dish and bake for around 50 minutes. Serve with avocado salad and bread.

Avocado salad
2 tablespoons mayonnaise
1 tablespoon mustard sauce
3 tablespoons crème fraiche or dairy sour cream
2 tablespoons lemon juice
salt and pepper
2 tomatoes, peeled, seeded and chopped
2 avocados, peeled, pitted and cubed
1 garlic clove, grated
¹/₂ red chili, minced
3 tablespoons fresh chopped coriander

Combine mayonnaise, mustard sauce and crème fraiche and season with lemon juice, salt and pepper in a bowl. Add the remaining ingredients and toss.

This salad is also good with plain grilled chicken legs.

Chicken wings
Count on 250 g (9 oz) raw wings per person

3 tablespoons mild chili sauce
1 teaspoon mustard
1 teaspoon wine vinegar
1 teaspoon Worcestershire sauce
1 tablespoon oil
1 garlic clove, minced
salt and pepper

Preheat the oven to 200°C (400°F). Arrange the chicken wings in an ovenproof dish. Combine the remaining ingredients in a small bowl and brush onto the chicken. Bake in the middle of the oven for around 30 minutes. Serve with salad, dip and good bread.

Fried boneless chicken breasts *for a crowd*

Preheat the oven to 180°C (350°F). Fry the chicken in butter or oil for 1-2 minutes per side. Transfer to an aluminum foil lined oven pan and bake for 13-15 minutes, depending on the size of the chicken breasts.

Chicken breasts *with sauce*
2 servings

2-3 boneless, skinless chicken breasts
salt and ground pepper
butter or oil

Fry the chicken in butter or oil for 3-4 minutes per side. Let them rest for a few minutes before serving.

Sauce
1 dl (¹/₂ cup) chicken stock
2 dl (1 cup) whipping or light cream
1 teaspoon Dijon mustard
2 tablespoons soy sauce
salt and pepper (optional)
2 teaspoons cornstarch stirred into 2 teaspoons cold water
1-2 dl (¹/₂-1 cup) bell pepper cubes
fried mushrooms

Chicken breasts with sauce

Combine stock and cream and heat to boiling. Stir in the mustard and soy sauce and season with salt and pepper. Whisk in the cornstarch and heat to boiling, whisking until smooth. Stir in the pepper and mushrooms and let the sauce simmer for a few minutes. Serve with chicken and potatoes.

Sweet-and-sour chicken
3 servings

3 boneless, skinless chicken breasts
1 garlic clove, minced
1 tablespoon grated fresh ginger
oil
½ bell pepper, in strips
10-15 string beans
1 can (6-8 oz) pineapple chunks in juice, drained (reserve the juice)
½ leek, sliced

Sweet-and-sour sauce
3 tablespoons soy sauce
1 dl (½ cup) pineapple juice (from the canned pineapple)
1 dl (½ cup) chicken stock
2-3 tablespoons tomato paste
1-2 teaspoons cornstarch stirred into
2 teaspoons cold water
1 tablespoon wine vinegar
1 tablespoon sugar

Stir-fried chicken with pineapple and sweet-and-sour sauce

Cut the chicken into thin strips and sauté with garlic and ginger in oil in a wok or large pan until the meat turns white. Add pepper, beans, pineapple and leek. Stir-fry for a few minutes until vegetables begin to soften slightly. Combine soy sauce, pineapple juice, stock, tomato paste and cornstarch mixture and pour over the meat. Heat to boiling. Season with vinegar and sugar. Serve with rice.

Chicken
with cabbage and creamy mushroom sauce
2 servings

2 boneless, skinless chicken breasts
butter or oil
salt and ground pepper
1 small head early cabbage

Creamy mushroom sauce
2 dl (1 cup) sliced mushrooms
½ onion, chopped
1 dl (½ cup) whipping cream
1 dl (⅓ cup) cooking water from cabbage
salt and pepper

Chicken with cabbage and creamy mushroom sauce

Sauté the chicken in butter or oil for 3-4 minutes per side. Let rest for a minute or two before serving. Halve the cabbage and cook for a few minutes in lightly salted water. Drain, reserving cooking liquid for sauce. Sauté the mushrooms and onion in butter. Add the cream and cooking liquid and simmer until slightly thickened. Season with salt and pepper.

Chicken with shrimp pasta
2 servings

2 boneless, skinless chicken breasts
salt and ground pepper
1 teaspoon minced red chili
1 teaspoon grated fresh ginger
oil

Sprinkle the chicken with salt, pepper, chili and ginger. Sauté in butter for 3-4 minutes per side. Let rest for a minute or two.

1 garlic clove, minced
2 ½ dl (1 cup) bechamel sauce
3 dl (1¼ cups) cooked corkscrew pasta
salt and ground pepper
100 g (4 oz) cooked, shelled shrimp, chopped

Chicken with shrimp pasta

Spicy chicken salad

1 tablespoon chopped fresh herbs

Sauté the garlic with the butter when making the béchamel sauce. Stir into the pasta and season with salt and pepper. Top with shrimp and sprinkle with herbs. Serve with chicken and fresh asparagus.

Spicy chicken salad
4 servings

4 boneless, skinless chicken breasts
1 teaspoon salt
$\frac{1}{2}$ teaspoon cumin
oil
150 g (5 oz) fresh green asparagus or string beans
150 g (5 oz) snow peas
2 carrots, sliced lengthwise with a cheese plane
1 red onion, thinly sliced
shredded lettuce

Dressing
3 dl (1$\frac{1}{4}$ cups) sour cream
1 dl (scant $\frac{1}{2}$ cup) plain yogurt
1 teaspoon curry powder
lemon juice
sugar

Cut the chicken into strips and sprinkle with salt and cumin. Sauté quickly in oil. Let cool. Blanch the asparagus and peas. Arrange all ingredients on a tray. Mix the sour cream, yogurt and curry powder with lemon juice and sugar to taste. Pour over the chicken or serve alongside. Serve with crusty bread.

Chicken in pastry *with apricot sauce*
4 servings

6 boneless, skinless chicken breasts
salt
2 tablespoons minced shallots
1 teaspoon minced red chili
1 teaspoon grated fresh ginger
1-2 tablespoons chopped fresh tarragon or 1 teaspoon dried
2 eggs
1 dl (scant $\frac{1}{2}$ cup) whipping cream
freshly ground pepper
butter
4 puff pastry sheets (US: 1 package frozen puff pastry, defrosted)

Cut 2 of the chicken breasts into chunks and place in a food processor. Add a little salt and pulse several times. Add shallot, chili, ginger, 1 egg and cream and process until well mixed. Season with ground pepper. Sprinkle the remaining chicken breasts with salt and pepper and sauté in butter for 2 $\frac{1}{2}$ minutes per side. Let cool. Preheat the oven to 225°C (425°F). (US: Divide the puff pastry into 4 pieces of equal size.) Roll the puff pastry to 3 mm thick. Halve each chicken breast lengthwise, but do not cut all the way through. It should open like a book. Fill with the chopped chicken mixture and fold over. Lightly beat the remaining egg. Place a stuffed chicken breast on each sheet of puff pastry. Brush around the edges of the pastry with beaten egg. Fold over the pastry, pressing the edges lightly together with a fork. Place the "packets" on a greased oven sheet and bake on the center shelf for around 15 minutes, until golden. Serve with apricot sauce.

Apricot sauce
2 onions, chopped
2 garlic cloves, minced
oil
2 bay leaves, crumbled

Chicken in pastry with apricot sauce

Chicken with basil

3 tablespoons curry powder (preferably a mixture of both strong and mild)
1 can (14 oz) apricots, drained and chopped
$^3/_4$ dl ($^1/_2$ cup) apple juice or apricot nectar
2 dl (1 cup) chicken stock
2 dl (1 cup) light cream
2 dl (1 cup) crème fraiche or dairy sour cream
1 teaspoon cornstarch stirred into 1 teaspoon cold water
salt and pepper

Fry onion and garlic in oil with the bay leaves and curry powder over low heat for around 10 minutes. Add the remaining ingredients and simmer for a few minutes. (If using sour cream, wait until the end to add it, as it may separate when boiled). Let cool slightly. Pour into a blender and puree until smooth. Strain into a clean saucepan.

If too thin, add cornstarch mixture and simmer until thickened. Season with salt and pepper. If using sour cream, stir in now, then reheat, but do not allow to boil.

Chicken *with basil*
4 servings

3 tablespoons shredded basil
1 garlic clove, minced
4 tablespoons ($^1/_4$ cup) cream cheese
4 chicken breasts
2 tablespoons oil
2 tablespoons honey
1 tablespoon soy sauce
salt and ground pepper

Preheat the oven to 180°C (350°F). Combine the basil, garlic and cheese. Loosen the skin on the chicken and insert the cheese mixture between the skin and the meat. Place the chicken in a greased ovenproof dish. Combine the remaining ingredients and brush over the breasts. Bake for around 30 minutes. Place under the grill for a few minutes just before serving for more color. Serve with rice, baked cherry tomatoes (bake for 3 minutes), and orange sections.

Turkey

The turkey is a newcomer to Norway. We can thank Englishmen living in Norway for its arrival – they had to have their Christmas turkey. That's also the time of year when Norwegians eat the most turkey. Half of all turkeys are sold between Christmas and the New Year.

For many years, turkey was sold "as is" – whole. After all, it was supposed to be roasted whole! Eventually, product developers realized the bird's

potential, and the number of turkeys sold as breasts, chops, sandwich fillers and sausages is increasing steadily.

Norwegian turkey schnitzel is really ground and breaded leg meat, with just over 10% fat. Turkey meatloaf is another popular dish here, served warm with vegetables and potatoes, or cold as sandwich filling. And of course, there is turkey ham. As more products are developed, consumption rises. One day, it may be just as easy to buy a turkey hotdog at a gas station as it is a regular hotdog.

Whole turkey

Whole turkey with skin contains 13.8% fat, without skin 1.6%. Norwegian turkeys weigh from 4 to 12 kg (8-26 lb), but 5-7 kg (11-15 lb) is the most popular size. The largest are sold only in specialty stores in the big cities. For the most part, turkey is sold frozen, but fresh birds are becoming more common.

Defrosting

To minimize fluid loss, a turkey should be defrosted in the refrigerator or in another cold place. A medium turkey takes around 48 hours to defrost. Defrost the turkey in its packaging, and remove the bag of giblets as soon as the bird is defrosted.

Cutting up the turkey

Press the leg-thigh out from the carcass and cut where it joins the back. Cut in two at the joint to separate the leg from the thigh. Cut along the breastbone and down along the wishbone. Cut out each breast by pressing the knife against the carcass down toward the wing on one side. Loosen the breast by cutting from the thigh toward the wing on the other. Remove the wings at the joints.

Helpful hint

Cut up a whole turkey and make several meals – roast one breast whole, slice the other into steaks, fry the wings and use the rest in stews. Cook stock with the carcass for soups and sauces.

Turkey breast

Boneless, skinless turkey breast is a delicacy. The lean, tender and mild-flavored meat is easy to prepare, and there's no waste at all. Roasted whole, it can be served warm with gravy and all the trimmings, or it can be served cold with fruit salad as part of a buffet. When sliced or cut into strips, it cooks in no time, so it's perfect for quick steaks and stir-fries.

Turkey breast is available frozen. marinated with and without skin and bone, and at holiday time, it can also be found fresh.

Turkey steaks are 2 cm ($^3/_4$") thick breast slices. Sauté them for around 3 minutes per side and let them rest for a couple of minutes before serving. They are great with a hearty wine sauce or a fruity orange sauce, sweet Cumberland sauce or a mild cream sauce. Choose side dishes to suit the sauce.

Turkey filet is the small muscle enclosed in the larger breast muscle. It is the finest part of the bird. Sauté carefully, until just cooked through, so that it doesn't dry out.

Turkey strips are perfect for quick meals. Stir-fry in a wok and serve with pasta, or use in salads.

Turkey stew meat – 6% fat

Cubed meat from the thigh is ideal for soups and stews.

Ground turkey

If you like lean sausages, turkey hotdogs are perfect. All the traditional Norwegian favorites can be found made with turkey. And there are cold cuts, too, as well as ground meat for burgers.

Roast turkey
– with or without stuffing

500 g (1 lb) per person
butter
salt and pepper

Defrost the turkey in the refrigerator (it should take 2-3 days). Remove the bag of giblets. Make stock for the gravy: Remove the fat and bloody bits from the giblets. Reserve the liver for another dish. Brown the giblets in butter, add cold water to cover and let simmer for 1-2 hours. Preheat the oven to 160°C (325°F). Fold the wing tips under back, so that the bird lies on them while roasting. Remove any bloody bits from the inside of the bird. Fill with desired "stuffing" (see following recipes) and close the opening with skewers or sew with cotton thread. Tie the legs together. Roast for 30 minutes per kilo (15 minutes per lb) plus 30-45 minutes, if filled with a raw stuffing. After 30 minutes roasting, add 5 dl (2 cups) hot water with 1 teaspoon chicken bouillon powder to the pan (add more later, if necessary). Baste with cooking juices several times during roasting. Let the turkey rest for 15-20 minutes before carving. Serve with potatoes, vegetables and cream sauce.

Walnut stuffing *with dried fruit*
1 onion
300 g (5-6 slices) white bread, crusts removed
butter

150 g (5 oz) walnuts
100 g (3 ½ oz) dried apricots
75 g (2 oz) dried figs
75 g (3 oz) prunes
1 apple
2 eggs
1 teaspoon salt
½ teaspoon pepper

Mince the onion, cube the bread and sauté in butter until the bread is golden brown. Transfer to a large bowl. Chop the walnuts, shred the dried fruit and grate the apple. Stir into the bread cubes. Whisk in the egg. The stuffing can either be spooned into the turkey or it can be baked in an ovenproof dish for the last 30-40 minutes of roasting time.

Prune and apple stuffing

250 g (9 oz) pitted prunes
4-5 apples, peeled and cut into wedges

Sausage stuffing

500 g (1 lb) loose turkey sausage
1 onion, minced
1 red or green bell pepper, diced
turkey liver, diced

Combine all ingredients. Spoon into the turkey. It should be no more than 3/4 full, as the stuffing expands during roasting. Count on 30-45 minutes longer cooking time when using this stuffing. The stuffing "stretches" the turkey.

Cream sauce

10 servings

1 1/2 liter (6 cups) turkey stock (+ chicken stock, if necessary)
1 1/2 dl (2/3 cup) flour
2 dl (1 cup) water
2 dl (1 cup) whipping cream
2 tablespoons port wine or red currant jelly
4 tablespoons (1/4 cup) soy sauce
salt and ground pepper

Measure the giblet stock, adding chicken stock if necessary. Heat to boiling. Place the flour and water in a jar. Tighten the lid and shake to blend. Whisk into the boiling stock. Let simmer for around 5 minutes. Add the remaining ingredients. Be sure to deglaze the turkey roasting pan with water, reheat, scraping the bottom, and add the juices to the sauce for more flavor.

Roast whole turkey breast

Preheat the oven to 180°C (350°F). Brush the meat with butter and sprinkle with salt and pepper. Insert a meat thermometer into the thickest part. Roast for 30-40 minutes, until the internal temperature reaches 69°F (156°F). Let the meat rest for 15 minutes before carving. By then, the internal temperature should be 72° (162°F). At this temperature, the meat is tender and moist. It is a good idea to tie larger breasts with cotton string. Brown them in butter before roasting in the oven.

Honey-sesame glazed turkey breast

4-6 servings

1 turkey breast, around 1 kg (2 1/4 lb)
1 teaspoon salt
ground pepper
2 tablespoons butter
2 dl (1 cup) white wine or cider
1 dl (1/2 cup) chicken stock
3 tablespoons melted honey
3 tablespoons soy sauce
1 garlic clove, minced
2 tablespoons sesame seeds

Preheat the oven to 180°C (350°F). Sprinkle the turkey with salt and pepper and brown in butter on all sides in a pan that tolerates oven heat. Add wine and stock and roast for around 30 minutes. Remove from the oven and pour off (and reserve) any cooking juices. Increase the heat to 225°C (425°F). Combine honey, soy sauce and garlic and brush onto the meat. Roast for 5 minutes. Brush the meat one more time and sprinkle with sesame seed. Roast for 5 minutes more. Let the meat rest for around 15 minutes. Carve and served with potatoes, orange sauce, steamed early cabbage, turnips and snow peas.

Orange sauce

2 shallots
1 tablespoon butter
1 teaspoon chopped red chili
2 dl (1 cup) strained cooking juices or stock and white wine
2 dl (1 cup) orange juice, strained
2 dl (1 cup) crème fraiche or dairy sour cream
grated orange zest
1/2 teaspoon salt
freshly ground white pepper

Honey-sesame glazed turkey breast with orange sauce

Mince the shallots and sauté in butter until shiny. Add the chili, cooking juices and orange juice and let simmer for around 10 minutes. Add crème fraiche and simmer a few minutes more. If using sour cream, reheat, but do not allow to boil. Season with orange zest, salt and pepper.

Peppered turkey

turkey breast slices, around 150 g (5 oz) per person
ground pepper mix (white, black, green and rose)
salt
butter

Dip the turkey into the pepper mix. Sprinkle with salt and sauté in butter for 2-3 minutes per side. Let the meat rest for a few minutes before serving. Serve with potato salad and tarragon sauce.

Potato salad with honey dressing

1 kg (2 ¼ lb) tiny potatoes (new potatoes)
1 endive
200 g (8 oz) mixed greens
2 yellow bell peppers
1 red onion, thinly sliced
chopped chives

Honey dressing

2 tablespoons honey
3 ½ tablespoons white wine vinegar
1 ½ teaspoons salt
1 dl (scant ½ cup) safflower oil
grated zest of 1 lemon
freshly ground pepper

Place the endive in cold water to retain crispness. Rinse the greens. Halve potatoes, slice large ones. Combine all ingredients in a bowl. Place all dressing ingredients in a jar, screw on the lid and shake. Pour over the salad.

Peppered turkey

Tarragon sauce

2 tablespoons butter
1 package béarnaise sauce mix
2 dl (1 cup) white wine
1 ½ dl (⅔ cup) light cream
1 egg yolk
2 tablespoons chopped tarragon

Melt the butter and add the sauce mix, wine and cream. Let simmer for a few minutes. Remove the saucepan from the heat and whisk in the egg yolk and tarragon. Serve immediately. Do not boil after the egg yolk is added or mixture may separate.

Turkey burgers

4-6 burgers

400 g (14 oz) ground turkey
1 teaspoon salt
$\frac{1}{2}$ teaspoon pepper
$\frac{1}{2}$ onion, minced
1 tablespoon potato starch
1 egg
3 $\frac{1}{2}$ tablespoons water
rosemary, oregano, garlic, chili or other spices
butter

Combine all ingredients in a bowl. Form into 4 or 6 round patties. Fry two at a time in butter over medium heat for 3-4 minutes per side, until cooked through. Serve with fried potatoes and a salad.

Helpful hint

For extra flavor, add chopped pickle, beets or grated carrot to the ground meat.

Turkey steaks *with herb cream*

4 servings

100 g (3 $\frac{1}{2}$ oz) feta cheese
2 tablespoons crème fraiche or dairy sour cream
1 garlic clove, minced
1 tablespoon chopped fresh oregano.
turkey breast slices, about 150 g (5 oz) each
butter
salt and lemon pepper

Mash the feta and stir in the crème fraiche, garlic and oregano. Sauté the turkey in butter for 2-3 minutes per side. Place a spoonful of herb cream on each turkey steak. Serve with fried potato wedges and stir-fried vegetables with soy sauce and sweet chili sauce.

Stir-fried vegetables

Use spring onions, baby corn, string beans, red onion, yellow squash, snow peas, red bell pepper, garlic, grated fresh ginger, a little salt and ground pepper. Cut the vegetables into bite-size pieces and sauté quickly in oil in a hot pan. (The cut-up vegetables can also be placed on doubled aluminum foil with a little butter and cooked on the grill.)

Turkey stew

4 servings

600 g (1 $\frac{1}{3}$ lb) turkey strips
butter
8 tiny onions
200 g (7 oz) mushrooms
5 dl (2 cups) chicken stock
$\frac{1}{2}$ teaspoon dry mustard
$\frac{1}{2}$ teaspoon ground paprika
1 tablespoon Worcestershire sauce
salt and pepper
3 tablespoons tomato paste
pinch sugar
3 dl (1 $\frac{1}{4}$ cups) sour cream or whipping cream
1 green and 1 red bell pepper, in strips
chopped parsley

Brown the turkey in butter. Transfer to a pot. Chop the onions and quarter the mushrooms and sauté lightly. Add to the pot with the stock and the other ingredients. Let simmer for a few minutes. Served rice or mashed potatoes with beets and pickles.

Turkey steaks with herb cream

Turkey stew

Turkey burgers

Boneless birds

400 g (14 oz) ground turkey
100 g (1 cup) breadcrumbs
1 egg
1/2 teaspoon salt
3 1/2 tablespoons water
2 tablespoons soy sauce

Spice blend

1/2 onion
1 garlic clove
1 teaspoon grated ginger
1/2 teaspoon grated nutmeg
1 tablespoon soy sauce
butter

Boneless birds

Chilidogs with macaroni casserole

Turkey dogs with mashed potatoes

Combine turkey with remaining ingredients. Divide into 4-6 oblong pieces and place them on moistened cooking parchment. Chop the onion and garlic and mix with the remaining ingredients. Place a little spice blend on each piece of meat and roll up. Seal the edges. Sauté on all sides in butter over medium heat. Serve with boiled potatoes, creamed vegetables and gravy.

Chilidogs *with macaroni casserole*
4 servings

8 dl (3 1/3 cups) cooked macaroni (3 dl/1 1/4 cups raw)
3 eggs
1 leek or 3 scallions, thinly sliced
3 dl (1 1/4 cups) grated cheddar cheese
1 teaspoon salt
1/2 teaspoon pepper
8 turkey chilidogs

Preheat the oven to 225°C (425°F). Combine macaroni, eggs, leek, 3/4 of the cheese, salt and pepper. Pour into a greased ovenproof dish. Slice the chilidogs and sprinkle over the macaroni. Top with the remaining cheese. Bake for 15-20 minutes, until thoroughly heated and golden brown.

Turkey dogs *with mashed potatoes*
4 servings

8 turkey hotdogs

Cut three slits through the skin of each hotdog. Fry without added fat over medium heat. Serve with mashed potatoes, relish and mustard.

Mashed potatoes

4-8 potatoes
2 dl (3/4 cup) milk
1 tablespoon chopped chives
1 garlic clove, minced
salt and pepper

Peel and cook the potatoes in boiling salted water until tender. Mash. Stir in the remaining ingredients.

Hens

Today's hens are much younger than they used to be. After around 18 months, hens are no longer efficient egg-layers, but their meat is still good to eat. It's cheap, healthy and tasty food.

Most hens go to the food-processing industry, but some grocery stores do sell them.

The fat on a hen sits just under the skin, and when cooked, it melts into the stock. After the stock is chilled, the fat rises to the top and is easily removed. There is a lot of good flavor in chicken fat, and it can be used for frying. It gives sauces and soups that little something extra. Hens are sold frozen and weigh around 1 kg (2 ¼ lb).

Poaching hens and chickens

It's easy to poach several hens or chickens at a time. Halve each one and place in a pot with enough water to just cover. Quarter 1 large onion and chop a carrot and add, along with 10 allspice berries, 10 cloves, 10 peppercorns, 2 bay leaves and 1 teaspoon salt per liter water. Let simmer at 90°C (195°F) for around 2 hours. Frozen hens need around 2 ½ hours, chickens around 1 hour. Remove the meat from the bones and strain the stock.

Chicken fricassee

6-8 servings

meat from 2 poached hens
6 carrots
1 large leek
2 parsley roots
1 celeriac

5 tablespoons (1/3 cup) butter
1¼ dl (½ cup) flour
1 ½ liter (6 cups) chicken stock or cooking liquid
from the hens
½-1 dl (⅓ cup) whipping cream
lemon juice
salt and pepper
chopped parsley

Chicken fricassee

Cut the meat into serving pieces. Peel and cut the vegetables into 1 cm (½") chunks. In a pot, melt the butter and stir in the flour. Let cook slightly. Heat the stock to boiling. Whisk in the boiling stock and add the cream, chicken and vegetables. Let simmer until the vegetables are tender, 10-15 minutes. Season with lemon juice, salt and pepper. Sprinkle with parsley and serve with boiled potatoes.

Helpful hint

If you don't have time to poach hens for the fricassee, you can make it with chicken, which take less time to cook. You can even simmer boneless, skinless chicken breasts in a good chicken stock with vegetables and make sauce from the stock. Fricassee in a flash!

Curried chicken

Use the above fricassee recipe, but add 1 teaspoon curry to the butter when making the sauce and do not add lemon juice. Serve curried chicken with root vegetables and rice.

Chicken in red wine sauce

4-5 servings

1 large chicken, around 1 ½ kg (3 ¼ lb)
3 ¾ dl (1 2/3 cups) red wine
2 garlic cloves, minced
1 bay leaf
2 tablespoons chopped fresh thyme or
1 teaspoon dried
100 g (3 ½ oz) salt pork
1 ½ teaspoons salt
¾ teaspoon white pepper
4 tablespoons (¼ cup) cognac (optional)
chicken stock
1 tablespoon tomato paste (optional)
around 20 tiny onions
250 g (8 oz) mushrooms
1½ tablespoons butter
1 tablespoon flour
fresh thyme

Cut the chicken into 8 pieces. Combine the wine, garlic, bay leaf and thyme in a bowl and add the chicken. Refrigerate overnight or let

Chicken in red wine sauce

marinate at room temperature for 4-5 hours. Remove the chicken and dry well. Pour the marinade into a pot and heat to boiling. Dice the salt pork and fry until all the fat has melted. Transfer the pork to the pot but leave the fat in the pan. Sprinkle the chicken with salt and pepper and brown in the fat. Pour over the cognac and

ignite. When the flames have died down on their own, transfer the chicken to the pot. Add enough stock to just cover the chicken. Add tomato paste for more color, if desired. Simmer over low heat for around 40 minutes, until tender. While the chicken is cooking, sauté the onions and mushrooms and add to the pot.

Knead the butter and flour together and whisk into the pot to thicken the sauce. Let simmer for 5 more minutes. Adjust the seasoning. Garnish with fresh thyme. Serve with potatoes, rice or bread.

Soups

Making stock

You can't make good soups and sauces without good stock! Stock is not as time- consuming to make as many think – and it's worth the effort. Make a lot and freeze it in small containers.

Chicken and hen carcasses, backs, wings and trimmings are perfect for cooking stock. Brown in butter with chopped carrot, celeriac, onion and leek. Add cold water to just cover. Heat to boiling, skimming frequently for a clear stock. Add salt, peppercorns, bay leaf and a parsley sprig. Let simmer for 1 hour or more. Strain.

Curried chicken soup

⅔ dl (¼ cup) lentils
2-3 onions
2 teaspoons curry powder
butter
1 liter (4 cups) chicken stock
1-2 dl (½-¾ cup) whipping cream
1 small can (⅔ cup) coconut milk
skinless and boneless meat from 1 poached hen or chicken
salt and pepper

Cook lentils according to package directions. Mince the onion and sauté with the curry powder in butter until shiny. Add stock, cream and coconut milk. Simmer until thickened. Cut the meat into bite-size pieces and add. Season with salt and pepper. For a more hearty soup, add cooked rice just before serving and heat through.

Curried chicken soup

Chicken soup *with potato dumplings*
4 servings

1 ½ liter (6 cups) clear chicken stock
2 carrots
½ rutabaga
½ celeriac
1 parsley root
1 leek
salt and pepper
skinless and boneless meat from 1 poached hen or chicken
chopped parsley

Make stock according to recipe on page 183. Peel and julienne the vegetables. Heat the stock to boiling and add the vegetables. Let simmer until tender. Season with salt and pepper. Slice the chicken. Serve the soup in bowls with chicken slices and dumplings. Garnish with chopped parsley. Serve with homemade bread or flatbread.

Potato dumplings
750 g (1⅔ lb) potatoes
1 ½ dl (⅔ cup) barley flour
1 ½ dl (⅔ cup) finely milled whole wheat flour
½ onion, chopped
1 teaspoon salt

Chicken soup with potato dumplings

Peel and coarsely grate the potatoes. Squeeze out some of the liquid. Stir in the remaining ingredients. Form dumplings with a tablespoon. Let the dumplings simmer in lightly salted water (1 teaspoon per liter/quart) for around 20 minutes.

Meat

– a basic food in the Norwegian diet

Lamb, pork and beef have all played a great role in the Norwegian diet. Fresh meat used to be regarded as a delicacy, and animals were slaughtered in connection with holidays and special occasions. Otherwise, people ate mostly salted or salted and dried meat. Today, we can get fresh meat year-round, and the choice is immense, but we still appreciate traditional products and dishes.

Pork

With pork, you can make delicious dinners in no time. Juicy, tender pork has a mild flavor that can be varied with different seasonings.

Pork is lean. Visible fat is easy to remove, but wait until after the meat is cooked. Fat adds flavor, and you don't want to miss that. Do you believe that meat "absorbs" fat during cooking? Just the opposite is true. When fat reaches a certain temperature, it melts and runs into the pan. As long as you don't pour the cooking juices over the meat, the fat stays in the pan. The meat is so lean that you need to cook it right. Use medium to high heat and sauté the meat for a couple of minutes per side. Remove the pan from the heat and let the meat cook for another couple of minutes per side. If pork is cooked at too high heat or for too long, it dries out.

Pork is proof that lean meat doesn't have to be boring – and that not everything that tastes good is bad for you. Lean pork contains only 2-4% fat, and half of that is unsaturated fat, which is good for the heart.

Cuts of pork

Ground pork – 6% fat
Ground pork is a good alternative to ground beef. Use in recipes for ground beef.

Pork strips – 2-4% fat
These strips are usually cut from the leg. They are ready to cook, lean and tender and can be used in all kinds of dishes.

Pork chops
Rib and loin chops are easy to prepare. The fat is visible and easy to remove. Shoulder chops are more marbled with fat, which adds both flavor and juiciness. Chops can be fried, baked or grilled. Try marinating them for extra flavor.

Pork tenderloin – 3.6% fat
The tenderloin is the finest cut. Prepare whole or in medallions, but cook gently, and do not overcook. It's perfect when a little pink inside.

Boneless loin
Can be roasted whole or cut into medallions. Lovely, tender meat.

Pork round steak – 2-4% fat
This lean but juicy cut from the top round usually is sold in slices about (2 cm) ³/₄" thick. Either prepare as schnitzel or cut into strips or shreds for a quick main dish.

Pork - from trimmed, lean products to pork ribs and chops.

Ham hocks

There are three types of hocks: fresh, salted, and salted and smoked. They can be made into hearty dishes to satisfy big appetites. Serve with sauerkraut or mashed rutabagas and potatoes. Pork hocks are especially good in pea soup, stew and casserole dishes.

Boneless fresh ham with rind

Fresh ham with rind is available rolled in a net or just as it is. If you like crispy rind, don't buy one in a net. Score the rind well. Then it crisps more easily, and it's easy to cut into even slices.

Boneless pork rib or loin roast

Available with rind, which is cut into thin strips. This is the perfect roast and doesn't need to be rolled and tied.

Smoked pork loin

Lightly salted and smoked. Either poach or roast whole. When sliced, chops from the smoked loin are called "summer chops" as they're perfect warm weather food. Canadian bacon is boneless smoked pork loin.

Boneless ham roll

Lightly salted ham that's good in both hot and cold dishes. You can buy it either raw or cooked.

Trimmed beef for roasts, steaks and stews.

Beef

In Norway, beef refers to both veal and beef. When Norwegians refer to beef per se, they generally mean the more tender cuts. Norwegian beef is aged in a vacuum method before it is sent to the shops. Meat that is too tough for braising is trimmed and ground or processed. Veal is not readily available in Norway. It usually has to be ordered in advance.

For Norwegians, beef is usually associated with parties, candles, red wine, romantic dinners and visits to restaurants. And that is not without reason. Beef is used in a wide range of recipes, as juicy steaks, robust roasts and tasty stews.

Beef is lean, healthy meat, contrary to what many believe. It contains high-quality protein, iron, B-vitamins and zinc. Most steaks contain only 2-3% fat, but the side dishes often contain more.

Cuts of beef

Beef tenderloin – 3.7% fat
The tenderloin sits on the inside of the backbone. It can be roasted whole or cut into medallions. Filet mignon is the pointed end piece and is considered a delicacy. Tournedos are the next two or three steaks. Chateaubriand is the midsection and is often prepared for two people. The butted end of the tenderloin has many names and can be used in many dishes.

Strip loin of beef – 2.3% fat
The strip loin sits on the outside of the backbone. It can be roasted whole or cut into many slices of equal size.

Rib-eye or boneless rib of beef – 11.5% fat
Called entrecote in French and Norwegian, this cut is an extension of the strip loin on the front of the back. It is marbled with fat, which makes it juicy, tender and flavorful. This cut can be roasted whole or sliced and grilled as steaks.

Sirloin – 2.3% fat
The sirloin sits at the top of the rump and is the most tender part of the leg. It can be roasted whole or cut into slices or strips for quick dishes.

Top round – 1.7% fat
The top round is the largest muscle in the leg. It can be roasted whole or sliced and cut into strips for quicker preparation.

Rump – 3.7% fat
More of the same. Often rolled and tied for roasting.

Round steak – 2 % fat
Often roasted, but best braised or in stews.

Oxtail
Some feel that the tail is the best part of the animal. It requires long cooking time to break down the fibers, but it's worth the wait. The meat is fantastic and the stock is even better. It's easiest to prepare when sliced and cooked until the meat falls off the bones. Oxtail soup is a delicacy.

Shoulder (chuck), brisket and short ribs – 9.2 – 14.8% fat
Beef shoulder is juicy and flavorful meat, with a high proportion of meat to bone. The brisket and short ribs are good braised.

Arm, shank and bottom round – 4.4-8.8% fat
Arm and shank are front quarter meat. The meat is quite lean with bone. Bottom round is part of the leg, lean and boneless. These are not naturally tender cuts, so care must be taken in preparation. Both are best braised or in stews.

Lamb

Norwegian lamb is among the best in the world. Lam is tender and juicy with a distinctive flavor that comes from pastures along the coast or on mountain slopes.

Norwegian lamb is finely textured, tender meat. Mutton requires longer cooking time than lamb. Since mutton also has a stronger flavor, it is best in the classic dish *fårikål*, mutton and cabbage stew, and other braised dishes.

Norwegian lamb is the basis for many exciting dishes, but also for some of our most traditional holiday fare, including *pinnekjøtt*, dried ribs of mutton, and *smalahovud*, smoked lamb heads.

Herbs such as rosemary, thyme, basil, tarragon, parsley, chives and juniper berries are good with lamb. Other frequently used seasonings are garlic and bay leaves. Norwegian lamb tastes of

Norwegian nature, and we should used seasonings that enhance its natural flavor.

Cuts of lamb

Leg of lamb
Leg of lamb is tender and juicy. Roast it whole or bone it and make one large or two smaller roasts. It is also good cut into chunks and grilled or stewed. It can also be salted and dried or lightly salted and smoked.

Lamb roast with bone
The tailbone and the end of the shank should be removed. This makes it easier to carve the roast. The shank is a good "handle" for stabilizing the roast while carving. Cut lengthwise into thin slices.

Boneless lamb roast
A boneless rolled lamb roast packed in a net is prepared like an ordinary leg of lamb on the bone, but it requires less time in the oven and is much easier to slice and serve.

Sliced leg of lamb
Leg slices can be grilled or roasted like large chops, or they can be cut into chunks and braised. They are also excellent marinated.

Lamb shank
The lowest part of the leg of lamb is full of flavor, but it requires longer cooking time to be tender. Braise on top of the stove or cover with foil and roast in the oven.

Lamb chops
The rack or loin can be sliced into chops, either single or double. Lamb chops are best sautéed or grilled and are "fast food".

Saddle of lamb
If you want to impress your guests, serve a saddle of lamb. It is the rack of lamb with the ribs attached. The backbone is sawed off and the meat between the ribs is trimmed away. It roasts in no time.

The selection of ingredients is huge, the possibilities unlimited.

Lamb tenderloin
When only the very best is good enough. The lamb tenderloin is often the strip loin, as the filet itself is very small. The skin and fat are often trimmed away, but if you have a filet with skin, score it and place it under the grill right before serving.

Lamb ribs
The bony flanks and ribs are great for grilling. Season the ribs and steam first, then place on the grill. A special cut for rib connoisseurs.

Boneless lamb stew meat
This is boneless lamb with almost no fat, usually from the leg or shoulder. Great for stews, sautés and other delicate dishes.

Lamb stew meat with bones
After the leg and saddle are removed, you are left with the best meat. There's a lot of flavor in bone and fat. If you have time to wait, it becomes tender, juicy and tasty. A lot of the fat melts off and is easy to remove. *Fårikål*, lamb and cabbage stew, is a Norwegian classic.

Sliced lamb shoulder
This cut is sold both fresh and lightly salted. Fresh shoulder slices are used like stew meat on the bone. Lightly salted lamb is cooked in unsalted water and then served with potato dumplings all over western Norway.

Shaved lamb
Thin slices of leg or shoulder. In Norway, packages of frozen lamb shavings are sold in many supermarkets, or you can make them yourself from partially frozen meat. Use in quick sautés.

Ground lamb
Gound lamb is a must for moussaka and Greek lamb meatballs. Use as an alternative to ground beef for an extra flavorful dish.

Reindeer

Reindeer, moose, deer, and other game

Reindeer is one of our most exotic meats. It is a clean, natural luxury from Norwegian mountain plateaus. The meat is subjected to strict quality controls, as expected by Norwegian consumers. Game is a good choice for all occasions. Fortunately, in Norway, there is a good selection of reindeer meat at most meat counters. Other game is also available in season, but there are regional differences. Many Norwegians are enthusiastic hunters and freeze their own game.

Reindeer meat is famous for its unique, mild game flavor. But did you know that reindeer meat and other game are among the leanest meat you can find? The fat content is as low as 2-4%. The reason is completely natural – due to the wild landscape of Norway, with endless miles of grazing land filled with many kinds of moss, herbs and lichens. With this kind of menu and all

that exercise, game could well be the most natural of all meats.

Game is also extra nutritious, with protein, iron and B-vitamins. But still, most people choose game for its flavor.

Game is good for grilling, but because it is so lean, you can't leave it on the grill for long! Place the rack at mid-level over the coals, and turn the meat often. The meat should be pink and juicy inside.

Cuts of game

Game is very lean and needs proper handling to bring out peak flavor. Remember to brown it quickly, then let it finish cooking over low heat. It's important to let the meat rest before serving, so that the juices set.

Tenderloin
This is the best and most tender cut, real festive food, with short cooking time.

Chops
Double chops are cut across the loin, so that both strip loin and tenderloin sit on the bone. Great for sautéing and grilling.

Roast
A boneless rolled roast is every bit as good as roast beef. The meat is juiciest when cooked quickly, as it is very lean.

Steaks
Top round of reindeer, moose, deer or roedeer is unbelievably tender. Use it for steaks, in sautés or stews.

Shaved reindeer
Thin shavings of reindeer meat or other game. This lean meat should be cooked when still partially frozen to retain its juices.

Chopped or ground reindeer and moose
Coarsely chopped and ground meat can be varied endlessly. Use instead of other ground meat for less traditional variations on a theme.

Roasts

Roasts are usually cooked in the oven, but some reindeer and moose roasts are also good when braised on top of the stove. There are even some recipes for roast pork and veal prepared in this manner.

Lightly salted and smoked meats, such as leg of lamb and ham, also can be simmered in water. The water should be no hotter than 80°C (175°F). These roasts can also be wrapped in aluminum foil and baked in the oven.

It's important to use a meat thermometer for good results. Make sure to insert it into the thickest part of the meat. It should never touch bone, as that affects the temperature. This measures the temperature in the center of the meat, so that you know when it has finished cooking. The central temperature for roasts and filets will rise a few degrees while the meat rests before carving. How much it rises depends on how high the oven temperature was and how long the meat was in the oven.

Seasonings

Roast pork is good if it is rubbed with salt and pepper before roasting, especially if it's done several hours ahead of time. That can be enough in itself, but the addition of herbs also enhances the flavor. Sage and parsley are especially good with pork.

For many, garlic is a must with lamb, but don't use so much that you overwhelm the natural flavor of the meat. Rosemary is another herb that is good with lamb, as well as salt and pepper, of course. Other seasonings for lamb are oregano, thyme and parsley. Exotic spices such as coriander, cumin and curry complement lamb, but be careful not to use too much.

Be generous when seasoning beef roasts. A mixture of peppers and paprika are both good. Parsley and thyme are also good with beef.

Rosemary, thyme and juniper berries are excellent with reindeer and moose.

Marinades

All roasts can be marinated before cooking. The purpose of marinating is to add flavor to the meat, but marinating can also help to tenderize meat. Acidic liquids, such as vinegar, wine, lemon juice, buttermilk and yogurt are used. The acid starts the tenderizing process and helps the meat to stay fresh longer. Since salt draws moisture from the meat, it should not be used in marinades. Small pieces of meat require shorter marinating time than large. If the meat is going to be browned that same day, you can leave the meat at room temperature. If it's going to be used the next day or later, it should be refrigerated.

It's a good idea to place the meat in a plastic bag. Add the marinade and press out the air before tying the bag together. To be safe, put the bag of meat into another plastic bag to make sure that it doesn't leak, or place the bag in a bowl. Rotate the bag every so often. By using a bag for marinating meat, you can be sure that the meat is covered in marinade, and there are fewer utensils to wash.

Red wine marinade

4 tablespoons red wine
1 garlic clove, minced
1 tablespoon dried rosemary
2 bay leaves

Combine all ingredients. Use with beef, lamb and pork.

Mint Marinade

1 dl ($\frac{1}{2}$ cup) olive oil
1 dl ($\frac{1}{2}$ cup) dry white wine (or apple juice)
$\frac{2}{3}$ dl ($\frac{1}{4}$ cup) chopped fresh mint

Combine all ingredients. This marinade is especially good with lamb.

Honey marinade

2 tablespoons olive oil
1 tablespoon honey
2 tablespoons prepared mustard
2 garlic cloves, minced
2 teaspoons chopped fresh coriander
1 tablespoon lemon juice

Combine all ingredients. This marinade is especially good with pork and lamb.

Chili marinade

4 tablespoons ($\frac{1}{4}$ cup) oil
1 teaspoon chili oil or 1 teaspoon minced red chili
$\frac{1}{2}$ onion, sliced
1 tablespoon chopped fresh oregano
$\frac{1}{2}$ teaspoon coarsely crushed peppercorns

Combine all ingredients. This marinade is especially good with beef and lamb.

Garlic marinade

4 tablespoons ($\frac{1}{2}$ cup) oil
2 teaspoons lemon juice or 1 tablespoon white wine vinegar
2 garlic cloves, minced
3 peppercorns, crushed
1 teaspoon dried rosemary
1 parsley stalk, chopped
$\frac{1}{2}$ teaspoon dried thyme

Combine all ingredients. This marinade is especially good with lamb.

Herb marinade

3 $\frac{1}{2}$ tablespoons cognac
1 tablespoon oil
1 garlic clove, minced
1 teaspoon dried rosemary
$\frac{1}{2}$ teaspoon dried thyme
$\frac{1}{4}$ teaspoon dried basil
juice of $\frac{1}{2}$ lemon

Combine all ingredients. This marinade is especially good with beef and lamb.

Roast pork

with cider sauce and vegetables
8-10 servings

2 kg (4 ½ lb) boneless fresh ham, rind on
1 tablespoon salt
1 teaspoon pepper
2 carrots
2 onions
7 ½ dl (3 cups) water

Preheat the oven to 175°C (350°F). Rub the meat with salt and pepper. Insert a meat thermometer into the thickest part. Clean the vegetables and cut into chunks. Place in an oven tray with the meat. Roast until the internal temperature reaches 76°C (170°), 2 ½ –3 hours. Let the meat rest while preparing the side dishes. Just before serving, place under the grill to crisp the rind.

Cider sauce

6-8 servings

½ onion
1 leek
1 teaspoon oil
3 dl (1 ¼ cups) apple cider
6 dl (2 ½ cups) cooking liquid from roast
1 tablespoon cornstarch
3 ½ tablespoons cold water
1 teaspoon grated fresh ginger (or ½ teaspoon dried)
1 teaspoon lemon juice
½ teaspoon sugar

Finely chop the onion and leek and sauté in oil until soft and shiny. Add the cider and reduce by ⅔. Add the stock and reduce by ½. Stir the cornstarch into the water and whisk into the stock. Simmer until thickened. Season with ginger, lemon juice and sugar.

Vegetables

100 g (4 oz) snow peas
2 bell peppers, red and/or yellow
2 scallions
1 small broccoli stalk, parboiled for 1 minute, if desired.
1 tablespoon oil

Roast pork with cider sauce and vegetables

½ teaspoon salt
½ teaspoon pepper

Halve the snow peas, cut the peppers into strips, the scallions into rings and the broccoli into florets. Sauté in oil for a few minutes over medium heat. Sprinkle with salt and pepper.

Helpful hints
Roast fresh ham can be served in many ways and with all kinds of accompaniments. Try these:
– Sautéed apple wedges, Brussels sprouts and crispy bacon shreds
– Exotic fruits and mango chutney
– Sauerkraut and brown gravy

Roast veal

with white wine sauce and vegetables
4-6 servings

1 ½ kg (3 lb) veal roast
2 tablespoons flour
1 teaspoon salt
½ teaspoon pepper
2 carrots
½ leek
1 bunch parsley
2 garlic cloves

White wine sauce

6 tablespoons (⅓ cup) olive oil
1 dl (½ cup) dry white wine
5 dl (2 cups) veal stock

1 tablespoon cornstarch stirred into 1 tablespoon cold water

2 tablespoons chopped fresh sage

2 tablespoons capers

2 tablespoons oil

400 g (14 oz) fresh spinach

500 g (1 lb) chanterelles

butter

1 teaspoon salt

1/2 teaspoon coarsely ground pepper

Preheat the oven to 175°C (350°F). Rub the roast with a mixture of flour, salt and pepper. Finely chop the vegetables. Heat the olive oil in a cast iron pot and brown the meat on all sides. Add the vegetables, wine and stock. Insert a meat thermometer into the thickest part and place in the oven. Cooking time depends upon the dimensions of the roast. When the internal temperature reaches 62-65°C (150°F), remove the meat from the oven and let it rest for around 15 minutes. Strain the cooking liquid into a saucepan and heat to boiling. Whisk in the cornstarch mixture and cook until thickened. Just before serving, stir in the sage and capers. Rinse the spinach in cold water. Sauté the chanterelles in butter. Add the spinach and stir until wilted. Season with salt and pepper.

Roast lamb

6-8 servings

2 1/2 kg (5 lb) leg of lamb or 1 1/2-2 kg (3-4 1/2 lb) rolled boneless leg of lamb

3 garlic cloves

2 teaspoons salt

1/2 teaspoon coarsely ground pepper

1 teaspoon dried rosemary

5 dl (2 cups) boiling water

1 kg (2 1/4 lb) potatoes

1 leek

3 parsley roots

2 carrots

1 garlic clove

Roast veal with white wine sauce and sautéed vegetables

2 tablespoons olive oil
1 teaspoon salt
1/2 teaspoon coarsely ground pepper
1 teaspoon herbs de Provence

Au jus sauce

5 dl (2 cups) cooking liquid from roast
1 1/2 tablespoons cornstarch
2 tablespoons cold water
salt and pepper

Remove the tailbone with a small, sharp knife or buy a boned, rolled roast. Peel the garlic and cut into slivers. Make small slits in the meat and insert the garlic. Season with salt, pepper and rosemary. Insert a meat thermometer into the thickest part. It should not touch bone. Place in an oven tray and roast for around 2 hours, until the internal temperature reaches 65°C (150°F). After around 1 1/2 hours, add the boiling water. Peel and clean the potatoes and vegetables. Cut into coarse chunks. Mince the garlic. Heat the olive oil in a cast iron pot and sauté the vegetables with the seasonings for around 5 minutes. Cover and cook over low heat until almost done. Remove the meat from the oven, wrap in aluminum foil and let rest for around 15 minutes.

Roasted potatoes with thyme and garlic

10-12 potatoes of equal size
2 tablespoons oil
1/2 pot fresh thyme
2-3 garlic cloves, minced
100 g (3 1/2 oz) butter
2 tablespoons sea salt

Preheat the oven to 200°C (400°F). Scrub potatoes well. Do not peel. Arrange in a greased ovenproof dish. Sprinkle with strands of thyme and garlic. Thinly slice the butter with a cheese plane and place on the potatoes. Sprinkle with salt. Bake for 30-40 minutes, until tender.

Increase the oven temperature to 225°C (425°F). Pour off 5 dl (2 cups) cooking liquid for sauce. Transfer the vegetables to the roasting tray and bake for around 15 minutes, while the meat is resting and while the sauce is being prepared. Heat the cooking liquid to boiling, stir the cornstarch into the water and whisk into the stock.

Roast lamb with baked potatoes and vegetables

Cook until thickened. Correct the seasoning. Serve the lamb with the baked vegetables, potatoes and au jus.

Leg of lamb
– lightly salted and smoked
6-8 servings

2 1/2 kg (5 lb) lightly salted and smoked leg of lamb

Insert a meat thermometer into the thickest part of the roast. Place in a large pot with boiling water to just barely cover meat. Simmer until the internal temperature reaches 72°C (160°F). For added flavor, add sliced onion or leek. If you don't have a large enough pot, you can pack the meat in aluminum foil and "cook" it in a 125°C (250°F) oven. The internal temperature should still be the same. Serve with boiled potatoes and crisp-tender vegetables, or even creamed vegetables.

Helpful hint

For easy creamed vegetables, make a béchamel sauce, then add frozen vegetables and let simmer for around 10 minutes.

Leg of lamb – lightly salted and smoked

Reindeer roast

Reindeer roast

6 servings

1 ¹/₂ kg (3 lb) boneless reindeer roast, rolled and
tied
1 ¹/₂ teaspoons salt
1 ¹/₂ teaspoons pepper
2 carrots
1 onion
8 dl (3 ¹/₃ cups) water

Game sauce:

4 tablespoons (60 g/2 oz) butter
4 tablespoons (¹/₄ cup) flour
8 dl (3 ¹/₃ cups) cooking liquid
2-3 juniper berries, crushed

1 dl (¹/₂ cup) sour heavy cream
2-3 slices brown goat cheese (Ski Queen)
or 1 tablespoon crushed lingonberries
¹/₂ teaspoon salt
¹/₂ teaspoon pepper

Preheat the oven to 175°C (350°F). Rub the
meat with salt and pepper. Insert a meat thermometer into the thickest part. Place the meat in
an oven tray. Cut the carrots into thick slices and
the onion into wedges and add. Pour over the
water. Roast for around 1 ¹/₂ hours. When the
internal temperature is 65°C (150°F), the meat is
pink inside, when 70°C (160°F), it is gray. Let the
meat rest while you prepare the sauce. Melt the
butter in a saucepan and stir in the flour. Cook

until golden. Strain the cooking juices and add
gradually, whisking constantly. Heat to boiling,
lower the heat and simmer for around 10 minutes. Add the juniper, sour cream, cheese or berries. Reheat to boiling and season with salt and
pepper. Serve the roast with boiled potatoes,
broccoli or Brussels sprouts, sautéed mushrooms
and sauce.

Helpful hints

Poached pear halves filled with currant jelly are a
good accompaniment to this dish.

This recipe is also suitable for moose or deer.

Preparation of boneless meat and steaks

The four best cuts of beef, reindeer and moose – tenderloin, strip loin, rib eye and sirloin – are classified as steaks. Each animal has two of each of these cuts, which comprise only around 11 % of the meat on the animal. In Norway, meat is aged in vacuum packages, and it is not cut into steaks until it is fully aged.

Preparing tenderloin

If you plan to serve many guests, it is both impressive and practical to cook the tenderloin whole. It can be prepared in several ways, and if treated right, it's a juicy, tender piece of meat suitable for the most festive occasion.

This is what you do:
- Take the meat out of the refrigerator and let it rest at room temperature for around 30 minutes before cooking.

- Season whole roasts and place right in the oven.

- Brown tenderloins and roast beef quickly on all sides, then place in the oven.

- Use a meat thermometer to make sure that the meat is cooked to the right temperature. Cooking time depends on the temperature and the thickness of the meat.

- Roasts and tenderloins should always rest for 15-20 minutes before carving. The juices will set and the meat will be juicy and flavorful.

Cooking in a wok

Tender beef, pork and lamb cook well in a wok. Maintaining a high temperature is important. It can be difficult to reach a high enough temperature on a standard electric stove. Woks are supposed to be used over a gas flame. There are cast iron woks that reach a high enough temperature. It is important to use both a hot wok and hot oil when stir-frying.

This is what you do:
- Heat the wok before adding the oil. The oil spreads better and the ingredients don't stick to the pan.

- Brown the meat quickly. If you are browning a lot of meat, do it in small batches.

- Add the vegetables according to cooking times. Add those that require the most cooking time first. Don't overcook the vegetables or they get soggy.

- It is important to stir constantly and make sure that the wok does not cook dry.

Preparing steaks

How do you cook the perfect steak? The meat must be well aged. The best cuts are sirloin, rib eye, strip loin and tenderloin. Many prefer rib eye, because it is better marbled than tenderloin and is therefore extra juicy. No matter what, it is important to leave the fat on while cooking, as it adds flavor to the meat and makes it juicier. You can always remove it later. Tender, aged meat is often a darker red, with a matte surface, while very fresh meat is often lighter, with a shiny surface.

This is what you do:
- All the steaks should be approximately the same size, then they require the same cooking time.

- Take the meat out of the refrigerator and let it rest at room temperature for around 30 minutes before cooking.

- Sprinkle the steaks with salt and pepper immediately before adding them to the pan.

- Use high heat and let the butter turn golden brown before adding the steaks to the pan.

- Do not cook too much meat at one time. Then the pan cools down and the juices begin to leach out of the meat, causing the meat to stew rather than fry.

- When juice droplets form on top of the steaks, it's time to turn them. Do not pierce the meat with a fork when turning. Use a spatula instead.

- After a couple of minutes, droplets of juice form on top of the steaks. Then they are «medium» and should be removed from the pan. Let the steaks rest for a couple of minutes before serving.

- If you like your steak rare, cook it for only one minute per side. Medium needs around three minutes per side, while well-done meat requires one minute per side over high heat, then 4 minutes per side over low heat. Remember to turn the meat often.

Pork steaks *with orange jus*
4 servings

2 tablespoons butter
4 pork steaks (around 140 g (5 oz) each
1 teaspoon salt
$1/2$ teaspoon pepper
1 teaspoon dried rosemary or 2 tablespoons fresh
juice of 2 oranges

16 clusters tagliatelle
1 teaspoon oil
2 carrots
1 leek

Brown the butter in a heavy pan and fry the meat quickly on both sides over relatively high heat. Sprinkle with salt, pepper and rosemary. Then add the orange juice. Cover, remove the pan from the heat, and let the meat rest for around 10 minutes. Clean the vegetables. Cut the carrots lengthwise into thin slices with a

Pork steaks with orange jus

Steaks with mushroom-cream sauce

minutes, until somewhat thickened. Season to taste with soy sauce. Just before serving, sprinkle with chives. Serve with boiled potatoes.

Roast beef *with red wine sauce*
6 servings

1 ½ kg (3 lb) aged beef (rib eye, top round or sirloin)
1 ½ teaspoons salt
½ teaspoon pepper

Red wine sauce
1 small onion
½ carrot
1 garlic clove
1 tablespoon butter
½ teaspoon coarsely ground pepper
1 tablespoon tomato paste
2 tablespoons flour
3 ½ dl (1 ½ cups) red wine
3 dl (1 ¼ cups) beef stock
1 teaspoon salt
½ teaspoon dried thyme
2 tablespoons butter

Baked potato wedges
12 potatoes
3 tablespoons oil
1-2 teaspoons salt
2 teaspoons herbs de Provence or 2 tablespoons chopped fresh herbs (marjoram, rosemary, thyme and oregano

Preheat the oven to 175°C (350°F). Rub the meat with salt and pepper and insert a meat thermometer into the thickest part. If desired, roll and tie the meat. Roast for around 1 ½ hours, until the internal temperature reaches 55°C (130°F) for rare, 60°C (140°F) for medium. Let the meat rest for at least 10 minutes before carving. For the sauce, chop the vegetables and sauté in butter until soft and shiny. Add the pepper and sauté for a few more minutes. Stir in the tomato paste, sprinkle with flour and gradually add the wine and stock. Add salt and thyme and simmer for at least 15 minutes. The longer it cooks, the better it tastes. Strain, then whisk in the remaining butter. About 30 minutes before

cheese plane. Cut the leek into thin rings. Cook the pasta in water with oil to prevent sticking. Add the carrot and leek around 3-4 minutes before the end of the cooking time. Serve the pork steaks with pasta and vegetables. Pour over the orange flavored juices and serve with home-made bread and a salad.

Steaks *with mushroom-cream sauce*
4 servings

4 thick steaks (sirloin, rib eye, strip loin and tenderloin), around 180 g (6 oz) each
1 teaspoon salt
1 teaspoon pepper
2 tablespoons butter

Mushroom-cream sauce
250 g (9 oz) fresh mushrooms
2 tablespoons butter
½ teaspoon salt
½ teaspoon pepper
2 dl (1 cup) stock or bouillon
2 dl (1 cup) whipping cream
1 teaspoon soy sauce
2 tablespoons chopped chives

Sprinkle the steaks with salt and pepper and sauté in butter over medium heat until drops of juice appear on the top. Turn and cook until new drops of juice appear. Then the meat is medium. Prepare the sauce: Clean and slice the mushrooms. Brown butter in a pan and add the mushrooms. Cook until golden. Sprinkle with salt and pepper. Add stock and cream and heat to boiling. Let the sauce simmer for around 10

Roast beef with red wine sauce

serving, increase the oven temperature to 200°C (400°F). Scrub the potatoes and cut into wedges. Peel if old. Grease an ovenproof dish with the oil and arrange the potatoes evenly in the bottom. Sprinkle with salt and herbs. Bake for 20-30 minutes. Serve with the roast beef and sautéed vegetables.

Pork tenderloin
wrapped in Parma ham
4 servings

800 g (1 ³/₄ lb) pork tenderloin
¹/₂ teaspoon pepper
8 slices Parma or other dried ham
2 tablespoons oil

Ratatouille

2 onions
2 bell peppers
1 zucchini
2 garlic cloves
2 tablespoons oil
4 tomatoes or 1 can chopped tomatoes
1 tablespoon finely chopped fresh herbs (thyme, rosemary, oregano, parsley)
¹/₂ teaspoon salt
¹/₂ teaspoon pepper

Preheat the oven to 175°C (350°F). Rub the meat with pepper. Arrange the ham slices overlapping on a sheet of plastic wrap. Place the meat at one end and roll up. Tie at even intervals with cotton string. Brush with oil and place in an ovenproof dish. Roast until an instant thermometer reads 70°C (160°F). Start checking after 10

Pork tenderloin wrapped in Parma ham

minutes. For the ratatouille, clean and cut the onion into wedges, the peppers and zucchini into large cubes. Mince the garlic. Heat the oil in a saucepan and add the garlic. Sauté until golden, then add the vegetables, tomatoes and herbs. Let simmer for around 15 minutes, stirring occasionally. Season with salt and pepper. Serve with the meat and fried potato wedges.

Pork and tomato sauce *for pasta*
4 servings

1 onion
2 garlic cloves
1 can (14 oz) chopped tomatoes

Pasta with pork and tomato sauce

Pasta med skinke- og soppsaus

2 dl (1 cup) water
1 chicken bouillon cube
1 carrot
1 teaspoon salt
½ teaspoon pepper
500 g (1 ¼ lb) boneless pork
oil

Mince the onion and garlic and place in a saucepan with the tomatoes. Add the water and bouillon cube. Grate the carrot and add. Simmer for 15 minutes. Season with salt and pepper. Brown the meat in oil in two batches. Just before serving, add to the sauce and reheat. Serve over pasta with crusty bread and a green salad.

Ham and mushroom sauce
for pasta
4 servings

250 g (8 oz) cooked ham
150 g (5 oz) fresh mushrooms
1 tablespoon butter
2 dl (1 cup) vegetable stock
2 dl (1 cup) whipping cream
2 tablespoons minced parsley
½ teaspoons lemon juice
½ teaspoon salt
½ teaspoon pepper
pasta
grated parmesan cheese

Cut the ham into strips. Slice the mushrooms and sauté in butter until golden. Add stock and cream and reduce the mixture over high heat. When thickened, stir in the ham and parsley. Season with lemon juice, salt and pepper. Serve over pasta and sprinkle with parmesan cheese.

Pork wok
4 servings

500 g (1 ¼ lb) boneless pork
2-3 tablespoons sweet soy sauce (kecap manis)
1 garlic clove
1 teaspoon grated fresh ginger
¼ red chili
1 onion

1 leek
1 red bell pepper
1 carrot
250 g (8 oz) dried flat noodles
oil
1/2 teaspoon pepper
2 tablespoons chopped fresh herbs (coriander/
cilantro or parsley)

Cut the meat into strips and place in a glass
dish. Drizzle over the soy sauce. Mince the garlic,
ginger and chili and stir in. Marinate for at least
30 minutes. Slice the onion and leek. Shred the
pepper and carrot. Cook the noodles according
to package directions. Fry the meat quickly in oil
in two batches. Set aside. Sauté the vegetables
quickly, stir in the meat and then the noodles.
Season to taste with more soy sauce and pepper.
Sprinkle with herbs and serve immediately.

Fried ham sandwich

4 servings

1-2 garlic cloves
1 tablespoon olive oil
8 slices white bread
12 slices boiled ham
1 avocado, in thin wedges
8 lettuce leaves
1-2 tomatoes, sliced
1 teaspoon lemon juice
1/2 teaspoon coarsely ground pepper

Mince the garlic and sauté in olive oil. Add the
bread and fry on both sides. Remove from the
pan. Sauté the ham and avocado. Arrange lettuce and tomato on 4 slices of the bread. Top
with ham and avocado. Season with lemon juice
and pepper. Top with the remaining bread. Halve
on the diagonal. Eat while warm!

Helpful hint
Use different kinds of meat. Try shredded pork.
Sauté it in oil for 2-3 minutes.

Pork wok

Fried sandwich

Wiener schnitzel

Reindeer strips

with mushroom and cheese sauce
4 servings

500 g (1 ¼ lb) shaved reindeer
1-2 tablespoons butter
1 teaspoon salt
½ teaspoon pepper
150 g (5 oz) fresh mushrooms
200 g (7 oz) bacon-flavored cheese spread
2 dl (1 cup) game or beef stock
1 tablespoon chopped fresh thyme or rosemary
or 1 teaspoon dried

Defrost the meat slightly. Sauté in a hot pan with a little butter. Season with salt and pepper. Do not use too much salt, as the cheese is salty.

Quarter the mushrooms and add. Sauté lightly with the meat. Add the cheese and stock and stir until the cheese has melted. Cook over medium heat until well mixed. Sprinkle with herbs. Serve with boiled potatoes, Brussels sprouts and lingonberry compote.

Helpful hint
This dish tastes even better when topped with crispy bacon slices.

Any kind of game is also good in this dish, and you can shave it yourself. Defrost the meat slightly, then cut paper thin slices with a sharp knife. Fry in a hot pan.

Wiener schnitzel

4 servings

4 thin slices veal round steak, about 150 g (5 oz) each
1 egg
1 teaspoon salt
½ teaspoon pepper
1 dl (½ cup) fine breadcrumbs
1-2 tablespoons butter
100 g (3 ½ oz) butter
1 tablespoon minced fresh parsley
4 lemon slices
4 anchovy fillets

Pound the meat lightly. Beat the egg with salt and pepper. Dip the meat first in egg, then in crumbs. Brown the butter in a frying pan and fry the schnitzels for 2 minutes per side. Beat the butter and parsley together. Using plastic wrap, form into a sausage. Refrigerate until serving. Place a lemon slice on each schnitzel. Top with an anchovy fillet and a slice of lemon butter. Serve with boiled potatoes and peas.

Reindeer strips with mushroom and cheese sauce

Pork chops with fried onions

Chops

You can remove some of the fat from chops before frying, but the flavor is better when chops are cooked with their fat. Remember that fat melts away when the meat is fried. The fat can be removed after cooking, too. Fry chops for 2-3 minutes per side over medium heat. Lower the heat and continue cooking for 2-5 minutes depending upon the thickness of the chops.

Pork chops *with braised vegetables*
4 servings

4 pork chops
2 tablespoons oil
3 garlic cloves
1 teaspoon salt
½ teaspoon coarsely ground pepper
2 bell peppers, red and/or yellow
1 zucchini
1 dried pepper or 1 chili
3 tablespoons olives
1 ½ dl (²/₃ cup) white wine or cider

Sauté the chops in oil for 2 minutes per side over medium heat. Sprinkle with salt and pepper. Remove from the pan and keep warm. Cut the vegetables into strips and chop the chili. Sauté quickly in the same pan and add the wine. Top with the chops, cover and let simmer over low

heat for around 10 minutes. Serve with bread, rice or boiled potatoes.

Pork chops *with fried onions*
4 servings

4 pork chops
2 onions
1 red bell pepper
1 tablespoon butter
1 teaspoon salt
½ teaspoon freshly ground pepper
2 tablespoons butter

Peel and slice the onion. Cut the pepper into strips. Sauté onion and pepper in butter until golden. Remove from the pan and keep warm. Season the chops with salt and pepper and sauté them in butter over medium heat for 2-3 minutes per side. Lower the heat and continue cooking for 4-5 minutes. Serve with buttered potatoes and the fried onions and pepper.

Pork chops with braised vegetables

Lamb chops with pizzaiola sauce

Lamb chops *with pizzaiola sauce*

8 lamb chops
olive oil
1 teaspoon salt
$^1/_2$ teaspoon pepper
2 tablespoons shredded fresh basil or 1 teaspoon dried

Pizzaiola sauce

1 onion
2 garlic cloves
1 can (14 oz) chopped tomatoes
2 tablespoons tomato paste
1 dl ($^1/_3$ cup) pitted black olives

Brown the chops in oil in a hot cast iron pan for around 1 minute per side. Sprinkle with salt, pepper and basil. Lower the heat and continue cooking for 3-4 minutes. Clean and mince the onion and garlic. Sauté in oil until shiny, add the tomatoes and tomato paste, and reduce slightly. Just before serving, halve the olives and add. Serve the chops with the sauce, pasta, lemon wedges and crusty bread.

Smoked pork loin
with creamed vegetables
4 servings

1 – 1 $^1/_2$ kg (2 $^1/_4$ - 3 lb) smoked pork loin
1 teaspoon freshly ground pepper

Creamed vegetables

3 carrots
3 rutabaga slices
$^1/_2$ celeriac
2 dl (1 cup) water
$^1/_2$ teaspoon salt
1 tablespoon flour
1-2 dl ($^1/_2$ – 1 cup) milk
2 tablespoons butter
ground nutmeg

Preheat the oven to 175°C (350°F). Place the meat in an ovenproof dish and sprinkle with pepper. Insert a meat thermometer into the thickest part. Roast for 1 – 1 $^1/_2$ hours, until the internal temperature reaches 72°C (165°F). Let the meat rest for at least 15 minutes before carving into slices. While the meat is cooking, prepare the vegetables. Clean and cut the vegetables into 2 cm ($^3/_4$") cubes. Cook in the water (it should just cover the vegetables) with a little salt until tender. Place flour and milk in a jar and shake until blended. Pour in a thin stream over the vegetables, stirring well. Heat to boiling, add the butter and cook for 3-4 minutes. Season with a little nutmeg. Serve with boiled potatoes.

Helpful hint

This dish is good with béarnaise sauce or red wine sauce (see page 198, roast beef with red wine sauce).

Roast ribs of pork
4 servings

2 kg (4 $^1/_2$ lb) pork belly, with bones and rind
2-3 teaspoons salt
1 teaspoon pepper

Count on 500 g (1 lb) per person.

Score the rind

Cut through the rind and slightly into the fat with a sharp pointed knife. If you score the rind parallel with the bones, it will be easier to slice after roasting. If the ribs are frozen, it's a good idea to score the rind when still partially frozen, as that makes the task easier.

Seasoning

Rub the ribs with salt and pepper 1-3 days before roasting, being sure to get salt into every part of the roast. Place the ribs in an oven tray, rind down and cover with aluminum foil. Refrigerate until ready to roast. This gives the seasonings time to penetrate the meat.

Smoked pork loin with creamed vegetables

Roasting

Turn the ribs rind side up. Place an upside down dish under the ribs to raise them slightly in the middle (that way, the melted fat runs off). For even roasting, the ribs should be the same thickness on both sides. Pour over 2 dl (1 cup) water and cover the pan with aluminum foil. Preheat the oven to 230°C (450°F). Roast the foil-covered ribs on the center shelf for around 45 minutes. The ribs should "blow up" a little and the rind should crack. Remove the foil (but leave the dish) and lower the oven temperature to 200°C (400°F). Continue roasting for around 1¹/₂ hours. Sometimes the rind becomes crispy on its own. If this doesn't happen, move the pan to the top oven shelf and increase the temperature to 250°C (475°), or turn on the grill. Do not burn the rind. If parts of the rind are already crispy, cover them with foil. When all the rind is crisp, remove the meat from the oven and let it rest for at least 15 minutes before carving. The traditional Norwegian Christmas accompaniments, such as pork patties, pork sausages, apples and prunes, can be roasted in the pan with the ribs for the final 20 minutes of cooking time.

Serve the ribs with natural juices or brown gravy, sauerkraut or pickled red cabbage – and prunes, apples, lefse and lingonberry compote.

Helpful Hint

To avoid a mad rush before everyone comes for dinner, you can prepare the ribs earlier in the day. Let the ribs rest for a while before cutting into serving pieces. Place in an oven tray along with pork patties and sausages and reheat at 200°C (400°F) for 30 minutes.

Gravy

1 packet brown gravy mix
chopped fried shallots
rose and green peppercorns

For added flavor, use a packet of gravy mix to thicken the natural pan juices. Prepare according to package directions, but use pan juices (be sure to skim off the fat first) instead of water. Add shallots and peppercorns, if desired.

See recipe for pork patties on page 219.

Roast pork ribs with crispy crackling, sausage patties and link sausages – Norwegian Christmas dinner!

Roast dried ribs of mutton
4 servings

Count on 350 g (11 oz) mutton ribs per person

If you have a whole side of ribs, it's a good idea to cut between each rib for chops. Soak the ribs in cold water overnight. Change water several times. Place a metal rack or birch twigs (without bark) in the bottom of a large pot. Fill with water to the edge of the rack. Arrange the meat on the rack. Cover and simmer until the meat practically falls off the bones, around 2 hours. Check frequently – do not let the pan cook dry. For more color, the pinnekjøtt can be browned lightly in the oven. Arrange in an oven tray and place on the top shelf under the grill for around 5 minutes. If serving sausages alongside, steam them with the meat for the last 15-20 minutes. Serve pinnekjøtt on heated plates with coarsely ground sausages, mashed rutabagas, pan juices from the meat, boiled potatoes and mustard.

Roast dried ribs of mutton

Preparation of stewing cuts

Stewing or boiling cuts include oxtail, chuck, brisket, short ribs, arm, bottom round and eye of round. These cuts contain more connective tissue and do not become tender by the usual means. However, after long enough cooking, these too become tender and flavorful.

Boiled meat is an old tradition that also appears in newer trends. It's time-consuming, but it's worth it. This is lean, nutritious, good food. Boiling is a good way to cook cheap, tough meat from the front quarter. Boiling meat really means letting it simmer in water that's just under the boiling point. The ideal temperature is 80°C (175°F). At this temperature, connective tissue dissolves and the meat becomes tender and juicy. A higher temperature results in hard, dry meat. It's a good idea to check the water temperature with an instant thermometer now and then while the meat is cooking.

Count on 1 ½ liters water and 2 teaspoons salt per kilo (3 cups water and a scant teaspoon salt per lb) of meat. Cut the meat into serving pieces. Heat the water to boiling and add the salt. Add the meat and reheat to boiling. Skim well, so that the stock will be clear. Lower the heat and let the meat simmer at 80°C (175°F) until tender, around 2 hours. Meat on the bone is ready when it begins to separate from the bone. Add seasonings and vegetables according to taste or according to the recipe.

Helpful hint

If you cook the meat and refrigerate it until the next day, you have a good basis for a quick and easy dinner. Any fat that has melted off the meat is easy to remove. As long as you are taking the time to boil meat, you may as well make a large batch to use in many meals.

Beef is also sold in strips or chunks. As a rule, the strips are tender and easy to use in quick dishes. Chunks of stew meat are usually best in dishes that require a longer cooking time.

Hungarian goulash
4 servings

700 g (1 ½ lb) boneless beef from the shoulder
oil
1 teaspoon salt
1 ½ teaspoons pepper
2 tablespoons ground paprika
2 tablespoons flour
1 onion
1 red bell pepper
1 can (14 oz) chopped tomatoes
1 tablespoon tomato paste
6 dl (2 ½ cups) stock
¼ teaspoon caraway seeds
½ teaspoon chopped fresh marjoram
grated zest of ¼ lemon
1 garlic clove
1 tablespoon soft butter

Cube the meat and brown in oil in a hot pan in several batches. Transfer to a pot. Sprinkle with salt, pepper, paprika and flour. Peel and coarsely chop the onion and cube the pepper. Sauté onion and pepper until onion is shiny. Add to the pot. With the tomatoes, tomato paste and stock. Heat to boiling, cover, lower heat and let simmer for around 1 hour. Combine the remaining ingredients into a paste and whisk into the pot. Simmer for 10 minutes more. Readjust the seasoning. Serve with homemade bread or rice.

Hungarian goulash

Osso bucco

4-6 servings

150 g (5 oz) sun-dried tomatoes
100 g (3 ½ oz) dried mushrooms (such as porcini or chanterelles)
6 slices veal shank on the bone
3 tablespoons olive oil
2 onions
1 celeriac
2 carrots
3 cups dry white wine
1 teaspoon salt
1 teaspoon coarsely ground pepper
2 tablespoons chopped fresh parsley

Soak the tomatoes and mushrooms in water for around 2 hours. Brown the meat on both sides in oil in a heavy pan. Coarsely chop the vegetables, including the tomatoes and mushrooms, and add. Sauté for 3-4 minutes. Add the wine and cover. Lower the heat and let simmer for around 1 ½ hours. Sprinkle with parsley just before serving. Serve with hearty bread.

Swiss steak

Osso bucco

Swiss steak

4 servings

600 g (1 ⅓ lb) boneless beef round steak (or lamb or game)
4 tablespoons (¼ cup) flour
1 teaspoon salt
½ teaspoon pepper
2 tablespoons butter
1 onion
1 bay leaf
6 peppercorns

Cut the meat into 1 ½ cm (¾") slices. If the slices are too thin, the meat will become dry. Combine flour, salt and pepper. Dip the meat in the mixture, then brown in butter. Transfer to a pot. Slice the onion and brown lightly, then add to the meat with the bay leaf and pepper. Add

water to just cover the meat. Heat to boiling, stirring carefully. Cover, lower the heat and let simmer until tender, around 1 hour. Served with boiled potatoes, buttered vegetables and lingonberry compote.

Seamen's stew

4 servings

600 g boneless beef stew meat
butter
3-4 dl (1 ¼-1 ½ cups) water or stock
6 potatoes
2-3 carrots
1 thick slice rutabaga
1 parsley root

Seamen's stew

Cube the meat and brown on all sides in butter in small batches. Transfer to a pot and add the water or stock. Peel and cube the vegetables and add. Simmer over medium heat until meat and vegetables are tender, around 1 hour. Stir as little as possible to avoid breaking down the vegetables, but make sure that nothing burns. Season with salt and pepper. Serve with whole grain bread or flatbread and lingonberry compote.

If you are in a hurry, you don't have to brown the meat. You can also use leftover meat in this dish.

Boiled beef and soup
with onion sauce
4 servings

1 ¼ liters (6 cups) water
1 ¼ kg (2 ½ lb) chuck, arm, brisket or short ribs, with bone
1 teaspoon salt
1 small leek
3 carrots
100 g (4 oz) celeriac or parsley root
150 g (5 oz) cabbage
½ teaspoon pepper

Onion sauce
1 onion, finely chopped
5 dl (2 cups) beef stock
2 tablespoons flour
½ dl (¼ cup) cold water
2 teaspoons 7% vinegar
1 tablespoon sugar

Heat the water to boiling and add the meat, keeping the pieces as whole as possible. Reheat to boiling, skimming well. Add salt and the green part of the leek. Cover and let simmer until the meat is tender, about 1½ hours. Skim off any fat with a slotted spoon. Slice the remaining leek. Peel and cube the carrots and celeriac. Shred the cabbage. Add to the pot and simmer until tender, around 10 minutes. While the vegetables are cooking, remove around 5 dl (2 cups) cooking liquid for the onion sauce. In a saucepan, heat the cooking liquid and onion to boiling. Place flour and water in a small jar and shake. Whisk into the stock. Heat to boiling, lower the heat and let simmer for around 10 minutes. Season with vinegar, sugar, salt and pepper. Serve the soup first. Slice the meat and serve with boiled potatoes, soup vegetables and onion sauce.

Lamb fricassee
4 servings

1 kg (2 ¼ lb) lamb shoulder on the bone
6 dl (2 ½ cups) water
2 carrots
2 parsley roots
1 cauliflower
1 leek
6 dl (2 ½ cups) stock
4 tablespoons (¼ cup) flour dissolved in a little cold water
3 tablespoons fresh dill or 1 tablespoon dried
2 ½ tablespoons sour cream
1 tablespoon lemon juice

Cut the meat into serving pieces. Heat the water to boiling, then add the meat. Reheat to boiling, skimming well. Add the salt and let the meat simmer for around 45 minutes. Clean and cut the vegetables into chunks and add. Simmer for

Boiled beef and soup

Lamb fricassee

around 10 minutes, until the vegetables are tender. Prepare the sauce in the same pot or use a new saucepan. Heat the cooking liquid to boiling, whisk in the flour mixture. Simmer for around 10 minutes. Add the remaining ingredients, seasoning with a little salt and pepper, if necessary. Serve with boiled potatoes.

Lamb and cabbage stew
4 servings

1 ¹/₂ kg (3 lb) cabbage
1 ¹/₂ kg (3 lb) mutton or lamb shoulder on the bone, in chunks
2 teaspoons salt
4 teaspoons black peppercorns
3 dl (1 ¹/₄ cups) water

Cut the cabbage into wedges. Layer the meat and cabbage in a pot, sprinkling salt and pepper between the layers. The peppercorns can be placed in a tea-ball, if desired. Add the water. Heat to boiling, cover, then lower the heat and simmer over low heat until the meat is tender, 1 ¹/₂ - 2 hours. Serve piping hot on heated plates with boiled potatoes. For thicker pan juices, sprinkle 1-2 tablespoons flour between the layers of meat and cabbage.

Lightly salted ham hocks
A traditional Norwegian dish that's also found on the continent. This is a Norwegian variation of a well-known German dish.

4-6 servings

2 ³/₄ liter (11 cups) water, or enough to cover the meat
4 lightly salted and smoked ham hocks

Heat the water to boiling and add the hocks. Do not add salt. The meat should be completely submerged. Lower the heat, cover and cook at a slow simmer for around 3 hours. Preheat the oven to 225°C (425°F). Transfer the meat to a rack over an oven tray and roast for around 30 minutes, until the rind is golden and crispy. If not crispy enough, place under the grill for a few minutes. Serve with boiled potatoes, sauerkraut (see recipe below), mustard and pan juices.

Lamb and cabbage stew

Lightly salted ham hocks with dumplings

Stock and soups

A good soup is based on good stock. A bouillon cube can never replace the flavor of real meat. Making stock is time-consuming, but it's worth it. Stock freezes well. As long as you are making the effort, make a big pot of stock that you can use as the basis for many good meals.

Innherred soup

Light stock

1 kg (2 ¼ lb) beef bones, marrow bones, oxtails or meat on the bone
3 liters (12 cups) water
1 carrot, in chunks
1 celeriac slice
½ leek
½ onion
1 teaspoon black peppercorns

Rinse the bones under cold running water. Place in a large pot, add cold water to cover and heat to boiling, skimming often. Add the vegetables and seasonings and let simmer for 4-5 hours. Strain and let cool uncovered.

Helpful hint

During cooking, any fat in the meat melts into the stock. When the stock is chilled, the fat solidifies on top and is easy to remove. Stock freezes well. Use frozen stock within 3-4 months.

Brown stock

Use the same ingredients as in the previous recipe, but brown the bones first, either in a little butter in a frying pan or in a 250°C (475°F) oven for around 20 minutes. Then transfer to a large pot and follow the directions in the previous - recipe.

Innherred soup

This is a festive dish, traditionally served at christenings, confirmations and weddings in rural Norway.

8 servings

Stock
2 ½ kg (5 lb) mutton and beef on the bone
3 ½ liters (14 cups) water
2 ½ tablespoons salt
1 teaspoon ground ginger
1 teaspoon peppercorns
1 onion

Meatballs
400 g (14 oz) boneless mutton and beef
100 g (3 ½ oz) suet
1 ½ teaspoons salt
½ teaspoon white pepper
1 teaspoon flour
2 teaspoons potato starch
1 teaspoon grated onion
2 dl (¾ cup) light cream

Dumplings
4 tablespoons butter
6 tablespoons flour
1 dl (½ cup) boiling water
2 eggs
1 teaspoon sugar
½ teaspoon salt
½ teaspoon ground cardamom

It's a good idea to start this dish a day before serving. Begin with the stock. Remove the meat from the bones and cut into cubes. Reserve 400 g (14 oz) for the meatballs. Cut the bones into smaller chunks and place in a pot with the water. Heat to boiling, skimming well. Add the salt, pepper and ginger. Quarter the onion and add. Lower the heat, cover and let simmer for at least 2 hours. Strain. Simmer the meat in the stock until tender, 30-45 minutes. For the meatballs, grind the meat and suet with salt 3-4 times. For an extra fine texture, use a food processor. Add the flour, pepper and onion, and with the motor running, add the cream in a thin stream. Make small meatballs and poach in a little of the stock. For the dumplings, melt the butter and stir in the flour. Cook until the mixture leaves the sides of the pan. Beat in the boiling water. Lightly beat the eggs and whisk into the flour mixture. Season with sugar, salt and cardamom. Make small dumplings with a teaspoon. Cook in lightly salted (2 teaspoons salt per liter/quart) water until they rise to the surface. Just before serving, reheat the meatballs and dumplings in the soup. Serve with boiled potatoes, carrots and leeks and flatbread.

Grandmother's pea soup

Grandmother's pea soup

4 servings

200 g (8 oz) dried yellow peas
1 onion
1 celeriac slice
1 dried ham hock or bones from a leg of mutton
2 liters (8 ¼ cups) water
1 teaspoon dried thyme or 1 tablespoon chopped fresh
2 carrots
1 leek

Soak the peas in water overnight. Drain and return the peas to the pot. Coarsely chop the onion and celeriac and add with the meat. Add the water and thyme and heat to boiling. Lower the heat and let simmer for 2-3 hours. Around 20 minutes before the soup is ready, slice the carrot and leek and add. Remove the hock, cut off the meat, cut into bite-size pieces and return to the soup. Serve with potatoes and flatbread.

Helpful hint:
This soup can be made with all kinds of salted meat. Chose a cut on the bone for more flavor.

Soupy stew

4 servings

400 g (14 oz) boneless pork
1 garlic clove
1 tablespoon olive oil
6 dl (2 ½ cups) stock (1 bouillon cube + water)
1 liter (4 cups) frozen vegetables with potatoes
1 teaspoon herbs de Provence
¼ teaspoon salt
¼ teaspoon pepper

Soupy stew

Meat soup

Cut the meat into strips. Mince the garlic and fry in oil in a pot. Add the stock and heat to boiling. Add the meat, vegetables and herbs and let simmer for around 5 minutes, until the soup is slightly thickened. Season with salt and pepper. Serve with flatbread or crusty bread.

Meat soup

4 servings

800 g (1 ¾ lb) boneless front-quarter meat
1 liter (4 cups) stock
½ teaspoon dried thyme
1 onion
1 rutabaga
1 celeriac
1 leek
4 potatoes
½ teaspoon salt and pepper

Cut the meat into 3 cm (1 ¼") cubes. Cook in stock with thyme until tender, around 40 minutes. Clean and cut the vegetables into large chunks and add during the last 15 minutes of cooking time. Season with salt, pepper and more thyme, if desired. Serve with crusty bread or rolls.

Helpful hint
This soup is excellent when made with moose or reindeer.

Ground meat

Ground beef is the most popular ingredient there is. If you have ground beef in the house, you can make everything from classic Norwegian meat patties to the most exotic dishes.

Important facts about ground meat:

1. Norwegian ground meat is made from beef and contains at most 14% fat. A leaner variety, with maximum 6% fat, is also available. It is permitted to add 1% salt and up to 5% ice or ice water.

2. Ground meat should be used on the day of purchase. It will keep overnight in the refrigerator. Frozen ground meat keeps for around 3 months.

3. When frozen ground meat defrosts, juices are released. They should be stirred back into the meat. These juices contain proteins that bind the ground meat together when mixed with other ingredients.

4. Ground meat for stews and spaghetti sauce can be quick-thawed in the microwave oven. Ground meat for meat patties should be defrosted in the refrigerator overnight.

Ground meat is not supposed to contain any additives, although up to 5% ice or ice water can be added, and in some cases up to 1% salt. In Norway, it is also possible to buy forcemeat, ground meat that has been extended with liquid, seasonings and starch. If you want to make your own forcemeat, you need to mix the ground meat thoroughly with salt before adding liquid, which should be the same temperature as the meat. Then it won't separate so easily.

Spaghetti with bolognese sauce

Bolognese sauce
4 servings

1 onion
2 celery stalks
1 carrot
3 bacon slices
500 g (1 ¼ lb) ground beef
2 tablespoons tomato paste
1 can (14 oz) tomatoes
3 dl (1 ¼ cups) stock
½-1 teaspoon salt
½ teaspoon pepper
1 teaspoon dried oregano

Clean and chop the vegetables. Cut the bacon into shreds. Brown the ground beef without added fat over medium heat. Add the vegetables, bacon, tomato paste, tomatoes and stock. Let simmer for around 20 minutes. Add the seasonings. Serve over spaghetti and top with grated Parmesan cheese. Serve with a salad and garlic bread.

Helpful hint:
This sauce is also good on pizza. Cook it a little longer, so that more liquid evaporates and the filling is thicker.

Meat patties *with brown gravy*
4 servings

500 g (1 ¹/₂ lb) ground beef
1 ¹/₂ teaspoons salt
¹/₄ teaspoon pepper
¹/₄ teaspoon nutmeg
¹/₄ teaspoon ground ginger
2 ¹/₂ tablespoons potato starch
2 dl (³/₄ cup) water or milk
butter

Brown gravy
5 dl (2 cups) stock or cooking juices
1 onion, minced
3 tablespoons flour stirred into a small amount of cold water
salt, pepper
soy sauce

Mix the ground meat with salt until elastic. Stir in the seasonings and starch, mixing thoroughly. Gradually add the liquid, mixing it thoroughly into the meat before adding more. Form the meat mixture into round patties. Fry in butter over medium heat for about 5 minutes per side. Transfer to a pot and simmer in stock or water for around 10 minutes.

Strain the pan juices for gravy, add the onion and heat to boiling. Whisk in the flour mixture and heat to boiling, stirring constantly. Let simmer for 7-8 minutes, then season with salt and pepper. Serve with boiled potatoes and lingonberry compote.

Lean meat patties
4 servings

500 g (1 ¹/₄ lb) low fat ground beef
1 teaspoon salt
¹/₂ teaspoon pepper
1 ¹/₂ teaspoons potato starch
3-4 teaspoons water

Lightly mix the ground beef with the salt, pepper and starch. Stir in the water. Form into 8 flat patties. Make a checkerboard pattern on the surface with a knife. Fry over relatively high heat for 2 minutes per side. Lower the heat, then finish cooking for around 2 minutes per side. Serve with fried onions, boiled potatoes and stewed peas.

Helpful hint:
These patties can be made with moose or reindeer meat, then it's good to substitute cream for water. This meat is very lean and benefits from the added flavor and fat. Delicious side dishes include sautéed mushrooms, fried bacon and creamy game sauce. For an easy variation of creamed peas, cook frozen peas for around 2 minutes. Transfer to a blender, add 1-2 tablespoons of butter and puree. Season with salt and pepper.

Lasagna
4 servings

Meat sauce:
1 onion
1 carrot
100 g (4 oz) mushrooms
500 g (1 ¹/₄ lb) ground beef
¹/₂-1 teaspoon salt
¹/₂ teaspoon pepper
2 tablespoons tomato paste
3 dl (1 ¹/₄ cups) beef stock
1 can (14 oz) chopped tomatoes

Meat patties with creamed cabbage

Clean and chop the vegetables. Brown the meat in a dry pan. Sprinkle with salt and pepper. Add vegetables, tomato paste, stock and tomatoes. Let simmer for around 20 minutes.

Cheese sauce:

1 tablespoon butter
2 tablespoons flour
4 dl (1 ²/₃ cups) milk
1 dl (½ cup) grated mozzarella or Swiss cheese
1 teaspoon salt
½ teaspoon white pepper
¼ teaspoon nutmeg

Melt the butter and stir in the flour. Gradually whisk in the milk. Let simmer for around 10 minutes. The sauce should be rather thick. Stir in the cheese. Season with salt, pepper and nutmeg.

9 pre-cooked lasagna noodles
1-2 dl (½-1 cup) grated cheese

Preheat the oven to 225°C (450°F). Layer the lasagna noodles, meat sauce and cheese sauce in a greased pan, beginning with noodles and ending with cheese sauce. Top with grated cheese. Bake for 30-40 minutes. Let the lasagna rest for around 10 minutes before serving. Serve with Italian bread and a salad.

Lean meat patties

Lasagna

Moussaka

Moussaka

4 servings

2-3 eggplants
1 ½ teaspoons salt
2 tablespoons olive oil
2 onions
2 garlic cloves
1 bunch parsley
400 g (14 oz) ground lamb
2 dl (1 cup) stock
1 can (14 oz) chopped tomatoes
½ teaspoon dried thyme
½ teaspoon dried rosemary
½ teaspoon ground cinnamon

Bechamel sauce

2 tablespoons butter
3 tablespoons flour
4 dl (1 2/3 cups) milk
½ teaspoon salt
¼ teaspoon white pepper
2 eggs

1 dl (1/2 cup) grated mozzarella or Swiss cheese

Cut the eggplants into ½ cm (³/₁₆″) slices. Place on paper towels and sprinkle with salt on both sides. Let marinate for 1 hour, then rinse under cold water. Dry well. Brown lightly on both sides in oil. Drain on paper towels. Mince the onion, garlic and parsley and brown lightly. Add the meat and fry until golden. Add the stock, tomatoes with juice and seasonings. Let simmer over low heat for 25-40 minutes. Add more liquid if necessary. Preheat the oven to 225°C (450°F). For the béchamel sauce, melt the butter and stir in the flour. Whisk in the milk and add the seasonings. Cook until thickened. Whisk in the eggs. Layer the eggplant, meat sauce, béchamel sauce and grated cheese in a greased ovenproof dish, ending with cheese. Bake for around 30 minutes. Serve with crusty bread and a salad.

Taco casserole

with guacamole and salsa
4 servings

500 g (1 ½ lb) ground beef
1 tablespoon oil
1 leek
1 packet Taco Seasoning Mix
2 ½ dl (1 cup) water
1 can (14 oz) chopped tomatoes
1 can kidney or pinto beans
1 packet tortilla chips
1 dl (½ cup) grated cheddar cheese

Brown the meat in oil. Clean and slice the leek and add. Sprinkle with Taco mix and stir in the water and tomatoes. Simmer for around 10 minutes. Pour into a casserole. Drain and rinse the beans thoroughly and sprinkle on top, then cover with tortilla chips and grated cheese. Serve with guacamole, salsa, lettuce, sour cream and more chips.

Guacamole
2 ripe avocados
3 tablespoons lime juice
2 garlic cloves, minced
1 dl (⅓ cup) chopped scallion
1-2 tablespoons chopped fresh chili pepper
2 tablespoons chopped fresh coriander (cilantro)
½ teaspoon salt
¼ teaspoon pepper

Halve the avocado and remove the pit. Scoop out the flesh with a spoon and place in a bowl with the remaining ingredients. Mash with a fork to desired consistency – some like it coarse, others like a puree.

Salsa
1 can tomatoes
2 garlic cloves
½ green bell pepper, in chunks
1 pickled jalapeno
¼ teaspoon salt
¼ teaspoon coarsely ground pepper

Puree all ingredients in a blender until almost smooth.

Pork patties

6 servings

1 kg (2 ¼ lb) ground pork
1 tablespoon salt
2 cups milk
5 tablespoons (1/3 cup) potato starch
¼ teaspoon ground pepper
½ teaspoon ground nutmeg
¼ teaspoon ground ginger
oil

Brown gravy
4 tablespoons (¼ cup) butter
4 tablespoons (¼ cup) flour
8 dl (3 ⅓ cups) hot stock
1 teaspoon soy sauce
salt, pepper

Mix the pork thoroughly with the salt. Gradually stir in ⅔ of the milk. Start slowly, increasing gradually. Mix thoroughly. The mixture should become quite elastic with each addition of liquid. Add the starch and seasonings, then the remaining milk. Make round patties and brown in oil on both sides. Add a little water or stock and simmer until cooked through, 4-5 minutes.

Taco casserole with guacamole and salsa

Use the cooking juices to make gravy. Melt the butter and let it turn golden brown. Add the flour and cook until nut brown. Gradually whisk in the stock. Let simmer uncovered for around 10 minutes. Add the soy sauce. Season with salt and pepper if necessary. Serve with mashed potatoes and cooked vegetables.

Pork patties

Boneless birds

4 servings

500 g (1 ¼ lb) boneless beef, reindeer or moose, trimmed of all fat, in one piece
1 teaspoon salt
¼ teaspoon ground pepper
¼ teaspoon ground cloves

Filling:
Alternative 1: 100 g (4 oz) cubed bacon mixed with 1 dl (½ cup) chopped onion

Alternative 2: 100 g (4 oz) chopped fresh mushrooms mixed with 1 tablespoon chopped fresh herbs or 1 teaspoon dried herbs

Alternative 3: 150 g (5 oz) finely ground beef

3 tablespoons butter
4 dl (1 ⅔ cups) stock
½ dl (¼ cup) water
2 tablespoons flour

Cut the meat into thin slices. Combine salt, pepper and cloves and sprinkle over the meat. Prepare the filling of choice and place 1 tablespoon filling on each piece of meat. Roll up and fasten with wooden picks or tie with cotton string. Brown the "birds", seam side down, in butter over medium heat. Do not brown too many at once or the pan cools down too much. When all the "birds" are brown, return all to the pan. Add stock and simmer until tender, around

Cabbage rolls

30 minutes. Shake the water and flour in a jar to blend. Whisk into the pan. Heat to boiling and let simmer for around 10 minutes, until thickened. Serve with boiled potatoes and peas.

Cabbage rolls

4 servings

1 cabbage
400 g (14 oz) ground beef or pork
2 teaspoons salt
½ teaspoon pepper
1 tablespoon potato starch
1 small egg (optional)
3 dl (1 ¼ cups) milk
¼ teaspoon ground nutmeg

Bechamel sauce
1 tablespoon butter
2 tablespoons flour
2 dl (¾ cup) cooking liquid or stock
2 dl (1 cup) milk
½ teaspoon salt
¼ teaspoon ground nutmeg

Place the whole cabbage in boiling water for a few minutes to loosen the outermost leaves. Cut out the core and remove the leaves as carefully as possible so they don't tear. Trim the thick stalk. Let cool. Mix the ground meat with the salt until elastic. Add the pepper and starch. Whisk the egg into the milk and add gradually. Stir in the nutmeg. Place a spoonful of the meat mixture onto every cabbage leaf. Fold up around the meat and tie with string. If the rolls are placed in a "tight" pan, they don't need to be tied. Simmer in stock or lightly salted water for around 20 minutes. Remove from the cooking liquid and drain. Reserve the cooking liquid for the sauce. Melt the butter in a saucepan. Stir in the flour. Do not allow the mixture to brown. Whisk in the stock and milk. Heat to boiling, whisking constantly. Simmer for around 10 minutes. Season with salt and nutmeg. Serve with boiled potatoes and sauce.

Helpful hint
Cabbage rolls taste even better when browned. Cook until done, then fry until golden in butter over medium heat.

Boneless birds

Sausages

Tiny sausages, smoked sausages, pork sausages, cocktail wieners, knockwursts and traditional wieners, along with regional specialties, are Norwegian classics. They are still made in the traditional manner – in natural casings – and every sausage is twisted by hand.

A century ago, every farm used to make its own sausages. Although they are seldom made on farms these days, many regional sausages are made all over Norway, their recipes safe in the hands of professionals with both quality and tradition as bywords. Most of these traditional sausages are coarse in texture, full of flavor and full of meat!

A number of newer varieties have become popular in Norway in recent years. These generally are more highly seasoned than traditional Norwegian sausages.

Skinless hotdogs for grilling are a relatively new invention in Norway. They are made with skin, but it is removed after production. There are many sizes of hotdogs, and they come plain, of course, or flavored with cheese, bacon and even chili pepper.

Hotdogs have not always had a good reputation, and there are many jokes about the contents of hotdogs. But that is a thing of the past. Good raw materials are the beginning, and Norwegian hotdogs contain 14 kg (lb) of meat for every 20 kg (lb) of finished sausages.

All sausages labeled wiener, grill, smoked and unsmoked sausages, knockwursts, pork sausages and Christmas sausages are made according to strict specifications that must be followed if the sausage is to be labeled as such. The govern-

There are many varieties of sausages. Back from left: Small sausages, smoked sausages, pork sausages and cocktail sausages. Front from left: Tiny sausages, knockwursts and wieners.

ment agency that supervises all food production in Norway has very strict rules regarding sausage production. Norwegian sausages are made of beef, pork and/or lamb, with the addition of pork fat, salt, seasonings, starch and milk or water. The percentage of fat is not supposed to exceed 20% (most are 17-18%), except for Christmas sausages and finely ground pork sausages, which can have 25% fat, and Voss sausages, which can have 27%. The seasonings most frequently used in Norwegian sausages are pepper, nutmeg, ginger, cloves and allspice.

Storage and labeling

Smoked sausages keep better than unsmoked, because smoking is a means of preservation. Loose smoked sausages will keep for around a week in the refrigerator, while unsmoked should be used within 2-3 days. Vacuum-packed sausages have the longest storage time and are marked with a use-by date. Frozen sausages should be used within three months. All packaged sausages are required to list ingredients, fat content, storage recommendations and a use-by date.

Frying

Do sausages burst when you fry them? Sausages are best when fried over medium heat. It's a good idea to pierce the casing before frying, to keep them from bursting so easily. Use as little fat as possible and remove them from the heat as soon as they are brown on both sides. If cooked for too long, they become wrinkled and dry.

Simmering

Sausages should not be boiled. Ideally, they should be simmered. Heat the water to boiling, then lower the heat before adding the sausages. You can use an instant thermometer to check the water temperature. 80°C (175°F) is suitable for all kinds of sausages. Thin sausages require short simmering – around 10 minutes. Plump sausages, such as smoked sausages and finely ground pork sausages, should be simmered for around 20 minutes. If the sausages are frozen, they will need 5-10 minutes additional cooking time.

Steaming

It's practical and easy to steam sausages on a bed of vegetables or on a rack. Fill water to the edge of the vegetables or the rack. Top with sausages and cover. This method works well if the sausages need to be kept warm for a while. This way, they don't get watery.

Grilling

Whether you grill in the oven or outdoors, you should make several slits in each sausage, or you can pierce the skin with a skewer. Turn frequently, so they don't burn. It takes only a couple of minutes to cook a sausage on a hot grill.

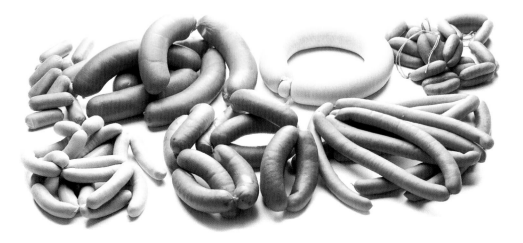

Sausage omelet
4 servings

2 smoked sausages
1 small red bell pepper
4 mushrooms
2 tablespoons butter
8 eggs
1 dl (¹/₃ cup) water
1 ¹/₂ teaspoons salt
2 tablespoons chopped chives

Cube the sausages and pepper. Slice the mushrooms. Fry in butter. Remove from the pan and set aside. Beat the eggs with water and salt and pour the mixture into the pan. Cook until the omelet is set in the center. Arrange the filling on one side of the omelet and fold the other half over. Sprinkle with chives. Serve with a salad and bread.

Helpful hint
Other kinds of sausages, including dried ones can be used in this dish.

Sausage omelet

Curried sausage *with apples*
4 servings

2 apples
1 onion
2 tablespoons butter
2 teaspoons curry powder
600 g (1 ¹/₃ lb) sausages (frankfurters or bratwurst)

Cube the apple and cut the onion into wedges. Fry in butter, then sprinkle with curry powder. Keep warm. Fry the sausages. Serve with mash potatoes and garnish with fresh herbs.

Curry sausage with apples

Christmas cold cuts

Lamb roll

1 kg (2 ¼ lb) lamb flank + shoulder meat
½ teaspoon ground pepper
½ teaspoon ground ginger
1 ½ tablespoons salt
¼ teaspoon sodium nitrate (for a fresh color)
1 teaspoon sugar
2 ½ teaspoons powdered gelatin

Remove any bones from the meat. Cut the meat
into a flat rectangle (around 20 cm/8" long). Any
trimmings can be rolled with the meat. Combine
the remaining ingredients and sprinkle over the
meat. Roll up tightly. Start from the roll with the
most meat. Use wooden picks to hold together,
then sew with cotton thread, starting at the
thickest end. Refrigerate for 24 hours, so that
the seasonings can penetrate the meat. Pack the
roll in a linen towel and tie with string. Place in
boiling unsalted water and let simmer at 80°C
(175°F) for around 1½ hours (cooking time
depends on the thickness of the roll). Remove
from the water and let the meat rest for 10-15
minutes. Place under pressure. If you don't have
a press, place the roll on a cutting board. Place a
new board on top with something heavy on top
of it (a brick or a kettle of water, around 6 kg/13
lb). Let rest overnight. The roll can be stored in
weak salt brine for 10 days. The raw roll can be
frozen.

Weak salt brine
5 liter (quarts) water
300 g (1 cup) salt
1 tablespoon sugar

Combine all ingredients and stir until dissolved.
Meat stored in this liquid keeps fresh for around
10 days.

Beef roll

1 beef flank
800 g (1 ⅔ lb) beef flank or skirt steak
200 g (7 oz) pork fat, in thin slices
1 ½ tablespoons salt
1 teaspoon sugar
1 teaspoon ground pepper
1 tablespoon ground ginger
1 small onion, minced
2 teaspoons powdered gelatin

Trim the flank into a rectangle. Cut trimmings
and beef into 1 cm (3/8") thick strips. Layer
meat and fat so that the flank just encloses the
filling. Sprinkle seasonings, onion and gelatin
between the layers. Roll up and fasten with
picks. Sew the roll together with strong thread.
Begin in the center and sew toward both ends.
Tie with cotton string to maintain its shape.
Place in a plastic bag and refrigerate for 24
hours. Cook and press as in the previous recipe.

Pork roll

1 – 1 ¼ kg (2 ¼ - 2 ¾ lb) pork belly
1 tablespoon salt
1 teaspoon ground pepper
1 teaspoon ground cloves
½ teaspoon ground allspice
1 teaspoon ground ginger
1 tablespoon powdered gelatin

Cut the meat into three layers that stay connected, like a zig-zag: Place on a cutting board, rind
side down. Using a sharp knife, cut the upper-
most layer, but do not cut all the way through
the end. Turn the meat with the rind up and cut
the next layer almost down to the rind, but do
not cut all the way through the end. Unfold the
connected layers. The rind should be at the end
of the piece of meat. If the meat is very fatty,
place some thin slices of pork on it. Combine the
remaining ingredients and sprinkle over the entire piece of meat. Roll up, starting from the side
opposite the rind, so that the rind ends up on
the outside. Tie with cotton string and pack in a
linen cloth. Twist cotton string all around the roll.
Place in boiling water, reheat to boiling and simmer at 80°C (175°C) for 1½ -2 hours, depending

Lamb roll

Beef roll

Pork roll

upon the thickness of the roll. Press as in the previous recipe. Store in brine (recipe, page 223).

Pickled pork belly

3 liter (quarts) water
4 tablespoons salt
1 kg (2 ¼ lb) pork belly
1 tablespoon whole cloves.

Heat water and salt to boiling. Add the pork, lower the heat and let simmer at 80°C (175°F) for around 1½ hours. Remove the meat and let cool for around 10 minutes. Fold in half, rind side out and place under a weight overnight. Stud the rind with whole cloves and place in brine for 3-4 days. Store in a weak brine solution with other kinds of Christmas cold cuts.

Salt brine

This brine gives meat a well-rounded flavor. Meat rolls and headcheese should soak for at least 24 hours, depending on how salty you want them to taste and how much seasoning you have used in them.
500 g (18 oz) salt
5 liters (21 cups) water
2 tablespoons sugar
6 bay leaves

Traditional head cheese

½ medium pig's head
1½ tablespoons salt
1 teaspoon pepper
½ teaspoon ground cloves
½ teaspoon ground allspice
1 teaspoon ground ginger
2 teaspoons powdered gelatin

Loosen the meat from the lower jaw all the way in to the joint and remove the bone. Loosen the meat from the upper jaw from the front and toward the eye and cut over. Place the head in cold running water (or change water frequently) for 6-8 hours or overnight. Place the head in a large pot and add boiling water. Simmer for 2-2½ hours. Cut the meat off the head while still

warm. Try to keep the rind as whole as possible. Chop small pieces of rind and sprinkle them between the layers. Cut meat and fat into thin slices or strips and keep separate. Combine the remaining ingredients in a separate bowl. Place a clean linen towel or several layers of cheesecloth in a bowl with high sides. Cut a round of rind and place it in the bottom. Layer meat and fat in the bowl. Sprinkle each layer with spice mixture and chopped rind. When all the meat and fat are used up, top with another round of rind. Fold the cloth over the meat and fasten with skewers. Tie with string around the entire package in a wheel and spoke pattern. Return to the cooking liquid and let simmer at 80°C (175°F) until heated through, around one hour. Do not allow the liquid to boil. Immediately place under a weight, light to start out, heavier as it cools. Store in a weak brine.

Liver paté

1 kg (2 ¼ lb) beef or pork liver
500 g (1 ¼ lb) ground pork
1 onion, quartered
3-4 tablespoons breadcrumbs
1 tablespoon salt
½ teaspoon ground pepper
½ teaspoon ground allspice
½ teaspoon ground cloves
½ teaspoon ground nutmeg
3 eggs
1 ½ dl (⅔ cup) milk

Preheat the oven to 170°C (350°F). Grease a 2-liter (8 cup) loaf pan. Place everything except the eggs and milk in a food processor with a steel blade. Puree until almost smooth. Whisk the eggs and milk together and add gradually with the motor running. Process until smooth. Pour into the pan. Bake for around 1 hour. The paté should feel firm when pressed. Serve with hearty bread, pickles and onions. Top with crispy bacon for extra flavor.

Liver paté

Dried meats

Dried meats were popular years ago because drying was a reliable method of preservation. Meat has been treated this way for hundreds of years in Norway, and there are also traditions for serving this kind of meat. Classic accompaniments are potato salad, green salad, flatbread and sour cream porridge. A great deal of dried meat is used in sandwiches. In recent years, Norwegians have adopted dishes from the Mediterranean, such as tapas and pasta dishes, which are also served with dried meats.

Dried meats are just as good on a romantic evening for two as they are for a large party. Dried meat is easy to use, tasty and can be varied in many ways. It keeps well and is easy to bring along on a picnic. It's also good to have around for unexpected company. Dried ham can be fried lightly for extra flavor and crispness.

Count on 150 g (5 oz) dried meat per person with simple accompaniments such as salad, flatbread and sour cream. Dried ham is the most popular, so it's a good idea to calculate half of all the dried meat served will be ham. For 10 people, you should serve 750 g (1 2/3 lb) dried ham, 250 g (9 oz) dried leg of mutton, 250 g (9 oz) salami, and 250 g (9 oz) other types of dried sausage. If the side dishes are very filling, you won't need quite as much dried meat.

Side dishes
– a wealth of possibilities

In recent years, side dishes have become a more important part of the meal. We have been eating salads for a long time now, and they give us the opportunity to try different kinds of vegetables, fruit and berries, nuts and cheeses. We have also become more versatile in our use of potatoes. Now we eat them fried, baked, creamed and mashed, in addition to boiled. Potatoes go with just about everything. We also have long traditions of serving bread with food. Although we have now opened our kitchens to dishes from many lands, we still enjoy breaking good bread along with meat or fish.

Potatoes

Baked potatoes
4 servings

4 large potatoes
salt

Preheat the oven to 200°C (400°F). Wash the potatoes well. Cut an x in each potato. Place in an ovenproof dish. Bake until soft all the way through, from 60 to 80 minutes. Remove the potatoes from the oven and let rest for a few minutes. Break open at the x, or cut through. Spoon on desired filling.

Filling:
– Sour cream and crisp bacon bits
– Sour cream and shrimp, crab or lobster
– Herb butter
– Mushroom sauce
– Pickled herring, beets, onion and sour cream
– Bacon, tomato, cucumber and sour cream
– Grated cheese
– Blue cheese blended with butter

Garlic butter
3 tablespoons butter
2 garlic cloves
chopped parsley and/or chives

Beat the butter until soft. Mince the garlic and add with the parsley. Place on plastic wrap and form into a roll. Freeze until solid. Slice and serve with baked potatoes. Garnish with parsley.

Mushroom sauce
50 g (2 oz) fresh mushrooms
1 teaspoon lemon juice
2 dl (1 cup) sour cream
3 tablespoons minced parsley
1 tablespoon minced oregano
salt and pepper

Finely chop the mushrooms and combine with the remaining ingredients, seasoning with salt and pepper to taste.

If you can't get fresh oregano, use 1 teaspoon dried.

Baked potatoes

Scalloped potatoes

Baked potato wedges

Preheat the oven to 200°C (400°F). Wash and dry the potatoes well. Cut into wedges and arrange on an oven tray. Drizzle with oil, tossing to coat. Sprinkle with ground paprika, salt, pepper and your choice of herbs. Bake until potatoes are tender, around 30 minutes.

From left: Baked potato wedges, potatoes boulangère and rösti

Rösti

Count on 200 g (8 oz) potato per person. Peel, wash and coarsely shred the potatoes. Press out the water. Heat oil in a skillet and spread a handful of potato over the pan. Fry until golden brown on one side. Ease the potato cake onto a lid to simplify turning onto the other side and fry until golden. Season just before serving. Excellent with both fried meat and fish.

You can sprinkle rösti with grated cheese and serve it on its own with bacon.

Scalloped potatoes
4 servings

8 potatoes
2 garlic cloves
1 teaspoon salt
½ teaspoon pepper
2 ½ dl (1 cup) whipping cream
grated cheese

Preheat the oven to 200°C (400°F). Peel and slice the potatoes. Peel and mince the garlic. Arrange in a greased ovenproof dish. Sprinkle with salt and pepper. Pour cream over potatoes. Bake for 20 minutes. Remove from the oven and sprinkle with cheese. Bake for around 40 minutes, until potatoes are tender.

You can also add minced onion, leek or bell pepper. Half and half or even milk can be used instead of cream. Cooking time is lowered if the potatoes are parboiled in cream/milk for a few minutes.

Scalloped potatoes
with mushrooms
4 servings

4 potatoes
200 g (8 oz) fresh mushrooms
1 garlic clove
200 g (1 ¾ cups) grated cheese
½ teaspoon salt
½ teaspoon pepper
3 dl (1 ¼ cups) half and half

Preheat the oven to 200°C (400°F). Peel and slice the potatoes, slice the mushrooms and mince the garlic. Layer with cheese (reserving a little to sprinkle on top) in a greased ovenproof dish. Sprinkle with salt and pepper. Pour half and half over potatoes. Sprinkle with remaining cheese. Bake for around 1 hour.

Scalloped potatoes
with onion and peppers
4 servings

4 potatoes
$\frac{1}{2}$ bell pepper
$\frac{1}{2}$ onion
$\frac{1}{2}$ dl ($\frac{1}{4}$ cup) whipping cream
$\frac{1}{2}$ dl ($\frac{3}{4}$ cup) milk (or just use 2 $\frac{1}{2}$ dl/1 cup half and half total liquid)
ground paprika
grated cheese

Preheat the oven to 200°C (400°F). Peel and thinly slice the potatoes. Finely chop pepper and onion. Cook the potatoes in cream and milk for 2-3 minutes. Stir in pepper and onion. Transfer to a greased ovenproof dish. Sprinkle with paprika and cheese. Bake for 20-40 minutes.

Use any color pepper you like, or even a mix.

Potatoes boulangère
4 servings

1 kilo (2 $\frac{1}{4}$ lb) potatoes
200 g (8 oz) onion
oil
salt and pepper
5 dl (2 cups) stock

Preheat the oven to 200°C (400°F). Peel and slice the potatoes and onion. Sauté quickly in oil and sprinkle with salt and pepper. Transfer to an ovenproof dish. Pour the stock over the potatoes. Cover and bake for 10 minutes. Turn the potatoes and bake until tender, around 15 minutes.

Vegetables

Green spaghetti sauce
4 servings

200 g (8 oz) fresh spinach leaves
2 garlic cloves
3 tablespoons olive oil
1 $\frac{1}{2}$ dl ($\frac{2}{3}$ cup) basil leaves, packed well
3 tablespoons pine nuts
salt and pepper

Rinse and dry the spinach well. Mince the garlic. Lightly sauté in a little of the oil. Transfer to a food processor and add basil and pine nuts. With the motor running, add the remaining oil and puree until smooth. Season with salt and pepper. Serve over pasta with grated Parmesan cheese.

Norwegian ratatouille
4 servings

6 tomatoes
300 g (10 oz) zucchini
1 red bell pepper
1 green bell pepper
2-3 onions
2 garlic cloves
oil
2 tablespoons tomato paste
salt and pepper
minced parsley

Peel and dice the tomatoes. Dice the zucchini and peppers. Mince the onion and garlic. Sauté onion and garlic in oil until shiny. Add remaining vegetables and tomato paste. Simmer until tender. Season with salt and pepper and sprinkle with parsley.

Norwegian ratatouille

Mashed rutabagas
4 servings

1 kg (2 $\frac{1}{4}$ lb) rutabaga
1 liter (4 cups) water
$\frac{1}{2}$ teaspoon pepper
2 teaspoons salt
$\frac{1}{2}$ dl ($\frac{1}{4}$ cup) stock

Peel and slice the rutabaga. Cook until tender in lightly salted water. Drain, then mash. Season with pepper, salt and stock from the pinnekjøtt.

Carrot cream
4 servings

$\frac{1}{2}$ teaspoon dried dill
$\frac{1}{2}$ teaspoon dried basil
2 teaspoons chopped parsley
1 teaspoon chopped chives
3 dl (1 $\frac{1}{4}$ cups) cottage cheese
3 dl (1 $\frac{1}{4}$ cups) grated carrot

Stir seasonings into cottage cheese. Fold in the carrots.

Delicious with bread or as a side dish with fish or meat. Store covered in the refrigerator.

Potato puree

Use 2 medium potatoes per serving

4 servings

1 kg (2 ¼ lb) potatoes
2 dl milk
100 g (3 ½ oz) butter
salt and white pepper
grated nutmeg

Peel and cook the potatoes in unsalted water until tender. Drain and mash. Stir in milk and butter. Reheat and season with salt, pepper and nutmeg.

Norwegian sauerkraut

4 servings

1 ¼ kg (2 ½ lb) cabbage, finely shredded
2 apples, peeled, cored and thinly sliced
125 g (4 oz) butter
1 ½ teaspoons salt
125 g (⅔ cup) sugar
1 teaspoon caraway seed
2 dl (1 cup) water
1 dl (½ cup) 7% vinegar

Layer cabbage and apple slices in a pot with butter, sprinkling each layer with seasonings. Add water and let simmer for around 1 hour. Add vinegar to taste, adding more sugar and salt as necessary. Good with roast pork ribs and meat cakes.

Pickled red cabbage

4 servings

1 kg red cabbage, finely shredded
2 apples, peeled, cored and thinly sliced
100 g (3 oz) butter
2 ½ tablespoons salt
2 teaspoons caraway seed
2 ½ dl (1 cup) water
3 ½ tablespoons vinegar
sugar

Layer cabbage and apple slices in a pot with butter, sprinkling each layer with seasonings. Add water and vinegar (or use the same amount of red currant juice). Let simmer for around 1 hour. Add sugar to taste. Good with roast pork ribs and meat cakes.

Stewed peas

4 servings

500 g (1 lb) dried green peas
60 g (2 oz) butter
1 tablespoon salt
1 teaspoon sugar
white pepper

Rinse peas and soak in cold water overnight. Let simmer in soaking water until tender. If too much water, drain off any excess. Add salt, sugar, pepper and butter. Good with *lutefisk* and meat cakes.

Creamed carrots

4 servings

4-5 carrots, in chunks
2 tablespoons butter
3 tablespoons flour
3 dl (1 ½ cups) 2% milk
1/2 teaspoon salt
grated nutmeg

Cook the carrots until tender. Melt the butter and stir in the flour. Gradually add the milk, simmering until thickened. Season with salt and nutmeg. Vegetable cooking liquid can be substituted for some of the milk. Stir the carrots into the sauce. Serve immediately.

Mashed roots

4 servings

4 carrots, in chunks
1 potato, in chunks
3 slices rutabaga, in chunks
2-3 tablespoons milk or light cream

2 tablespoons butter
salt, pepper, grated nutmeg, minced parsley

Cook the vegetables until tender. Reserve the cooking liquid. Mash the vegetables, adding cooking liquid and milk to desired thickness. Stir in the butter and season with salt, pepper and nutmeg. Garnish with parsley

Vegetable fricassee

4 servings

200 g (7 oz) carrots, diced
150 g (5 oz) rutabaga, diced
50 g /2 oz) celeriac, diced
1 small leek, sliced
2 tablespoons butter
4 tablespoons (½ cup) flour
3 dl (1 ½) vegetable cooking liquid
1 dl (scant ½ cup) milk
salt, white pepper, grated nutmeg

Cook the vegetables in lightly salted water until almost tender. Melt the butter and stir in the flour. Gradually add stock and milk. Combine vegetables with sauce and season with salt, white pepper and grated nutmeg.

Creamed cabbage

750 g (1 ⅔ lb) cabbage
2 tablespoons butter
4 tablespoons (1/4 cup) flour
4 dl (1 ⅔ cups) milk (or 3 parts milk and 1 part cabbage water)
½ teaspoon salt
pinch grated nutmeg

Shred the cabbage and cook in lightly salted water until tender. Drain the cabbage, reserving 1 dl (1/2 cup) of the cooking liquid. Melt the butter and stir in the flour. Gradually whisk in the milk (or milk and cabbage water). Heat to boiling, stirring constantly. Let simmer for around 5 minutes, then season with salt and nutmeg. Stir the cabbage into the sauce and reheat to boiling.

Salads

Potato-egg salad
4 servings

4 large boiled potatoes, boiled
4 hard-cooked eggs
$^{1}/_{2}$ red onion (or regular onion)
1 bunch dill

Dressing
2 tablespoons sour cream
3 tablespoons mayonnaise
juice of 1 lemon
$^{1}/_{2}$ teaspoon salt
$^{1}/_{2}$ teaspoon pepper

Peel and cube the potatoes. Quarter the eggs.
Mince the onion and dill. Arrange on a platter or
in a bowl. Combine ingredients in dressing and
pour over. Sprinkle with dill.

Low–fat sour cream and mayonnaise can be
used in this dish. This salad is delicious with fried
fish.

Warm potato salad
4 servings

1 $^{1}/_{2}$ kg (3 lb) potatoes
3 dl (1 cup) sour cream
2 teaspoons low-fat milk
1 teaspoon salt
$^{1}/_{2}$ teaspoon pepper
1 tablespoon chopped chives

Boil the potatoes. Let cool slightly. Cut into
cubes. Combine remaining ingredients and pour
over the potatoes. Toss well. Garnish with more
chives.

This salad is delicious with cured or grilled meat.

Blue dot salad

Blue dot salad
4 servings

1 leaf lettuce
$^{1}/_{2}$ seedless cucumber
2 celery stalks
1 grapefruit
10 blue grapes

Dressing
2 tablespoons sour cream
4 tablespoons ($^{1}/_{4}$ cup) cottage cheese

Shred the lettuce and arrange in a bowl. Cut the
cucumber into chunks. Thinly slice the celery.
Peel and divide the grapefruit into sections.
Halve each section. Halve the grapes. Mix the
dressing. Layer ingredients (except for the
grapes) and dressing in the bowl. Top with the
grapes.

This salad is good with meat and fish.

Potato-egg salad

Tomato salad

Tomato salad
4 servings

lettuce
6 tomatoes
1 onion
1 dl (¹/₂ cup) fresh bean sprouts
fresh basil

Dressing
4 tablespoons (¹/₄ cup) olive oil
1 tablespoon red wine vinegar
1 tablespoon fresh lemon juice
1 teaspoon prepared mustard
salt and pepper

Arrange lettuce leaves in a bowl. Thinly slice tomatoes and onion and layer in the bowl with sprouts and basil. Mix dressing and pour over salad.

Add 1 minced garlic clove to dressing, if desired.

Easy slaw
4 servings

250 g (8 oz) rutabaga
2 apples
¹/₂ leek

Dressing
3 tablespoons oil
1 tablespoon vinegar
¹/₂ teaspoon salt

Peel and grate the rutabaga. Dice the apple and thinly slice the leek. Layer the ingredients in a salad bowl. Mix dressing and pour over salad. Toss.

Winter salad
4 servings

¹/₂ kg (1 lb) cabbage
1 onion
2-3 celery stalks
1 apple

Dressing
3 tablespoons low-fat sour cream
3 tablespoons low-fat mayonnaise
1 tablespoon lemon juice
1 teaspoon sugar
pinch chili powder

Shred the cabbage. Mince the onion. Thinly slice the celery. Dice the apple. Combine. Mix dressing and pour over salad. Toss.

Grated carrots and crushed pineapple are also good additions to this salad.

Cucumber salad
4 servings

1 seedless cucumber
1 teaspoon salt
2 tablespoons white vinegar
2 tablespoons water
1 tablespoon sugar
minced parsley

Slice the cucumber with a cheese plane. Sprinkle with salt. Combine vinegar, water and sugar and pour over. Sprinkle with parsley.

This salad is good with all fish dishes.

Easy slaw

Waldorf salad

Waldorf salad

4 servings

100 g (4 oz) cabbage
100 g (4 oz) grapes
2 apples
2 pineapple rings
2 celery stalks
1 dl (½ cup) chopped walnuts

Dressing
1 dl (½ cup) whipping cream
1 dl (½ cup) mayonnaise
1½ teaspoons fresh lemon juice
2 teaspoons sugar

Shred the cabbage. Halve the grapes, removing any seeds. Dice the apples and pineapple. Thinly slice the celery. Combine with nuts. Whip the cream. Fold in the mayonnaise, lemon juice and sugar. Pour over the salad, mixing gently to combine. Serve on a platter garnished with grapes, pineapple chunks and chopped nuts.

Waldorf salad is excellent with turkey and chicken, baked ham, tongue and roast beef, and it can be made ahead of time.

Dressings

Sour cream dressing

2 dl (1 cup) sour cream
prepared mustard
lemon juice
salt and pepper

Mix ingredients together.

Garlic dressing

1 garlic clove
2 tablespoons wine vinegar
salt and freshly ground pepper
4 tablespoons (¼ cup) olive oil

Mince garlic and combine with vinegar, salt and pepper. Whisk in oil until emulsified.

Mustard dressing

This recipe uses raw egg yolk. Use only safety-checked eggs.

1 egg yolk
1 tablespoon Dijon mustard
1 tablespoon wine vinegar
salt and pepper
4 tablespoons (¼ cup) olive oil

Whisk egg yolk with mustard, vinegar, salt and pepper. Whisk in oil until emulsified.

Mild sour cream dressing

2 dl (1 cup) sour cream
2 tablespoons mayonnaise
1 tablespoon fresh lemon juice
1 tablespoon chopped scallions or chives
salt and white pepper

Combine sour cream and mayonnaise. Whisk in remaining ingredients, seasoning to taste with salt and pepper.

Low-fat sour cream and mayonnaise can be used in this dressing.

Blue cheese dressing

2 dl (1 cup) sour cream
1 tablespoon fresh lemon juice
75 g (2 ½ oz) blue cheese
2 tablespoons chopped chives

Stir sour cream and lemon juice together. Crumble cheese and add. Fold in chives.

Spring dressing

6 tablespoons olive oil
2 tablespoons fresh lemon juice
1 garlic clove, minced
salt and freshly ground pepper
Combine all ingredients in a jar and shake well.

Vinaigrette

2-3 tablespoons olive oil
1 tablespoon wine vinegar or fresh lemon juice
¼ teaspoon salt
⅛ teaspoon white pepper

Combine all ingredients in a jar and shake well.

The usual proportions in vinaigrette are 3 tablespoons oil to 1 tablespoon vinegar. For less oily flavor, reduce the amount of oil to 2 tablespoons. Store all dressings in the refrigerator.

Norwegian holiday tables

– celebration of traditions

The difference between everyday and holiday can be found in all cultures, and this is normally emphasized through the foods we eat. Wedding cakes go with weddings, and lamb at Easter. The drinks that accompany festive foods are also important. Beer served with aquavit often means that it's a special day.

In some situations, festive food is completely different from everyday food. Few eat roast deer or reindeer in the middle of the week. These meals are served on special occasions. Other times, it is the situation that determines whether it's a Christmas cod or merely the everyday version, as the food is virtually the same. Occasionally, foods that once were served only on holidays are now considered everyday food. Few today would label fish pudding as festive food, but in the middle of the 19th century, it was considered a refined dish. The opposite is also true, as formerly everyday foods have been elevated to festive food. Festivals connected with traditional dishes such as *lutefisk*, fermented fish, *gamalost* and *smalahove* (sheep heads) all are examples of this.

Throughout the year, we participate in festive and formal occasions. Everything from May 17 (Norway's Constitution Day), birthdays, Easter, weddings and Christmas to the more informal, when friends and colleagues meet for a pleasant evening. Food plays a central role in all of these occasions. For some of these meals, the menu is traditional, the same every time. You don't think

about what to serve on Christmas Eve – it's the same every year. Other times we can experiment with new dishes and serve our guests something we tasted on our last vacation.

Many Norwegian festive tables are seasonal, but there are also variations that are served year-round. Few would even think about serving *lutefisk* for a summer party, but it's perfect for autumn and the weeks leading up to Christmas. A grill evening is definitely a summer party, though some enthusiasts may serve grilled food in the winter. Just about everything can be grilled, which is why a grill party can be successful for both birthdays and casual parties with friends on late summer evenings. Salmon, cucumber salad and a bowl of strawberries and cream lead many to think about both May 17 and other festive occasions during the spring and summer months. When we set a shellfish table, with huge bowls of crabs, lobster and crayfish, it's often in the late summer and fall. Fall is also the best time for game such as moose, deer and ptarmigan, as well as the all-time Norwegian favorite, lamb and cabbage stew.

Even though some of the tables we sit around are often seasonal, they can also be set at different times of the year. A table set with cured meat, herring, marinated and smoked fish or cheese is always a good occasion for a feast.

There are many Norwegian festive tables that can be the basis for exciting social and culinary experiences. The food becomes the center of attention, and everyone can enjoy the company and the cuisine. Just do it – set the table!

Christmas table

Many associate the Christmas table with huge restaurant buffets in the weeks before Christmas, but in this case, we are thinking about the food served in private homes during the holiday. The departure point is usually special Christmas food, such as roast ribs of pork, pork patties, smoked ribs of mutton, smoked lamb and turkey. In addition, there's usually ham, headcheese, lamb roll, liver paté, pig knuckles, smoked or marinated salmon or trout, herring dishes and eggs in some form or another.

There's generally an assortment of cheeses on the Christmas table, while anyone with a sweet tooth can enjoy almond ring cakes, Christmas cookies and caramel pudding.

Cured meat table

Cured meats have always been festive food, equally popular with all generations. A cured meat table is therefore perfect for a family party where different generations are assembled. At a festive cured meat table, you will usually find cured ham, dried leg of mutton, salami, mutton sausage, black sausage, flatbread, lefse, sour cream, scrambled eggs and creamed potatoes.

With new generations come new side dishes alongside traditional cured meats. Olives, nuts, sun-dried tomatoes, pies and fresh salads – all of these things go well with cured meat and are

Cured meats have long been served on special occasions, and everyone loves them

good examples of how impulses from abroad can be combined with Norwegian traditions.

In addition, there are many cured white meats that make the table even more interesting.

Herring table

Sometimes we use the expression "fish and herring", and in this way, we consider herring something special. What is special about herring is its versatility and the great breadth of herring products. Herring is sold fresh, cured, spiced, warm-smoked and cold-smoked, often as both whole fish and fillets. Each one of these offers a wealth of possibilities. Soaked and cleaned spiced and cured herring fillets are the bases for many delicious dishes. The fillets can be sliced and mixed with different vegetables, spices and sauces. On a well-appointed herring table, we

Assorted shellfish: Lobster, oysters, sea urchins, sea snails, horse mussels and blue mussels

usually can find most of these dishes – pickled herring, tomato herring, mustard herring, curried herring and glazier's herring – in addition to different salads and perhaps a couple of hot herring dishes. Whole grain bread, onion, pickled beets, butter and sour cream all belong on the herring table. here are a few recipes for some herring dishes that can be the basis of a herring table.

Shellfish table

Toward Christmas and throughout the winter and spring, shellfish is at its very best. We should take advantage of this by making a spread of shellfish in the winter. It can be simple and exclusive with half a large lobster per person, served with bread, mayonnaise, a little lettuce, lemon and good wine. Or serve a wide variety of everything good from the sea: Lobster, crab,

shrimp, crayfish, scallops, mussels, oysters and sea urchins. All of these can be served cooked and chilled, but you can also serve some hot dishes.

Tomato herring, herring salad and glazier's herring

Tomato herring
4-6 servings

¹/₂ dl (¹/₄ cup) soy oil
100 g (4 oz) tomato paste
2 ¹/₂ dl (1 cup) sugar
1 dl (¹/₂ cup) pineapple juice
1 dl (¹/₂ cup) 7% vinegar
ground pepper
6 spiced herring fillets
1 onion
2 dl (1 cup) pineapple chunks
2 tablespoons chopped fresh dill

Heat the oil and tomato paste to boiling. Remove from heat. Add sugar and stir until melted. Let cool, then add pineapple juice, vinegar and pepper. Cut the herring into diagonal slices. Slice the onion. Layer onion, pineapple herring and dill in a bowl or jar. Pour over the tomato mixture. Cover and refrigerate for at least 24 hours before serving.

Herring salad
4 servings

1 dl (¹/₂ cup) sour cream
100 g (¹/₂ cup) mayonnaise
vinegar or pickle juice
sugar
4-6 spiced herring fillets, diced
1 small apple, diced
¹/₂ dl (¹/₄ cup) diced pickled beet
1 boiled potato, diced
¹/₂ onion, minced
¹/₂ dl (¹/₄ cup) minced pickle

Combine sour cream and mayonnaise, seasoning to taste with vinegar and sugar. Combine remaining ingredients. Pour over dressing, mixing carefully.

Sherry herring
4 servings

6 cured herring fillets
milk
1 dl (¹/₂ cup) sherry
¹/₂ dl (¹/₄ cup) water
3 tablespoons 7% vinegar
1 dl (¹/₂ cup) sugar
7-8 peppercorns, crushed
2 red onions, sliced
3-4 tablespoons chopped fresh dill

Let the herring soak in milk for at least 2 hours. Rinse in cold water, then dry well. Cut into 1-2 cm (1") diagonal slices. Combine sherry, water, vinegar, sugar and pepper. Layer herring, onion and dill in a bowl or jar. Pour over sherry mixture. Cover and refrigerate for at least 24 hours before serving.

Glazier's herring
4 servings

4-6 cured herring fillets
milk
4 dl (1 ²/₃ cups) water
3 ¹/₂ dl (1 ¹/₂ cups) sugar
2 dl (⁷/₈ cup) 7% vinegar
1 red onion, sliced
1 horseradish, thinly sliced
1 small carrot, thinly sliced
1 teaspoon mustard seed
1 bay leaf

Let the herring soak in milk for at least 2 hours. Heat water and sugar to boiling. Let cool, then add vinegar. Rinse fillets in cold water, then drain well. Cut into 1-2 cm (1") diagonal slices. Layer herring, onion, horseradish and seasonings in a bowl or jar. Pour over the marinade. Cover and refrigerate for at least 24 hours before serving.

Good desserts
– of the old-fashioned kind

A generation ago, dessert was part of every dinner. Today, we are fortunate if we get dessert after Sunday dinner. Dessert is the sweet finale that gives an extra dimension to a meal. For many, special desserts are associated with childhood memories. We can dream about stewed prunes with cream, semolina pudding with red berry sauce or homemade chocolate pudding with vanilla sauce, just to name a few. Serve dessert after a meal and notice how good it feels.

Marte Knipe from Røkenes farm

Marte Knipe *from Røkenes farm*
4-6 servings

1 liter (quart) milk
¾ dl (⅓ cup) tapioca
½ dl (3 tablespoons) raisins
½ dl (3 tablespoons) blanched almonds
1 tablespoon sugar
3-4 drops rum extract

Heat the milk and tapioca to boiling, whisking constantly. Let simmer for around 15 minutes. Stir in the remaining ingredients. Transfer to a bowl and let cool completely. Serve with mashed strawberries or red berry sauce and sprinkle with blanched almonds.

Red dessert
4-6 servings

3 dl (1 ¼ cups) red berry juice (if using concentrate, dilute to drink strength)
3 dl (1 ¼ cups) water
around 60 g (3 tablespoons) semolina
1 tablespoon sugar

Heat the juice and water to boiling. Whisk in the semolina. Let simmer over low heat for around 15 minutes. Whisk in the sugar. Transfer to a bowl and let cool completely. Serve with vanilla sauce (see page 253).

Red dessert with vanilla sauce

Rhubarb soup with vanilla ice cream

Rhubarb soup
4-6 servings

1 liter (4 cups) water
300 g (1 ¼ cups) sugar
1 vanilla bean
500 g (1 lb) rhubarb
1 tablespoon finely shredded mint
sliced strawberries
vanilla ice cream

Heat water and sugar to boiling. Split the vanilla bean lengthwise and scrape out the seeds. Add bean and seeds to sugar syrup and let simmer for around 15 minutes.

Wash, peel and cut the rhubarb into chunks. Add to the syrup with the mint and remove from the heat. Cover and let steep until cold. Remove the vanilla bean. Serve with strawberries and ice cream. Garnish with mint leaves, if desired.

Prune compote
4 servings

150 g (5 oz) pitted prunes
8 dl (7 1/3 cups) water
125 g (5/8 cup) sugar
1 teaspoon vanilla extract
2 ½ tablespoons potato starch (or cornstarch)

Soak the prunes in the water overnight. Simmer in the soaking water until tender. Stir in the sugar and vanilla. Shake the starch and 2 table-spoons water in a jar. Whisk into the compote. Let cool, then transfer to a bowl. Serve with cream or whipped cream.

Trondheim soup
4 servings

5 dl (2 cups) round or short grain rice
1 liter (4 cups) water
1 tablespoon flour
1 dl (⅓ cup) milk
1 dl (⅓ cup) raisins
2 tablespoons sugar
1 dl (½ cup) sour cream or whipping cream

Simmer the rice in the water until barely tender. Shake the flour and milk in a jar. Whisk into the rice soup and cook until thickened. Add the raisins and simmer for 5-10 minutes more. Add sugar to taste. Remove from the heat and add the sour cream or whipping cream.

Red berry compote

4-6 servings

1 liter (4 cups) red berry juice (if using concentrate, dilute to drink strength)
³/₄ dl (¹/₃ cup) tapioca
2 tablespoons sugar

Combine juice and tapioca in a saucepan and heat to boiling, stirring constantly. Let simmer for around 15 minutes. Stir in the sugar. Remove from the heat and let cool. Serve with half and half or vanilla sauce.

Barley cream

4 servings

1 dl (¹/₂ cup) pearl barley
2 ¹/₂ dl (1 cup) whipping cream
2 teaspoons sugar
3 drops almond extract

Soak the barley in cold water overnight. Drain. Cover with new water and simmer the barley for around 1 hour, until tender. Strain and let cool. Whip the cream and sugar and fold in the barley. Add almond extract to taste and serve with fresh berries or mashed berries.

Barley cream

Constitution dessert

4-6 servings

200 g (8 oz) pitted prunes
200 g (8 oz) rhubarb, cleaned and cut into 2 ¹/₂ cm (1") chunks
3 dl (1 ¹/₄ cups) water
2 dl (1 cup) sugar
1 tablespoon potato starch (or cornstarch)
¹/₂ dl (¹/₄ cup) water

Combine prunes, rhubarb, water and sugar and heat to boiling. Simmer until the fruit is almost tender. Remove several prunes for garnish. Shake potato starch with 3 tablespoons cold water in a jar. Whisk in a stream into the compote. Simmer over low heat until thickened, stirring constantly. Cool completely. Serve with vanilla sauce or whipped cream.

Constitution dessert

Fruit salad

Fruit salad

7-8 servings

3 oranges
3 kiwi fruit
200 g (8 oz) purple grapes
100 g (4 oz) chopped almonds
3 red apples
2 bananas
1 can (300g/11 oz) pineapple chunks packed in juice

Peel oranges and kiwi. Halve the grapes and remove the seeds. Toast the nuts in a dry pan until golden. Let cool. Cut apple, orange sections and kiwi into chunks. Peel the banana and cut into chunks. Combine all fruit with the pineapple and juice. Let marinate for at least two hours in the refrigerator before serving. Sprinkle with nuts and serve with raw cream or herbed vanilla sauce (see page 235).

Baked apples

4 servings

75 g (⅓ cup) butter
150 g (1 cup) flour
1-2 tablespoons water
4 medium apples
2 tablespoons ground almonds
2 tablespoons sugar
1 egg yolk
2 tablespoons currants
1 tablespoon confectioner's sugar
beaten egg white

Baked apples

Cream pudding

with the seam down. Brush with the remaining egg white. Bake for around 20 minutes. Serve warm with vanilla sauce (page 253) or whipped cream.

Cream pudding
6-8 servings

8 gelatin sheets
6 dl (2 ½ cups) whipping cream
4 tablespoons (¼ cup) sugar

Soak the gelatin in cold water for around 5 minutes to soften. Whip the cream with the sugar. Squeeze excess water from the gelatin and melt in ½ dl (3 ½ tablespoons) boiling water. Let cool slightly, then stir into the whipped cream. Rinse a 1-liter (4 cup) ring mold with cold water and pour in the cream mixture. Refrigerate until set. Unmold on a platter and fill the center with fruit salad or fresh berries.

Strawberry dessert
5-6 servings

1 liter (4 cups) strawberries
sugar
½ liter (1 pint) vanilla ice cream
1 liter (4 cups) strawberry yogurt

Clean the berries and mix with sugar. Layer berries, ice cream and yogurt in a bowl and stir carefully together.

Cut butter and flour together with a pastry blender. Add water and mix lightly together. Form into a ball and let rest for around 1 hour. Preheat the oven to 200°C (400°F). Peel and core the apples. Combine almonds, sugar, egg yolk, currants and confectioner's sugar and spoon into the holes in the apples. Roll the dough into a large sheet. Divide into 4 squares and place an apple on the center of each. Fold the dough over the apples, overlapping at the top. Glue together with egg white. Place in a greased baking dish (not too close together)

Strawberry dessert

Veiled country lass

Norwegian eggnog

This dessert contains raw eggs. Use only safety-checked eggs.

4 servings

4 eggs
4 tablespoons (¼ cup) sugar
chopped fruit or berries (optional)

Beat eggs and sugar until thick and lemon-colored. Fold in chopped fruit, if desired. Pour into glasses and serve with a spoon.

For children
Sprinkle with chopped chocolate or chocolate drink powder.

For grown-ups
Stir in 2 tablespoons cognac.

Troll cream

4-6 servings

7 ½ dl (3 cups) lingonberries
1 ½ dl (½ cup) sugar
1 egg white
lingonberries

Combine all ingredients in a food processor and process until thick and stiff. Transfer to a dessert bowl and sprinkle with berries. Garnish with fresh herbs, if desired. Serve with vanilla sauce and crispy cone cookies.

Veiled country lass

4 servings

5-6 apples
75 g (⅓ cup) sugar
2 dl (1 cup) water
3-4 dl (1 ½ cups) dry breadcrumbs
4 tablespoons (¼ cup) sugar
2 tablespoons butter
2-3 dl (1 cup) whipping cream

Peel and core the apples and cut into chunks. Cook in sugar water until just tender. Let cool. Combine bread, sugar and butter in a frying pan and cook until golden and crisp. Let cool. Whip the cream until light and fluffy. Layer the apple compote, crumbs and cream in a glass bowl. Garnish with chopped almonds, if desired.

Troll cream

Norwegian eggnog

Rice cream

4-6 servings

3 dl (1 ¼ cups) whipping cream
1 tablespoon sugar
1 teaspoon vanilla extract
3-4 dl (1 ½ cups) rice porridge
50 g (⅓ cup) chopped almonds

Whip the cream, sugar and vanilla until light and fluffy. Mix in the porridge and almonds. Serve with raspberry coulis or homemade red berry sauce.

Cloudberry cream

6 servings

5 dl (2 cups) whipping cream
1 teaspoon sugar
2 ½ dl (1 cup) lightly sweetened cloudberries

Whip the cream and sugar until light and fluffy. Carefully fold in the berries.

Chocolate pudding

4 servings

2 tablespoons cocoa
100 g (¾ cup) cornstarch
1 dl (⅓- ½ cup) sugar
1 liter (4 cups) milk
125 g (4 oz) semi-sweet chocolate
1 teaspoon vanilla extract

Combine cocoa, cornstarch and sugar in a saucepan. Whisk in the milk. Heat until boiling, stirring constantly. Break the chocolate into small pieces and add, stirring until melted. Stir in the vanilla. Transfer to a rinsed bowl or mold. Refrigerate. Serve in the bowl or on a platter. Garnish with whipped cream or serve with vanilla sauce or half and half.

Rice cream

Chocolate pudding

Palace dessert

4 servings

3 dl (1 ¼ cups) whipping cream
1 dl (½ cup) chocolate sauce
10-12 meringues
10-12 almonds, chopped and toasted until golden

Whip the cream until light and fluffy. Layer cream and meringues and drizzle with chocolate sauce. Sprinkle with nuts.

Cloudberry cream   *Palace dessert*

Semolina pudding

Heavenly dessert

Semolina pudding
4 servings

1 liter (quart) milk
1 ¼ dl (½ cup) semolina
1 tablespoon sugar
1 egg
3 drops almond extract

Combine milk and semolina in a saucepan and heat to boiling, stirring constantly. Let simmer for around 15 minutes. Whisk sugar and egg in a bowl. Whisk in a little hot porridge, then whisk that mixture back into the saucepan of porridge. Reheat to boiling, stirring constantly. Add almond extract to taste. Transfer to a bowl and sprinkle with a little sugar. Let cool and serve with red berry sauce.

Heavenly dessert
This dessert contains raw eggs. Use only safety-checked eggs.

6 servings

5 gelatin sheets
2 eggs
1 dl (½ cup) sugar
1 dl (½ cup) sherry or orange juice
3 tablespoons chopped almonds
3 tablespoons chopped candied cherries
2 tablespoons chopped chocolate
3 dl (1 ¼ cups) whipping cream

Soak the gelatin in cold water for around 5 minutes. Beat eggs and sugar until thick and lemon-colored. Squeeze excess water from the gelatin and melt in 3 tablespoons boiling water. Combine sherry with the gelatin and stir in the almonds, cherries and chocolate. Fold the egg mixture into the gelatin. Whip the cream and fold into the egg mixture. Pour into a glass bowl and sprinkle with more nuts, chocolate and berries.

Royal cream
This dessert contains raw eggs. Use only safety-checked eggs.

6 servings

1 basket strawberries
2 tablespoons sugar
50 g (⅓ cup) chopped almonds, toasted
4 gelatin sheets
2 eggs
4 tablespoons (¼ cup) sugar
1 teaspoon vanilla extract
3 dl (1 cup) whipping cream

Place the strawberries in a glass bowl and sprinkle with sugar and almonds. Soak the gelatin in cold water for around 5 minutes to soften. Beat the eggs, sugar and vanilla until light and lemon-colored. Squeeze excess water from the gelatin and melt in 3 tablespoons boiling water. Let cool slightly. Whip the cream. Lightly combine the egg mixture with the gelatin, then fold in the whipped cream. Spread the mixture over the berries and refrigerate until stiff. Garnish with more berries, if desired.

Caramel pudding
6-8 servings

2 dl (¾ cup) sugar
6 dl (2 ½ cups) milk or evaporated milk
3 dl (1 ¼ cups) whipping cream
3 tablespoons sugar
8 eggs
1 ½ teaspoons vanilla extract

Pour the sugar into a 1½-liter (6 cup) loaf pan and place it on the burner over medium heat. Heat until the sugar has melted and turned a warm golden brown. Pour it into the pan, moving the pan to coat the bottom evenly with the caramel. Heat the milk, cream and sugar to boiling. Let cool. Whisk the eggs, then whisk them into the milk mixture. Stir in the vanilla. Strain the mixture into the glazed loaf pan. Preheat the oven to 125°C (250°F). Let the pan rest for around 10 minutes before cooking, so that any air bubbles in the mixture can deflate.

Royal cream

Caramel pudding

Queen Maud cream

Place in a water bath and bake for 2-3 hours. Toward the end of the cooking time, check with the back of a wet spoon, to see if the surface has set, which means that the pudding is cooked. Let cool in the pan, then refrigerate overnight. Unmold onto a platter before serving.

Queen Maud cream

This dessert contains raw eggs. Use only safety-checked eggs.

5 gelatin sheets
3 ½ tablespoons port wine
5 egg yolks
5 tablespoons (⅓ cup) sugar
6 dl (2 ½ cups) whipping cream
100 g (3-4 oz) semi-sweet chocolate, grated

Soak the gelatin in cold water for around 5 minutes to soften. Squeeze excess water from the gelatin and melt in 3 ½ tablespoons boiling water. Stir in the port wine. Beat the eggs and sugar until light and lemon-colored. Whip the cream. Lightly combine the egg mixture with the gelatin, then fold in the cream. Layer in a glass bowl with the chocolate. Refrigerate until set.

Mocha Bavarian cream

This dessert contains raw eggs. Use only safety-checked eggs.

6 gelatin sheets
1 dl (⅓ cup) hot strong coffee
3 eggs
6 tablespoons sugar
4 dl (1 ⅔ cups) whipping cream
100 g (3-4 oz) semi-sweet chocolate, grated

Soak the gelatin in cold water for around 5 minutes to soften. Squeeze excess water from the gelatin and melt in the hot coffee. Let cool slightly. Beat the eggs and sugar until light and lemon-colored. Whip the cream. Lightly combine the egg mixture with the gelatin, then fold in the cream and the chocolate, or layer the chocolate with the coffee mixture. Pour into a pretty

Mocha Bavarian cream

serving bowl and sprinkle with more grated chocolate. Refrigerate until set.

Cloudberry parfait
4 servings

4 egg yolks
50 g (¼ cup) sugar
4-6 tablespoons sugared cloudberries or cloudberry jam
2-3 tablespoons cloudberry liqueur or cognac (optional)
3 dl (1 cup) whipping cream

Whisk egg yolks and sugar in a bowl to combine, then place over a saucepan of boiling water. Whisk until light yellow and creamy. Do not let the temperature rise too high or the eggs will scramble. Remove the bowl from the pan and place it in cold water. Whisk constantly until the mixture is almost cold. Fold in the cloudberries and the liqueur, if desired. Whip the cream until almost stiff. Fold the cream into the cloudberry mixture. Add more berries or sugar as necessary.

Cover the bottom of a springform pan with plastic wrap. Pour over the parfait mixture. Freeze overnight. Remove from the freezer around 20 minutes before serving. Remove from the pan and transfer to a platter. Garnish with whipped cream and some pretty cloudberries. Serve with cookies and warm cloudberries.

Basic recipe for ice cream
This dessert contains raw eggs. Use only safety-checked eggs.

4-6 servings

4 egg yolks
2 eggs
100 g (⅞ cup) confectioner's sugar
5 dl (2 cups) whipping cream

Suggestions for flavoring:
2 dl (⅞ cup) jam or berries

Beat egg yolks, eggs and sugar until light and lemon-colored. Whip the cream. Fold the cream

Berry ice cream

into the egg mixture. Fold in the desired flavoring. Pour into a mold and freeze, stirring occasionally when the ice crystals begin to form, or freeze in an ice cream machine.

Cloudberry parfait

Pralines-chevre ice cream
with puff pastry
4-6 servings

200 g (1 cup) sugar
1 dl (scant ½ cup) water
100 g (3 ½ oz) *Snøfrisk* (fresh chevre)
1 ½ dl (⅔ cup) whipping cream
2-3 tablespoons almond praline
5 eggs
2 sheets (US: ½ package) frozen puff pastry

Melt half the sugar in a saucepan until golden. Add water and cook to a syrup. Melt the cheese in the syrup and add 1 dl (³⁄₈ cup) of the cream. Let cool slightly and stir in the praline. Beat the eggs and the remaining sugar until light and lemon-colored. Whip the cream. Fold the cheese mixture into the egg mixture, then fold in the cream. Pour into a mold and freeze, stirring occasionally when ice crystals begin to form, or freeze in an ice cream machine. The ice cream should be frozen for at least 6 hours. Defrost the puff pastry and cut large circles with a cookie cutter. Bake according to package directions. Let cool. To serve, place a pastry circle in a bowl. Top with ice cream, then arrange berries and a good fruit sauce all around.

Praline-cherre ice cream with puff pastry

Vanilla ice cream

4-6 servings

5 dl (2 cups) milk or light cream
1 dl (scant 1/2 cup) sugar
1/2 vanilla bean, split lengthwise, seeds scraped out
4 egg yolks

Place milk, sugar, vanilla seeds and bean in a saucepan and heat to boiling. Whisk the egg yolks and add the hot milk in a thin stream, beating constantly. Return the mixture to the heat and heat, stirring constantly, until slightly thickened. Do not allow to boil or the eggs will scramble. Refrigerate overnight. Strain the mixture into a mold and freeze, stirring occasionally when ice crystals begin to form, or freeze in an ice cream machine. Serve with egg liqueur sauce, at right.

Dessert sauces

Fruit sauce

4-6 servings

4 dl (1 2/3 cups) water
4 dl (1 2/3 cups) berry juice concentrate
2 1/2 tablespoons potato starch

Combine all ingredients in a saucepan and heat to boiling. Whisk until shiny.

Strawberry sauce

4-6 servings

200 g (1/2 basket) strawberries
2 1/2 dl (1 cup) water
100 g (1/2 cup) sugar

Clean the berries. Place in a blender with water and sugar and puree until smooth. Heat to boiling, then strain.

Chocolate sauce

4-6 servings

175 g (6 oz) semi-sweet chocolate
1 tablespoon strong coffee
1 tablespoon cognac
2 1/2 dl (1 cup) whipping cream

Break the chocolate into bits and place in a saucepan with the remaining ingredients. Heat to boiling. Remove from the heat and stir until smooth.

Vanilla cream

4 servings

2 gelatin sheets
4 egg yolks
2 tablespoons sugar
1 1/2 dl (2/3 cup) milk
2 1/2 dl (1 cup) whipping cream
2 teaspoons vanilla extract

Soak the gelatin in cold water for 5 minutes to soften. Beat egg yolks and sugar until light and lemon-colored. Combine milk, cream, and egg mixture and heat carefully until the mixture thickens slightly. Squeeze excess water from the gelatin and melt in 3 tablespoons boiling water. Stir into the egg yolk mixture and let cool. Stir in the vanilla. Refrigerate until serving.

Vanilla sauce

4 servings

5 dl (2 cups) milk
2 eggs
2 tablespoons sugar
1 teaspoon cornstarch
2 teaspoons vanilla extract

Heat the milk to boiling. Whisk the eggs with the sugar and cornstarch. Whisk in the hot milk. Pour back into the pan and whisk until thickened. Stir in the vanilla. Let cool completely before serving.

Egg liqueur sauce

4 servings

2 1/2 dl (1 cup) vanilla sauce
1 dl (scant 1/2 cup) egg liqueur

Combine vanilla sauce and egg liqueur to taste.

Eggnog

This is a classic recipe for a good drink that also can be used as a sauce over ice cream or fruit.

12 servings

6 eggs
1 1/2 dl (2/3 cup) sugar
12 dl (5 cups) milk
1 1/2 dl (2/3 cup) cognac
1 teaspoon vanilla extract
5 dl (2 cups) whipping cream
grated nutmeg

Whisk the eggs and sugar in a saucepan and whisk in the milk. Stir over low to medium heat until thick enough to coat a spoon (be patient, this takes time). Remove from the heat, stir in the cognac and place in a cold water bath, stirring until cool. Stir in the vanilla. Refrigerate for at least 3 hours or overnight. Whip the cream and fold into the eggnog. Sprinkle with nutmeg.

Raw cream

4 servings

This dish contains raw egg yolks. Use only safety-controlled eggs.

3 egg yolks
3 tablespoons sugar
2 1/2 dl (1 cup) whipping cream

Beat the egg yolks and sugar until light and lemon-colored. Whip the cream. Carefully fold the cream into the egg yolk mixture. This is good with fruit and berries.

Baked goods

– the scent of childhood

Homemade baked goods are wonderful treats on busy days. Baking is a form of mental hygiene – it helps you to relax and enjoy life. The pleasure derived from serving a homemade cake is well worth the trouble.

Plum pie

60 g (¹/₂ cup) butter
2 ¹/₂ dl (1 cup) flour
1 dl (scant ¹/₂ cup) confectioner's sugar
100 g (¹/₂ cup) cottage cheese

1 liter (4 cups) plums
1 ¹/₂ dl (²/₃ cup) sugar
2 eggs
2 dl (scant 1 cup) half and half or coffee cream
1 teaspoon vanilla extract

Preheat the oven to 200°C (400°F). Cut the butter into the flour and sugar until the texture of coarse crumbs. Knead in the cottage cheese.

Press the dough into the bottom and up the sides of a greased (bottom only) cake pan, around 26 cm (10") in diameter. Prick the pastry with a fork and bake for 10 minutes. Let cool. Lower the oven to 180°C (350°F). Halve the plums, removing the pits and arrange in the bottom of the pie shell. Sprinkle with some of the sugar. Whisk the egg with the remaining sugar, cream and vanilla until blended and pour over the plums. Bake for 45 minutes. Serve warm, lukewarm or cold with whipped cream, ice cream or vanilla custard. This pie can be frozen.

Carrot cake

4 eggs
2 ¹/₂ dl (1 cup) sugar
¹/₂ teaspoon vanilla extract
3 ¹/₂ dl (1 ¹/₂ cups) flour
1 tablespoon cinnamon
2 teaspoons baking soda
¹/₂ teaspoon salt
1 dl (scant ¹/₂ cup) melted butter

4 dl (1 ²/₃ cups) finely grated carrots

Plum pie

Cream cheese frosting
135 g (4 oz) cream cheese
125 g (7/8 cup) confectioner's sugar
1 teaspoon vanilla extract

Preheat the oven to 180°C (350°F). Beat the egg, sugar and vanilla until thick and lemon-colored. Combine flour, cinnamon, baking powder and salt and add alternately with the butter. Fold in the carrots. Pour into a greased 23 cm (9") round pan. Bake for around 1 hour. Cool completely. Beat all ingredients in the frosting until smooth and spread over the cake. Garnish with grated carrot, if desired. This cake can be frozen but without frosting.

Carrot cake

Apple cake

Apple cake

150 g (1 cup) flour
150 g (³/₄ cup) sugar
1 teaspoon baking powder
150 g (5 oz) cold butter
2 eggs
4-5 tart apples
2 tablespoons sugar
1 teaspoon cinnamon
3 tablespoons chopped almonds

Preheat the oven to 180°C (350°F). Combine flour, sugar and baking powder in a bowl. Cut in the butter. Whisk in the eggs and mix to form an even-textured dough. Press into the bottom of a 24 cm (9") round pan. Peel, core and cut the apples into wedges and press into the dough. Sprinkle with sugar, cinnamon and almonds. Bake for around 30 minutes. Serve warm with whipped cream, sour cream or ice cream.

Make another kind of apple cake by changing the filling in a Prince's cake. Instead of almonds, confectioner's sugar and egg whites, use:
1 dl (scant ¹/₂ cup) sugar
5 apples, peeled, cored and cut into wedges
2 teaspoons cinnamon

Prince's cake

125 g (4 oz) butter
100 g (¹/₂ cup) sugar
2 egg yolks
2 tablespoons milk
250 g (1 ²/₃ cups) flour
1 teaspoon baking powder

Filling

200 g (7 oz) almonds
150 g (1 cup) confectioner's sugar
2 egg whites

Beat butter and sugar until light and fluffy. Add egg yolks one at a time, beating well after each. Add the milk. Combine flour and baking powder and knead into the dough. Cover with plastic wrap and refrigerate for one hour. Chop the almonds in a food processor. Add the confectioner's sugar and egg whites and process until relatively smooth and even-textured. Preheat the oven to 180°C (350°F). Roll out ²/₃ of the dough to fit in the bottom and up the sides of a 22 cm (9") springform pan. Pour in the filling. Roll the remaining dough into a 3 mm sheet. Cut into 1 ¹/₂ cm (9/16") strips and arrange in a lattice pattern over the filling. Place another strip around the edge of the cake to cover the ends of the strips. Brush with beaten egg. Bake for 45-50 minutes. The cake should be a little soft inside, so do not overbake. Cool in the pan.

Jelly roll

4 eggs
1 ¹/₄ dl (¹/₂ cup) sugar
2 dl (scant 1 cup) flour
¹/₄ teaspoon baking powder

Filling

2-3 dl (1 cup) raspberry or other jam
or whipped cream with chopped fresh berries or chocolate shavings

Preheat the oven to 200°C (400°F). Beat eggs and sugar until light and lemon-colored. Sift together flour and baking powder and fold into the egg mixture lightly but thoroughly. Spread into an oven tray lined with baking parchment. Bake on the center shelf for 8-10 minutes. Sprinkle sugar on another sheet of baking parchment and turn the cake out onto the sugared paper. Roll up lightly. Let cool somewhat. Unroll, spread with filling and roll back up, using the parchment to help. Pack the cake tightly in plastic wrap and refrigerate, seam down, until serving. Garnish with whipped cream

Cream puffs *with lingonberry cream*
12-16 puffs

125 g (4 oz) butter
2 ½ dl (1 cup) water
125 g (⅞ cup) flour
4 eggs

Lingonberry cream
6 dl (2 ½ cups) whipping cream
2-3 dl (1 cup) lingonberry compote

Preheat the oven to 200°C (400°F). Cut the butter into cubes and place in a saucepan with the water. Heat to boiling. Add the flour and stir vigorously until the dough forms a ball. Remove from the heat when the dough leaves the sides of the pan. Let cool slightly. Beat in one egg at a time. It is important to beat well after each egg. The batter should be thick enough to retain its shape. Line an oven sheet with baking parchment. Form mounds of batter with a tablespoon and place on the paper. Bake for 20-25 minutes. Do not open the oven door or the puffs will deflate. Transfer to a rack and let cool. Whip the cream and fold in the berries. Halve the puffs and fill with the cream just before serving. These puffs are also good plain with confectioner's sugar, and of course, you can substitute any other berries for lingonberries.

Jelly roll

Cream puffs with lingonberry cream

Tart with pastry cream, fruit and berries

Tart *with pastry cream, fruit and berries*

Pastry
3 ½ dl (1 ½ cups) flour
1 dl (scant ½ cup) confectioner's sugar
125 g (4 oz) butter, in pats
1 egg

Pastry cream
1 vanilla bean or 1 teaspoon vanilla
4 dl (²/₃ cups) milk
6 egg yolks
½ dl (¼ cup) sugar
1 tablespoon cornstarch
1-2 dl (1 cup) whipping cream
fruit and berries

Place pastry ingredients in a food processor and process until the dough forms a ball. Remove from the processor, pack in plastic wrap and refrigerate for 30 minutes. Preheat the oven to 200°C (400°F). Press the dough into a 22 cm (9") springform pan. Prick with a fork and bake for around 10 minutes. Let cool.

For the pastry cream, split the vanilla bean and scrape out the seeds. Place in a saucepan with the milk, egg yolks, sugar and cornstarch. Heat, stirring constantly, until thickened. Do not allow to boil. Cool quickly by immersing the pan in a larger pan of cold water, stirring occasionally. When completely cold, whip the cream and fold into the egg mixture. Pour into the tart shell and garnish with fruit and berries.

Sponge cake base

30 g (2 ½ tablespoons) sugar and 30 g (3 ½ tablespoons) flour per egg
1 teaspoon baking powder

4 eggs is the norm for a one-layer sponge cake base. They should be at room temperature. Preheat the oven to 160°C (320°F). Beat eggs and sugar until thick and lemon-colored. Sift flour and baking powder together and fold into the egg mixture. Pour into a greased 23 cm (9") springform pan and bake for 30-40 minutes. Cool slightly, then remove from the pan. Cool completely on a rack.

Bavarian cream

This recipe contains uncooked eggs. Use only safety-checked eggs.

6 gelatin sheets
3 eggs
1 dl (scant ½ cup) sugar
3 dl (1 ¼ cups) whipping cream

Flavors
- 3 ½ tablespoons lime juice + 1 pot lemon verbena, chopped
- 1 ½ dl (2/3 cup) raisins soaked in 1 dl (scant ½ cup) rum + seeds from a split vanilla bean
- 250 g (9 oz) berries, such as strawberries, raspberries, lingonberries, black currants or blackberries

Soften the gelatin in cold water for 5 minutes. Beat eggs and sugar until light and lemon-colored. Squeeze excess water from gelatin and melt in 3 ½ tablespoons boiling water, stirring

Bavarian cream cake

Marzipan cake

until completely dissolved. Combine gelatin with one of the flavors and stir into the egg yolk mixture. Whip the cream and fold into the egg yolk mixture. Pour into a large bowl or into individual bowls and refrigerate until stiff.

Marzipan cake

6 eggs
2 dl (⅞ cup) sugar
3 dl (1 ¼ cups) flour
1 teaspoon baking powder
orange juice
1 basket strawberries, chopped
1 recipe Bavarian cream flavored with lime

3 dl (1 ¼ cups) whipping cream
500 g (1 lb) marzipan

Preheat the oven to 160°C (320°F). Beat eggs and sugar until light and lemon-colored. Sift flour and baking powder together and fold into the egg mixture. Pour into a greased 26 cm (10") springform pan. Bake for 45 minutes. Remove from the pan and let cool on a rack. Divide into three layers horizontally and moisten with juice. Place one layer on a serving plate. Spread with Bavarian cream and chopped strawberries. Repeat, then top with remaining layer. Roll out the marzipan and drape over the cake. Cut off excess marzipan at bottom.

Helpful hint
Before decorating the cake, place some parchment paper under the sponge base to keep the plate clean.

Success torte

Success torte

Nut base
150 g (1 cup) confectioner's sugar
150 g (1 ⅓ cups) ground almonds or hazelnuts
4 egg whites

Cream filling
4 egg yolks
1 dl (scant ½ cup) whipping cream
125 g (⅔ cup) sugar
1 teaspoon vanilla extract
150 g (5 oz) butter, in pats

60 g semisweet chocolate (optional)
Combine confectioner's sugar and nuts. Stiffly beat the egg whites and fold into the nut mixture. Pour into a 24 cm (9") springform pan. Bake for 30-35 minutes. Let cool. Whisk together egg yolks, cream, sugar and vanilla in a large saucepan. Heat, whisking constantly, until thickened. Remove from the heat and stir in the butter in pats. Whisk until creamy and even-textured. Refrigerate (or freeze for a while after it is cooled completely). Place the cake on a serving platter. Spread with pastry cream, forming into mounds, Garnish with chocolate slivers, if desired.

Melt the chocolate and spread onto plastic sheeting. Freeze. Break into bits and use to decorate the cake.

Almond ring cake
18 rings

500 g (5 cups) finely ground almonds
500 g (3 ½ cups) confectioner's sugar
4 egg whites

Icing
½ egg white
75 g (½ cup) confectioner's sugar
½ teaspoon lemon juice

Combine the almonds and the sugar. Add egg whites to form a stiff dough. Pack in plastic wrap and let rest overnight. Preheat the oven to 200°C (400°F). Roll into finger-thick lengths, or use a cookie press with a wide round tip. Arrange in greased cake rings (can be purchased in specialty stores), making sure that the ends, where joined, are as seamless as possible. Place the rings on oven sheets and bake for around 10 minutes. Cool completely before tapping out of rings. Make a small cone of paper and cut off the tip. Combine ingredients in the icing and spoon into the cone. Pipe zigzags of frosting onto each ring and stack immediately. Almond cake rings freeze well.

Candy cookie cake
This recipe contains uncooked eggs. Use only safety-checked eggs.

375 g (13 oz) coconut fat
375 g (13 oz) semi-sweet chocolate
6 tablespoons (⅜ cup) strong coffee
4 eggs
3-4 tablespoons sugar

Almond ring cake

2 tablespoons cognac (optional)
16 plain butter cookies
chopped walnuts
colored marzipan, in small balls
gumdrops

Line a loaf pan with plastic wrap. Melt the coconut fat and let cool slightly. Melt the chocolate
and stir in the coffee. Lightly beat the eggs and
sugar together. Add the chocolate and cognac,
mixing until smooth. Gradually add the coconut
fat, mixing until smooth. Layer chocolate mixture
with cookies, nuts, marzipan and gumdrops.
Refrigerate until set. Unmold and garnish with
more gumdrops and nuts. This cake keeps well
and can be frozen.

Light chocolate cake

7 dl (3 cups) sugar
300 g (10 oz) soft butter
5 dl (2 cups) milk
4 eggs
8 dl (3 $\frac{1}{3}$ cups) flour
2 teaspoons vanilla extract
4 teaspoons baking powder
2$\frac{1}{2}$ tablespoons cocoa

Preheat the oven to 180°C (350°F). Place all
ingredients into a bowl and mix with an electric
mixer until smooth. Pour into a greased oven
tray. Bake for 30-40 minutes. When completely
cool, spread with a light chocolate frosting.

Chocolate roll

The combination of chocolate·and lemon cream
is piquant and lovely. It's even prettier when
served with colorful fresh berries

3 eggs
1 $\frac{1}{2}$ dl ($\frac{2}{3}$ cup) sugar
1 $\frac{1}{4}$ dl ($\frac{1}{2}$ cup) flour
4 tablespoons ($\frac{1}{4}$ cup) cocoa
$\frac{1}{2}$ teaspoon baking powder

Lemon cream
This recipe contains uncooked egg yolk. Use only
safety-checked eggs.
100 g (3 $\frac{1}{2}$ oz) butter

Chocolate roll with berries

100 g ($\frac{2}{3}$ cup) confectioner's sugar
1 egg yolk
1 teaspoon grated lemon zest
lemon juice

Preheat the oven to 240°C (450°F). Beat eggs
and sugar until light and lemon-colored. Sift
together the remaining ingredients and fold into
the egg mixture. Pour into a greased oven tray.
Spread the batter in an even layer right to the
edges of the pan. Bake in the center of the oven
for 6-8 minutes. Sprinkle a kitchen towel or
parchment paper with sugar. Turn the cake out
onto the sugar and roll up lightly. Let cool completely. Beat the butter and sugar until light and
fluffy. Beat in the egg yolk and lemon zest. If the
mixture is very thick, add a few drops of lemon
juice to achieve desired consistency. Unroll the
cake, fill with lemon cream and roll up. Wrap in
plastic and refrigerate until serving.

Light chocolate cake

Chocolate fondant

Serve this dessert cake warm so that it's still soft and moist inside. It's wonderful when drizzled with espresso syrup and served with ice cream.

300 g (10 oz) semisweet chocolate
250 g (9 oz) butter
2 dl (⅞ cup) sugar
5 eggs
3 dl (1 ½ cups) flour
1 teaspoon baking powder
1 teaspoon vanilla extract

Preheat the oven to 180°C (350°F). Melt chocolate and butter together in a large saucepan. Stir in the sugar and let cool slightly. Whisk in one egg at a time, then fold in the dry ingredients. Pour into greased individual molds or into a 23 cm (9") springform pan. Bake for 30-35 minutes. Do not overbake or the cake will dry out. Serve immediately for a runny center. If the cakes are allowed to cool completely, they will set.

Espresso syrup

2 dl (1 cup) strong coffee
½ dl (¼ cup) sugar

Combine coffee and sugar in a small saucepan and reduce over high heat until thick and syrupy. Add more sugar, if needed. Pour half of the syrup over the cakes as soon as they are removed from the oven but are in their pans. Wait until the syrup is absorbed, then drizzle over the rest.

Lemon cheesecake

Base

3 dl (1 ¼ cups) flour
3 tablespoons sugar
125 g (4 ½ oz) cold butter
1 egg yolk

Filling

250 g (9 oz) cream cheese
3 dl (1 ⅓ cups) dairy sour cream
3 eggs
1 egg white
3 tablespoons sugar
grated zest and juice of 1 lemon

Preheat the oven to 200°C (400°F). Place flour and sugar in a food processor. With the motor running, add the butter in pats, processing until coarse. Add the egg yolk and pulse to combine. Press the dough into the bottom and 3 cm (1 ¼") up the sides of a greased 24 cm (9") springform pan. Prick with a fork and bake for around 12 minutes. Remove from the oven. Lower the temperature to 160°C (320°F). Combine the remaining ingredients and beat with an electric mixer until smooth. Pour over the base. Bake until set, around 1 hour.

Chocolate fondant

Kvæfjord cake

150 g (5 oz) butter
125 g (²⁄₃ cup) sugar
5 egg yolks
150 g (1 cup) flour
1 teaspoon baking powder
5 tablespoons (¹⁄₃ cup) milk

Meringue

5 egg whites
180 g (scant 1 cup) sugar
100 g (1 cup) chopped almonds

Filling

2 dl (¾ cup) whipping cream
1 teaspoon vanilla extract
5 dl (2 cups) vanilla pastry cream (purchased or homemade)

Preheat the oven to 175°C (350°F). Beat butter and sugar until light and fluffy. Add one egg yolk at a time, beating well after each. Combine flour and baking powder and add alternately with the milk, beating until smooth. Pour into an oven tray lined with baking parchment. Beat the egg whites until almost stiff. Gradually add the sugar, beating until very stiff. Spread the meringue over the cake batter and sprinkle with almonds. Bake for around 25 minutes. Cool and halve the cake. Place one half on a serving platter, meringue side up. Whip the cream and vanilla and fold into the pastry cream. Spread over the cake base. Top with the other cake, meringue side up.

Lemon cheesecake

Kvæfjord cake

All seven kinds!

Is there anything more Norwegian than baking seven different kinds of cookies for Christmas. Every country has its own special kinds of cookies, but serving seven different small, dry cookies on the same table, preferably on the same plate, is very special and very Norwegian. There are many more than seven recipes for Christmas cookies, and every home has its own traditional favorites. The aroma of baking is something very special, it makes us remember times gone by, and for many, there is no such thing as Christmas without syrup snaps, pepper nuts and all the other cookies.

Serina cakes

150 g (5 oz) butter
250 g (1 ¾ cups) flour
2 teaspoons baking powder
100 g (½ cup) sugar
1 egg
1 teaspoon vanilla extract
egg white
pearl sugar or crushed sugar cubes

Preheat the oven to 200°C (400°F). Blend the butter, flour and baking powder with a pastry blender until crumbly. Add the sugar, egg and vanilla. Mix lightly but thoroughly. Roll into a long sausage. Cut into small pieces. Roll each piece into a ball and place on baking parchment or on a greased baking sheet. Press the balls down with a fork, brush with egg white and sprinkle with pearl sugar. Bake for around 10 minutes. Cool on a rack and store in an airtight tin.

Pepper nuts

500 g (1 lb) butter
500 g (1 lb) sugar
2 dl (½ cup) whipping cream
1 tablespoon ginger
2 teaspoons cinnamon
1 ½ teaspoons pepper
1 teaspoon cardamom
1 teaspoon baking powder
2 teaspoons baking soda
1 kg (2 lb) flour

Beat butter and sugar until light and fluffy. Add the remaining ingredients, mixing well. Cover with plastic and refrigerate overnight. Preheat the oven to 190°C (375°F). Roll the dough into finger-thick sausages. Cut into small pieces and roll each into a ball. Place on a greased baking sheet and bake for 12-13 minutes.

Berlin wreaths

2 egg yolks, hardcooked
2 egg yolks, raw
125 g (⅝ cup) sugar
250 g (1 cup) butter, softened
300 g (2 cups) flour
1 egg white
pearl sugar or crushed sugar cubes

Mash cooked and raw egg yolks together. Add sugar and beat until light and fluffy. Add butter and flour alternately. Refrigerate for around 1 hour. Preheat the oven to 180°C (350°F). Roll the dough into 10 cm (4") long thin sausages. Form into wreaths, crossing the ends. Place on baking parchment or onto a greased baking sheet. Brush with egg white and sprinkle with pearl sugar. Bake for around 10 minutes. Cool on a rack and store airtight.

Sand cakes

200 g (7 oz) butter
100 g (½ cup) sugar
250 g (1 ¾ cups) flour
100 g (1 cup) ground almonds
1 egg

Beat butter and sugar until light and fluffy. Add the remaining ingredients, mixing well. Refrigerate for 1 hour. Preheat the oven to 175°C (350°F). Grease "sandkake" (small fluted tartlet) tins. Press the dough into the tins. The dough should be very thin. Place on a baking sheet and bake for 10-15 minutes. Let cool slightly before removing from the tins. Cool on a rack. Store airtight or freeze.

Handy hint
These cookies are good year-round. Fill with whipped cream and fruit or berries for dessert.

White cookie *people*

100 g (3 ½ oz) butter, melted and cooled
3 dl (1 ¼ cups) sugar
2 dl (⅞ cup) milk
1 teaspoon hornsalt (ammonium carbonate) or 1 tablespoon baking powder
1 liter (4 cups) flour

Combine butter, sugar, milk, hornsalt and half the flour, mixing well. Mix in the remaining flour to a stiff dough. Cover with plastic and refrigerate overnight. Preheat the oven to 175°C (350°F). Roll out the dough to a ⅜" thick sheet. Cut figures and place on a greased baking sheet. Bake for around 7 minutes. They should not turn color. Cool completely before decorating with colored frosting.

Pepper nuts

Christmas cookies. Front from left: Vanilla crescents, a platter with ladyfingers, Finnish sticks, deer antlers, German slices and cookie stacks, spice cake (round), Christmas yeast bread, Christmas fruit cake and chocolate cookie cake. Center from left: Cake doughnuts, almond ring cake, rosettes, almond cake sticks dipped in chocolate, platter with goro, poor man's cookies, coconut macaroons, sand cakes, butter cookies and cookie cones. Back from left: Gingerbread house, white cookie men and women, and lefse with spread.

Syrup snaps

1 ¹/₂ dl (²/₃ cup) whipping cream
150 g (¹/₂ cup) dark corn or sugar syrup
150 g (³/₄ cup) sugar
100 g (3 ¹/₂ oz) butter
450 g (1 lb) flour
¹/₂ teaspoon ground pepper
¹/₄ teaspoon ground ginger
¹/₄ teaspoon ground anise
¹/₄ teaspoon ground cinnamon
³/₄ teaspoon hornsalt (or 2 teaspoons baking powder)

³/₄ teaspoon baking soda
blanched almonds

Heat cream, syrup and sugar to boiling. Add the butter and cool until lukewarm. Transfer to a large mixing bowl. Sift in the dry ingredients and mix with a dough hook until smooth. Cover and refrigerate overnight. Preheat the oven to 175°C (350°F). Using small amounts of dough (leave the rest in the refrigerator), roll into thin sheets. Cut into diamonds with a pastry wheel. Place half an almond in the center of each. Place on a

greased oven sheet and bake for around 5 minutes. Let cool on a rack and store airtight or freeze.

Helpful hint
For a shiny surface, brush with egg white before baking. The cookies will be shiny

Cookie stacks

2 egg yolks
2 tablespoons whipping cream
250 g (1 ¼ cups) sugar
250 g (8 oz) butter, softened
500 g (1 lb) flour
3 egg whites
250 g (1 ⅔ cups) confectioner's sugar
250 g (8 oz/2 ⅓ cups) ground almonds

Beat egg yolks, cream and sugar until thick and lemon-colored. Add butter and flour alternately, mixing well. Cover and refrigerate for at least 1 hour. Beat the egg whites until almost stiff. Gradually add the sugar and beat to a thick meringue. Stir in the almonds. Preheat the oven to 175°C (350°F). Roll the dough into a thin, rectangular sheet. Cut into strips, 2x12 cm (3/4x5"), with a pastry wheel and place on a greased baking sheet. Place a strip of almond mixture down the center of each cookie. Bake for around 10 minutes. Cool on a rack. Form a tower by stacking 2 cookies in 1 direction, then 2 in the other.

Goro

¾ dl (1/3 cup) whipping cream
1 egg
1 teaspoon vanilla
125 g (⅔ cup) sugar
500 g (1 lb) flour
1 teaspoon cardamom
325 g (11 oz) butter

Whip the cream. Beat the egg and sugar until thick and lemon-colored. Stir in the cream and vanilla. Set aside a small amount of the flour for rolling out, and combine the dry ingredients. Cut in the butter and stir in the egg mixture, mixing until smooth. Cover and refrigerate for at least 2 hours. Roll out a small amount of the dough at a time and cut pieces with a pastry wheel to fit a goro iron. Bake until crisp and golden. Cool on a rack and store airtight or freeze.

Helpful hint
Make a paper template the exact size of your goro iron, to place on the dough when cutting it out.

Cones

4 eggs
250 g (1 ¼ cups) sugar
250 g (8 oz) butter, melted
250 g (1 ¾ cups) flour
1 teaspoon cardamom

Beat eggs and sugar until thick and lemon-colored. Stir in the remaining ingredients, mixing well. Grease the "krumkake" iron for the first cookie only. Bake until golden over low heat. Form into a cone while still warm. Cool on a rack and store airtight or freeze.

Helpful hint
Place the warm cookies over an upturned cup to make baskets to fill with berries and whipped cream.

Poor man's cookies

5 egg yolks
5 tablespoons (⅓ cup) sugar
5 tablespoons (⅓ cup) whipping cream
1 tablespoon cognac
¼ teaspoon cinnamon
¼ teaspoon ground cardamom
1 egg white
350 g (2 ⅓ cups) flour
shortening or oil

Beat egg yolks and sugar until thick and lemon-colored. Whip the cream and fold into the egg yolk mixture with the cognac and spices. Beat the egg white until stiff and carefully fold in. Add just over half the flour, mixing well. Cover and let rest overnight. Use the remaining flour (as little as possible) for rolling out. Using small amounts of dough, roll into thin sheets. Cut out diamonds with a pastry wheel. Make a slit in the center of each diamond and pull one corner of dough through the slit. Fry several at a time in hot fat until golden, 2-3 minutes.

Deer antlers

4 eggs
250 g (1 ¼ cups) sugar
125 g (4 oz) butter
3 tablespoons cognac
1 teaspoon hornsalt (or 1 tablespoon baking powder)
1 teaspoon cardamom
600 g (4 cups) flour
shortening or oil

Beat eggs and sugar until thick and lemon-colored. Melt the butter and add with the cognac, hornsalt, cardamom and half the flour. Cover and refrigerate overnight. Use the remaining flour for rolling. Using a small amount of dough at a time, form into finger-thick rings. Cut three notches in each and deep-fry, a few at a time, in hot shortening or oil until golden, 3-4 minutes. Drain on paper towels.

Strull

2 ½ dl (1 cup) dairy sour cream (do not use low-fat) or whipping cream
100 g (⅔ cup) sugar
100 g (⅔ cup) flour
3 – 3 ½ tablespoons water

Whip the sour cream or cream with the sugar and stir in flour and water. Let the batter rest for around 30 minutes. Place a spoonful of batter in the middle of a "krumkake" iron and make very thin wafers. Roll up around a wooden spoon handle as soon as they are done. Cool on a rack and store airtight or freeze.

Helpful hint
The batter should be so thin that the cookies are lacy and crisp. Roll the dark side out, or the cookies will look gray. These can also be made into baskets, just like the previous recipe.

Cones

Rosettes

100 g (²/₃ cup) flour
1 egg
1 ½ dl (²/₃ cup) milk
1 teaspoon melted butter
1 tablespoon sugar
shortening or oil

Combine ingredients for the batter and let rest for 20 minutes. Heat the shortening. Dip the iron first into the hot fat, then into the batter. Do not let the batter go over the edge of the iron. Hold the iron in the fat until the cookies are golden. Carefully remove the cookies with a fork and drain on paper towels. Sprinkle with confectioner's sugar before serving. These freeze well.

Helpful hint
Rosettes are a lovely dessert when served with whipped cream and homemade jam.

Doughnuts

3 eggs
250 g (1 ¼ cups) sugar
5 dl (2 cups) dairy sour cream
(do not use low-fat)
1 ½ dl (2/3 cup) milk
4 teaspoons hornsalt
2 teaspoons cardamom
750-1000 g (5-7 cups) flour
shortening or oil

Beat eggs and sugar until thick and lemon-colored. Whip the sour cream. Combine all ingredients, cover and refrigerate overnight. Roll into a 1 cm (³/₈") thick sheet. Cut out doughnuts and deep-fry, a few at a time, in hot shortening or oil until golden, 3-4 minutes.

Mini jelly doughnuts

Deep-fry the doughnut holes. Fill with a little jam and roll in confectioner's sugar. These are also good without filling. These freeze well.

Helpful hint
This dough is rather loose. Roll out a little at a time on a flour-covered board.

It's easy to make six different sweet yeast pastries from one basic dough. Back from left: Prune twist, lingonberry cake and apple twist. Front from left: Marzipan bread, coconut horns and filled sweet buns.

Sweet yeast breads

Basic sweet yeast dough
(large portion)
You can make six different sweet breads with this dough

1 liter (quart) milk
100 g (3 ½ oz) fresh yeast
2 eggs
3 dl (1 ¼ cups) sugar
2 teaspoons baking powder
4 teaspoons cardamom
300 g (10 oz) butter
3 liters (12 ½ cups) flour

Heat the milk to lukewarm. Crumble the yeast into the milk and stir in the eggs. Combine sugar, baking powder and cardamom in a large bowl. Cut the butter into cubes and knead into the sugar mixture. Add the milk and gradually knead in the flour with a dough hook until it forms a ball. Cover and let rise until doubled.

Apple kuchen *–variation 1*

⅙ of the basic dough, risen once

Filling
2 ½ dl (1 cup) vanilla pastry cream (purchased or homemade)
3 apples
1 dl (scant ½ cup) sliced almonds

Grease a 20x25 cm (8x10") pan. Roll the dough into a rectangle large enough to fit and place in the pan. Spread with vanilla cream. Cut the apples into wedges and arrange over the cream. Sprinkle with almonds. Cover and let rise for around 20 minutes. Preheat the oven to 200°C (400°F). Bake for around 35 minutes. Cool on a rack. Serve lukewarm, with a drizzle of powdered sugar glaze and whipped cream alongside.

Prune kuchen *– variation 2*

⅙ of the basic dough, risen once

Filling
2 ½ dl (1 cup) vanilla pastry cream (purchased or homemade)
150 g (5 oz) pitted prunes
75 g (2 ½ oz) walnut halves

Grease a 20x25 cm (8x10") pan. Roll the dough into a rectangle large enough to fit and place in the pan. Spread with vanilla cream and arrange prunes and walnuts over the cream. Cover and let rise for around 20 minutes. Preheat the oven to 200°C (400°F). Bake for around 35 minutes. Cool on a rack. Serve lukewarm, with whipped cream alongside.

Coconut horns *– variation 3*
12 horns

⅙ of the basic dough, risen once

Filling
125 g (4 oz) cream cheese
1 dl (scant ½ cup) coconut
1 dl (scant ½ cup) sugar
2 teaspoons cinnamon
1 dl (scant ½ cup) raisins (optional)
chopped mint
beaten egg

Divide the dough in two and roll each into a circle. Cut each circle into three triangles. Combine all ingredients in the filling and spread over the triangles. Roll up. Place on baking parchment, cover and let rise for around 20 minutes. Preheat the oven to 225°C (425°F). Brush with egg. Bake for around 15 minutes. Cool on a rack.

Lingonberry cake *–variation 4*

⅙ of the basic dough, risen once

Filling
2 ½ dl (1 cup) vanilla pastry cream (purchased or homemade
2 ½ dl (1 cup) lingonberries
2 tablespoons sugar
beaten egg

Roll out the dough to a 30x35 cm (12x14") rectangle. Spread with vanilla cream and sprinkle with berries and sugar. Roll up from the long side. Cut into 12 pieces and arrange in a greased 23 cm (9") springform pan. Cover and let rise for around 30 minutes. Preheat the oven to 200°C (400°F). Brush with egg and bake for around 30 minutes. Let cool on a rack. Serve lukewarm, preferably with a drizzle of confectioner is sugar glaze.

Marzipan length *– variation 5*

⅙ of the basic dough, risen once

Filling
4 tablespoons (1/4 cup) vanilla pastry cream (purchased or homemade)
250 g (8 oz) marzipan
1 dl (scant ½ cup) shelled pistachio nuts

Beaten egg
confectioner's sugar glaze
coarsely chopped pistachio nuts

Roll the dough into a 30x35 cm (12-14") rectangle. Spread the vanilla cream in a strip down the middle and cover with thin slices of marzipan. Sprinkle with nuts. Make 10 diagonal cuts in the dough from each side toward the middle (toward the filling) and drape the dough strands over the filling alternately from each side to enclose it completely. Cover and let rise for 30 minutes. Preheat the oven to 200°C (400°F). Brush with egg and bake for around 20 minutes. Let cool on a rack and serve lukewarm with confectioner's sugar glaze and top with nuts.

Filled rolls – *variation 6*
12 rolls

1/6 of the basic dough, risen once

Filling
Candy covered chocolate or chocolate chips
Beaten egg
Confectioner's sugar glaze

Divide the dough into 12 pieces of equal size and form round balls. Make a hole in each and fill with 6 candies or chocolate chips. Close the hole and place the rolls on a greased oven tray, hole down. Cover and let rise for 30 minutes. Preheat the oven to 225°C (245°F). Bake for around 13 minutes. Cool on a rack. Serve lukewarm with confectioner's sugar glaze. Garnish with more chocolate, if desired. These are even good without filling.

Coconut cream rolls
12-14 rolls

3 1/2 dl (1 1/2 cups) milk
50 g (1 3/4 oz) fresh yeast
100 g (3 1/2 oz) butter
1 dl (scant 1/2 cup) sugar
1/2 teaspoon cardamom
1 liter (4 cups) flour
1 portion egg cream, see page 258
confectioner's sugar, coconut

Heat the milk to 37°C (98°F). Dissolve the yeast in the milk. Melt the butter, cool slightly and add, along with the sugar and cardamom. Sift in the flour and knead into a soft dough. Cover and let rise until almost doubled. Roll smooth balls and press them down in the center. Place on an oven sheet and let rise until doubled. Preheat the oven to 250°C (450°F). Place a generous spoonful of egg cream in the center of each roll. Bake for 10-12 minutes. Let cool on a rack. Spread confectioner's sugar glaze on each roll and dip into a plate of coconut.

Astrid's wreath, sweet roll, princess cake and cinnamon rolls

100 g (3 1/2 oz) butter
3 1/2 dl (1 1/2 cups) milk
50 g (1 3/4 oz) fresh yeast
1 egg
100 g (1/2 cup) sugar
1 teaspoon cardamom
1/2 teaspoon baking powder
600 g (4 cups) flour

Melt the butter and add the milk. Dissolve the yeast in the milk mixture and stir in the egg. Sift together the dry ingredients and add. Knead until smooth and elastic. Cover and let rise until doubled, at least 45 minutes. Form the dough into the desired shape.

Astrid's wreath

Filling
200 g (2 cups) ground almonds
150 g (1 cup) confectioner's sugar
1 egg white
1–2 tablespoons water

Topping
Vanilla or rum cream

Roll the dough into a 75x20 cm (30x8") length. Combine almonds, confectioner's sugar, egg white and water. Spoon the almond mixture along one long end. Roll together. Form into a

Coconut cream rolls

Astrid's wreath and cinnamon rools

"wreath" on a baking sheet. Cover and let rise for 20 minutes. Preheat the oven to 225°C (425°F). It's a good idea to place custard cups in the two "holes" during baking so that the pretzel doesn't spread out and run together. Brush with beaten egg, sprinkle with pearl sugar or sliced almonds and bake for around 20 minutes.

Sweet roll

Filling
Vanilla or rum cream

Topping
currants
sugar
cinnamon

Form the dough into two lengths and place them on an oven sheet. Make a groove down the center of each and fill with pastry cream. Sprinkle with currants, cinnamon and sugar. Cover and let rise for 20 minutes. Preheat the oven to 225°C (425°F). Brush with egg and bake for 15-20 minutes.

Princess cake and cinnamon rolls

Filling
100 g (3 ½ oz) butter, softened
2 teaspoons cinnamon
3 tablespoons sugar
vanilla cream
raisins

Divide the sheet into thirds. Roll one into a circle and place in the bottom and up the sides of a 24-26 cm (10") spring form pan. Roll the other two pieces into 60x30 cm (24x12") rectangles. Spread each length butter and sprinkle with a mixture of cinnamon and sugar. Spread with a little vanilla cream, sprinkle with raisins and roll up lengthwise. Cut the rolls into 3-4 cm (1 ½") slices. Place some rolls, cut side down, in the dough-lined pan. Top with vanilla cream. Place the remaining rolls on an oven sheet. Cover and let rise for 20 minutes. Preheat the oven to 225°C (245°F). Brush with egg and bake the cinnamon rolls for 12-15 minutes and the cake for 40 minutes.

Christmas bread
2 loaves

125 g (4 oz) butter
5 dl (2 cups) milk
50 g (1 ¾ oz) fresh yeast
125 g (⅝ cup) sugar
650 g (4 ⅓ cups) flour
1 teaspoon cardamom
150 g (5 oz) raisins
citron (optional)
beaten egg

Melt the butter and add the milk. Dissolve the yeast in the milk mixture. Stir in the sugar. Knead in the flour and cardamom, kneading until the dough is smooth and elastic. Cover and let rise until doubled, around 40 minutes. Turn out onto a floured board and divide in two. Divide the raisins (and citron) evenly between the two and knead into two large round balls. Using a sharp knife, cut a line around the edge of the balls and press them down in the center, to prevent them

from cracking so easily. The dough can also be placed in greased 2-liter (quart) loaf pans. Cover and let rise for 30-40 minutes. Preheat the oven to 175°C (350°F). Bake on the lowest shelf for 20-40 minutes. Let cool on a rack.

Sweet wort bread
2 loaves

50 g (3 tablespoons) butter
1 dl (scant ½ cup) dark corn syrup
2 ½ tablespoons brown sugar
3 1/3 dl (1 ⅙ cups) wort beer (non-alcoholic)
2 dl (⅞ cup) milk
50 g (1 ¾ oz) fresh yeast
300 g (2 cups) finely ground rye flour
500 g (3 ⅓ cups) flour
1 teaspoon salt
1 teaspoon ground cloves
½ teaspoon allspice
½ teaspoon pepper
50 g (2 oz) raisins

Melt the butter and stir in the syrup and sugar. Add the beer and milk and stir the yeast into the lukewarm liquid. Combine the dry ingredients, but reserve a little flour for rolling out the dough. Knead until smooth and elastic, adding as much flour as necessary for a smooth dough. Let rise until doubled, around 30 minutes. Knead in the raisins, then divide the dough in half. Form each into a round loaf. Cover and let rise for 30 minutes. Preheat the oven to 210°C (420°F). Prick each bread with a fork and bake for 45-60 minutes. Brush with water just before they are finished cooking for a shiny surface.

Christmas bread

Sweet wort bread

Yeast baking

– wonderfully delicious and deliciously healthy

There's nothing like the aroma of freshly baked bread, and few things taste better. Bread has been the foundation of life since the beginning of civilization. The cultivation of grain influenced the hunter-gatherers to form settlements. In the beginning, grain was most often used to make gruel. But the path from gruel to flatbread is not long. Perhaps it all began when some gruel boiled over and spilled onto a hot stone. Maybe someone forgot a bowl of gruel, and it began to ferment. And then the fermented gruel was thrown onto the fire. That could well have been how the first bread was made

There are many positive things to be said about bread. It keeps well, it transports well, and it can be dried and stored for a long time. It's easy to serve, and once baked, it can be the basis for a very quick meal.

"Bread and water" is a good enough diet. Such a shame that it landed in prison! But bread is versatile enough to have a place both in prisons and at rich men's tables. And as if that weren't enough, in Christianity, bread has been elevated symbolically to represent the body of Christ, and in the Lord's prayer, "give us this day our daily bread", it represents all food.

The Romans felt that people needed only two things, bread and circuses. And during the French revolution, the crowds of people shouted for bread.

In today's affluent society, bread no longer has the same importance, though in some countries, it is still the custom to offer guests bread and salt as a symbol of welcome. Maybe that's why real estate agents recommend sellers to bake bread before a showing. The aroma of freshly baked bread adds a homey touch to a house (and perhaps increases the price). And as if that weren't enough, baking bread is also good therapy. Everyone can help out, you can't rush it, and you can knead all your suppressed aggression into the dough. And – bread is good for you!

The baking process

If you are comfortable with the different steps that lead to the finished loaf, you can ultimately experiment and develop your own specialties. It's not magic. Anyone can learn to bake bread!

Measure, weigh and mix

Bread recipes are seldom so precise that you need to use a scale. However, it is much easier if you do have a good scale, especially if you are a beginner.

Start with the liquid, yeast and salt. Weigh the coarsest flour and stir that into the liquid as you weigh the rest. Add the finest flour last. If using very coarse flour, such as whole wheat, you might want to soak the grain (equal parts grain

Baking with heating elements over and under (regular bread)

Preheat the oven to 240°C (440°F). When the temperature has been reached, place the breads on the next to the bottom rack and lower the heat to 180-200°C (350-400°F). Most normal loaves take 30-45 minutes. Rolls are prepared in the same way, but baking time is 8-10 minutes.

Baking in a convection oven

Preheat the oven to 10°C (18°F) lower than stated in the recipe. If you are baking only one sheet of bread, you can use the "pizza" setting (circulating air plus heat from underneath), if your stove has this function.

Steam during the first part of baking results in a shinier, crispier crust. In a standard oven, you have to place an oven tray on the floor of the oven before preheating. After the bread is in the oven, pour 2 dl (1 cup) hot water into the pan and close the door immediately (watch out for the steam). You can also do this with a convection oven, but turn off the fan before adding the water.

If you plan to freeze the bread, bake it slightly less than usual. A hard, dark crust tends to separate more easily from the bread itself during the freezing and defrosting process than a light, soft crust.

The big question is often: Is the bread finished baking? In the recipes that follow, we have stated the normal baking time. It (and the temperature) should be regarded as a guide. No two ovens are completely alike, and a difference of 10-20°C (18-36°F) degrees is not unusual. There is also a difference in baking with hot air and baking in a normal oven. As a rule, the temperature in a hot air oven should be 10°C (18°F) lower than in a normal oven. All temperatures in this chapter refer to baking in a normal oven, not a convection oven.

Advice and hints

Look at the color of the crust to see if the bread is done or not. If in doubt, check the underside of the bread. The edges should not be too soft.

and water) overnight. Subtract soaking water from the total amount of liquid in the recipe.

Mix, knead, let rise

If you use a mixer with a dough hook, you should knead for 8-10 minutes. If kneading by hand, you will need 10-15 minutes of intense kneading. Knead until the dough becomes finely textured, smooth and elastic. Form it into a ball and place it in a bowl and cover with plastic wrap or a damp kitchen towel. Set it in a warm place to rest and rise for a specific time or until the dough has doubled in size. It's no disaster if it rises a little too much.

Shape

Then the dough has to be punched down, to release gas, and kneaded one more time until it is smooth and elastic. Then you divide it into the number of loaves, rolls or whatever you plan to bake. Use a little but not too much flour when forming the loaves. Wet your hands before working with very sticky dough. Place the bread on a baking sheet or in a pan and let it rise one more time.

Rise

Rising should take place in a warm (preferably close to 40°C/100°F) and preferably humid place. Brush or spray the dough with water to hinder the crust from becoming too dry. You can also brush with oil, make a tent of plastic wrap or cover with a damp kitchen towel. If you plan to bake the breads in loaf pans, just put the entire pan in a plastic bag, blow it up and seal it as airtight as possible. If your stove is relatively new, you can let the dough rise in the oven. Set it on 40°C (100°F) and pour a cup of boiling water into an oven tray on the floor of the oven. Make sure that your oven fan is turned off. The dough should rise for 30-45 minutes, depending on the temperature and how long the dough got to rest. Remove the breads from the oven around 5 minutes before they are finished rising, and then preheat the oven to the desired temperature.

Tap the bread lightly. It should sound hollow if finished baking.

If the bread has a soft crust, check with a cake tester. If uncooked dough sticks to the tester, the bread needs more time in the oven.

If you are really in doubt, use an instant thermometer. Stick it into the bread toward the end of the baking time. The end should be as close to the center of the bread as possible. Coarse, heavy bread should be baked until it reaches an internal temperature of 96°C (205°F), light whole grain bread should be 94°C (204°F) and white bread 92°C (198°F).

Bread baked in colored loaf pans requires less time in the oven than bread baked in shiny tins. Remove the loaves from the pans and return the bread to the oven for the last 10 minutes of baking time.

Rolls and other small baked goods made with yeast are finished when they are a golden color.

There are many ways to get a shiny crust. The most important thing is to let the bread rise in a humid room and to leave as little flour as possible remaining on the surface. Starting the baking process with a cup of boiling water in a tray on the oven floor is another good idea. You can also brush or spray water onto the bread before baking (but don't use too much water). After baking, you can brush the bread with a mixture of 1 egg, 1 pinch salt and 1 tablespoon of water or a mixture of potato starch and hot water. Some people use black coffee or a mixture of syrup and water.

The most popular ingredients

Wheat

Wheat is the most important bread grain. There are usually several varieties available in the shops. Ordinary white flour, all-purpose flour, is used in both bread and cakes. Cake flour is self-explanatory. Whole-wheat flour is available both coarsely and finely ground. Both are typical bread flours, but the latter can be used in crackers and in some cakes, on its own, or together with all-purpose flour. All textures of whole-wheat flour contain the whole grain, with all its fiber, vitamins and minerals. Whole-wheat kernels or cracked wheat are the coarsest types. The grain is lightly crushed, so that it can absorb water and become edible.

Rye

Rye is the next most important grain in Norway. It's available finely ground and diluted with some wheat flour, or as whole-grain flour, both coarsely and finely ground. Rye adds flavor and makes moist bread that keeps well, but it makes sticky dough. Don't be tempted to make firm dough with rye flour. The bread won't be good. Finely ground whole rye flour makes wonderful bread. It's nutritious, good and easy to use in baking. Now and then you can find whole or cracked rye. Whole rye grain has to be soaked before use. Otherwise, it must be crushed before mixing into dough. In some places, you can find rolled rye, which is excellent for baking.

Barley

Barley can also be used in baking bread, but no more than 25% of the flour can be barley. Barley groats must be cooked and cooled before using in bread. Follow directions for whole grain. *Skjåk* flour, a regional specialty, is especially flavorful barley flour.

Oats

Finely ground oat flour can be used in the same proportion as barley flour. Oatmeal can be added directly to dough as long as there is enough liquid to moisten the dry grain. Oatmeal is also good as decoration on top of bread (brush with water and roll the loaf in oatmeal before baking). Whole oats have to be cooked and cooled before use. Oat bran can be used directly in dough, as long as the amount of liquid is adjusted accordingly.

Bran

Bran is the shell of the wheat kernel and is especially rich in fiber. Add to dough for extra fiber. Bran absorbs liquid very well, so increase the amount of liquid if adding bran to dough.

"Mixed grains"

There are mixtures of flour as well as bread mixes marketed by the different mills. These can vary greatly. Read the package directions.

Salt

Most people use ordinary table salt. Sea salt is also acceptable. Light salt can also be used, but it sometimes leaves an aftertaste. Bread dough made without salt is stickier and doesn't hold its shape well. If you bake bread without salt or with only small amounts of salt (less than 10-15 g ($^1/_2$ oz) per liter (quart) liquid), bake it in a pan.

Sugar

Sugar does not need to be added to regular bread dough. Small amounts are good for long-rising dough, as it helps fermentation. Add sugar to the flour, not to the liquid.

Syrup

Syrup is a better sweetening agent than sugar in sweet breads. Use dark corn or sugar syrup, as it contains more minerals than light syrup. Syrup helps to keep bread moist, so that it keeps better.

Honey

Honey is also a good sweetening agent for sweet breads.

Yeast

Fresh yeast is a living organism. It should be stored in the refrigerator and should not be allowed to dry out. Yeast is marked with a "use by" date. Yeast should not be frozen because it loses some of its rising power. Dry yeast is around four times stronger than fresh yeast, so when substituting for fresh yeast, use only one-fourth the amount stated in the recipe. Dry yeast should be stored in a dry place and it keeps well. Mix it into the flour before adding the liquid. Dough made with dry yeast should rest longer than dough made with fresh yeast. Dry yeast takes longer to "wake-up" and start rising.

Liquid

Any kind of liquid can be used in dough, alone or together with water. The most important liquid for dough is indeed water. Milk is a good number two. All kinds of milk can be used, but sour milk or cultured milk is especially good in dough containing rye flour. Bread baked with milk only is usually more compact and sweeter than bread made with water. Half water, half milk is a good alternative. Remember that whole milk and some cultured milks contain fat. You can compensate for this by adding less fat. Dry milk is excellent to use in baking. Dissolve the powdered milk in the water along with the yeast. The liquid should always be lukewarm (around 30-35°C/87-94°F) before adding the yeast, flour, etc.

Fat

Fat helps to make smooth dough, and it results in bread that keeps well. You don't have to add fat to bread dough; you can bake without it. The fat should be soft. All types of margarine, butter and oil are used in baking bread. Don't use the most expensive oils in bread, as they don't add flavor or texture. The usual amount added is 20-50 g (1 $^1/_2$-3 $^1/_2$ tablespoons) per liter (quart) liquid.

Other additions
Raisins

Raisins or sultanas are added right at the end, so they aren't crushed by kneading. Hard raisins should be soaked for a couple of hours before adding. They don't need to be washed. Add the amount you like. You can also add prunes, apricots or other dried fruit in small pieces instead of or in addition to raisins.

Citron, fruit, etc.

Citron are chunks of candied peel. Similarly treated lemon and orange peel are also available. Chopped sun-dried tomato, olives and garlic have recently become popular additions to bread in Norway.

Nuts

Walnuts are a popular ingredient. For a stronger flavor, toast the nuts before adding, or use walnut oil in the dough. The amount of nuts added is a matter of taste. Start with 150-300 g (5-10 oz) per liter (quart) liquid. All kinds of nuts can be used – hazelnuts, pecans, almonds, Brazil nuts, peanuts, cashews and pistachios, to name the most popular. All become more intense in flavor when toasted, and some become so strong that they should be used with care.

Seeds

Poppy seeds (blue and yellow) are the most popular seeds used in bread. They are sprinkled on the surface of white bread, and sesame seeds can be used in the same way. To make them stick, dip loaves in water first, then dip in the seeds or sprinkle with seeds. Flaxseed and sunflower seeds can be used in the same way, but in general, these two seeds are used in the dough itself. Flaxseed can be used directly from the package, but it's good to crush or chop sunflower seeds. Seeds do not alter the dough appreciably, so you can use as much or as little as you like. For a more intense flavor, toast the seeds before adding. Sesame seeds turn golden or light brown when toasted. In recent years, many new types of seeds have begun to appear on the market, including pumpkin seeds, millet and buckwheat. All can be used in bread.

Spices

Caraway is the best-known bread spice from the olden days. As with all spices, caraway seed should be crushed before adding to the dough. All kinds of spices can be used in bread, even blends. It's hard to state amounts. Taste your way to good dough. The flavor is more intense in the finished product than in the dough. You can also use fresh, finely chopped herbs instead of dried herbs.

Making your own recipes

There is no magic formula to baking bread. You can experiment and make your own special recipes. And should disaster strike, the loss is not great. Ordinary bread is made of water, yeast, flour and salt. You can make good bread with just those four ingredients, but it's fun and easy to make variations too. Here is some good advice:

If 50% of the total amount of flour is all-purpose flour, you can be quite sure of a good

result. With further experimentation, you can increase the proportion of coarse flour or other types of grain in steps. Use 20-25 g (3/4-1 oz) salt and 30-50 g (1-1 3/4 oz) fresh yeast per liter (quart) liquid. If you want to add fat to the dough, start with 1-2 tablespoons oil per liter (quart) liquid. Make sure that you write down the ingredients and quantities, just in case this is your "lucky bread".

Follow the general rules for rising and baking.

Smaller baked goods

Basic dough
You can make six different breads with this dough

100 g (3 ½ oz) butter
1 liter (4 cups) water
100 g (3 ½ oz) fresh yeast
2 teaspoons salt
around 3 liter (12 ½ cups) all-purpose flour

Melt the butter and add the water. Dissolve the yeast in the lukewarm liquid. Add salt and stir until the dough sticks together and leaves the sides of the bowl. Cover with plastic wrap and let rise until doubled, at least 30 minutes. Divide into six pieces of equal size and make the following variations:

Herb bread – *variation 1*
1 bread

⅙ of basic dough, risen once

Filling
1 ½ dl (⅔ cup) finely chopped spinach leaves
125 g (4 oz) garlic cream cheese
beaten egg
grated Jarlsberg cheese

Preheat the oven to 200°C (400°F). Roll the dough into a 25x35 cm (10x14") rectangle. Spread with cream cheese and sprinkle with spinach. Roll up from the long side. Place seam side down on a baking sheet lined with parchment paper. Cut diagonal slits in the roll with a sharp knife. Cover with plastic and let rise until doubled. Brush with egg, sprinkle with cheese and bake for around 35 minutes.

Cheese spirals with ham
– variation 2
9-10 spirals

⅙ of basic dough, risen once

Filling
9 thin turkey ham slices
2 dl (1 cup) grated Jarlsberg cheese
1 dl (½ cup) finely chopped chives
beaten egg
grated Jarlsberg cheese

Preheat the oven to 225°C (425°F). Roll the dough into a 20x30 (8x12") rectangle. Top with ham and sprinkle with cheese and chives. Roll up from the long side. Cut into 9-10 slices with a sharp knife. Place on a baking sheet lined with parchment paper. Cover and let rise until doubled. Brush with egg and sprinkle with cheese. Bake for around 12 minutes and let cool on a rack.

Peanut knots – *variation 3*
9-10 knots

⅙ of basic dough, risen once
1 ½ dl (⅔ cup) coarsely chopped salted peanuts
beaten egg
coarsely chopped salted peanuts

Preheat the oven to 225°C (425° F). Knead the peanuts into the dough. Divide into 9-10 pieces of equal size. Roll each piece into a finger-thick sausage around 12 cm (5") long. Form into a knot and place on a baking sheet lined with parchment paper. Cover and let rise for around 15 minutes. Brush with egg and sprinkle with peanuts. Bake for around 10 minutes and let cool on a rack.

Large horns – *variation 4*
4 horns

⅙ of basic dough, risen once
100 g (3 ½ oz) fresh chevre or cream cheese
4 tablespoons (¼ cup) chopped sun-dried tomatoes, drained

beaten egg
grated cheese
1 ½ teaspoons caraway seed

Preheat the oven to 200°C (400°F). Roll the dough into a circle, around 35 cm (14") in diameter. Divide into 4 parts and spread with cheese. Spoon 1 tablespoon chopped tomato on each and roll up to make large horns. Place on a baking sheet lined with parchment paper. Cover and let rise for 20 minutes. Brush with egg, sprinkle with cheese and caraway seed. Bake for 15-17 minutes and cool on a rack.

Basil horns– *variation 5*
8 horns

⅙ of basic dough, risen once
2 dl (1 cup) grated Jarlsberg cheese
1 dl (½ cup) shredded fresh basil
beaten egg
1 dl (½ cup) sunflower seeds

Preheat the oven to 225°C (425°F). Roll the dough into a circle, around 35 cm (14") in diameter. Divide into 8 triangles and sprinkle with cheese and basil. Roll up to make horns. Place on a baking sheet lined with parchment paper. Cover and let rise for 20 minutes. Brush with egg and sprinkle with seeds. Bake for around 12 minutes and let cool on a rack.

Carrot roll cluster– *variation 6*
8 rolls

⅙ of basic dough, risen once
2 dl (1 cup) grated carrots
beaten egg
sunflower seeds

Preheat the oven to 200°C (400°F). Knead the carrots into the dough. Divide into 8 pieces of equal size and form into balls. Place one ball in the center of a baking sheet lined with parchment paper. Place the remaining balls in a ring all around. Cover and let rise for 20 minutes. Brush with egg and sprinkle with seeds. Bake for around 15 minutes and let cool on a rack.

It's easy to make six different yeast breads from one basic dough. Back from left: Large crescents, herb bread and basil crescents. Front from left: Peanut knots, cheese twists with ham and carrot rolls.

Breakfast rolls

30 rolls

2 dl (1 cup) rolled oats
250 g (8 oz) cottage cheese
50 g (1 ³/₄ oz) fresh yeast
5 dl (2 cups) lukewarm water
1 teaspoon salt
13-14 dl (5 ¹/₃ – 5 ³/₄ cups) whole-wheat flour

Combine oats and cottage cheese and let sit overnight. Dissolve the yeast in the water and stir in the oat mixture, salt and most of the flour. Knead well, until the dough leaves the side of the bowl. Cover and let rise for 30 minutes. Punch down the dough. Turn out onto a floured board and knead in the remaining flour. Divide into 30 pieces of equal size and form into round balls. Place the balls on a greased baking sheet, cover and let rise for around 30 minutes. Preheat the oven to 230°C (450°F). Bake for around 20 minutes. Serve slightly warm. These freeze well. Reheat for 5-8 minutes.

Bread

Unless otherwise stated, make all bread according to the following directions:

– All ingredients should be room temperature.
– Liquid (water or milk) should be 35-37° C (94-98° F).
– Dissolve yeast and salt in the liquid.
– Stir after each addition of flour, so that coarse particles can absorb liquid.
– After kneading, let the dough rise until double in size. Punch down, knead again and divide into loaves.
– Final rising can take place in the oven set to 40°C (104°F) with a cup of boiling water in a tray on the oven floor.
– Place the breads into an oven preheated to 230-240°C (450-465°F). Lower the temperature to 180-200°C (350-400°F), and bake for 30-45 minutes.
– Fresh yeast is used in all recipes. If using dry yeast, use one-fourth the amount of yeast.
– Add dry yeast along with the flour.

Basic dough

The basic dough can be used as is, but it also can be used as a basis for variations. The advantage is that you can bake several types at once, because rising and baking times, as well as temperature, are the same for all the breads. This recipe yields around 3 kg (6 ½ lb) basic dough.

1 ¼ liter (5 cups) water
50 g (1 ¾ oz) yeast
25 g (4 teaspoons) salt
300 g (2 cups) whole-wheat flour (finely or coarsely ground)
300 g (2 cups) whole-rye flour (finely or coarsely ground)
around 1 ¼ kg (2 ½ lb) all-purpose flour
2 tablespoons oil

Prepare according to general directions.

Sunflower seed bread
– *variation 1*

1 kg (2 ¼ lb) basic dough
150 g (5 oz) sunflower seeds

Three-grain bread
– *variation 2*

1 kg (2 ¼ lb) basic dough
150 g (5 oz) rye kernels
2 ½ dl (1 cup) water
½ teaspoon salt
2 dl (scant 1 cup) flaxseed

Soak the kernels in the water for at least 15 minutes before kneading into the dough. Add extra all-purpose flour if necessary.

Whole-wheat bread
– *variation 3*

1 kg (2 ¼ lb) basic dough
3 ½ dl (1 ½ cups) wheat kernels
2 ½ dl (1 cup) water
½ teaspoon salt

Soak the kernels in the water for at least 15 minutes before kneading into the dough. Add extra all-purpose flour if necessary.

Walnut bread
– *variation 4*

1 kg (2 ¼ lb) basic dough
50-75 g (½ cup) chopped walnuts

Canary bread
– *variation 5*

1 kg (2 ¼ lb) basic dough
200-300 g (7-10 oz) drained and chopped sun-dried tomatoes
4 tablespoons (¼ cup) chopped fresh herbs, such as oregano, rosemary and/or coriander

Kneipp bread

Named after the famous Dr. Kneipp, this bread is coarser and more flavorful than any you can find in a store.

2 breads

1 liter (4 cups) water (or half water, half milk)
4 teaspoons salt
25 g (1 oz) fresh yeast
8 ½ dl (3 ½ cups) whole-wheat flour
5 dl (2 cups) whole-rye flour (finely or coarsely ground)
2 tablespoons oil (optional)
around 11 ½ dl (4 ¾ cups) all-purpose flour for a not too stiff dough

Fiber bomb

It would be hard to find a coarser bread than this one baked with whole grain flour and bran.

2 loaves

1 liter (4 cups) water
4 teaspoons salt
1 tablespoon 7% vinegar or lemon juice
1 ¾ dl (¾ cup) whole wheat kernels
4 ½ dl (1 ¾ cups) wheat bran
or 2 dl (¾ cup) oat bran + 2 ½ dl (1 cup) wheat bran
1 ¾ dl (¾ cup) finely ground whole-rye flour
3 ½ tablespoons flaxseed
3 ½ tablespoons sunflower seeds, lightly crushed
9 - 11 dl (3 ¾ 4 ⅓ cups) finely ground whole-wheat flour
50 g (1 ¾ oz) fresh yeast

Combine the first 8 ingredients and stir into a thick gruel. Let steep for at least one hour. Add some of the flour and crumble in part of the yeast. Stir until all flour is moistened. Stir in flour until around ¾ of the entire amount has been added. Stir as long as you have the strength, if stirring by hand, 10 minutes if using a machine. Cover with plastic and let rest for 30 minutes. Make a mound of most of the remaining flour on a board. Turn out the dough onto the flour. With floured hands, knead until the dough is smooth and elastic (stretch, fold together,

repeating as necessary). Divide the dough into two parts and shape each piece first into a ball and then into a loaf. Place in greased loaf pans. Set the oven thermostat at 40°C (104°F) with the oven tray on the lowest rill and the rack just under the center of the oven. When the oven has reached 40°C (104°F), place the pans on the rack and pour 1 cup boiling water into the oven tray. Close the door immediately. Let the breads rise for 30 minutes. Remove carefully from the oven. Increase the oven temperature to 220°C (425°F) (use the "pizza function" if your oven has one). When the oven has reached 220°C (425°F), place the pans on the rack and pour another cup of boiling water into the oven tray. Close the door, lower the temperature to 185°C (375°F), and bake for 40-45 minutes. Remove the breads from the pans immediately and cool on a rack.

Aromatic French bread

2-4 loaves

6 ½ dl (2 ⅔ cups) cold water
1 tablespoon salt
25 g (1 oz) fresh yeast
2 teaspoons soft butter
15 dl (6 ¼ cups) all-purpose flour

Knead (at low speed in a machine) for 10 minutes. Place the dough in a plastic bag, knot it and refrigerate overnight. Divide the dough into 4 parts. Make round breads and place on floured baking parchment. Cover with plastic and let rise for 2-3 hours. Preheat the oven to 245°C (475°F) with a baking sheet inside to get hot. Carefully turn the loaves onto the hot baking sheet. Reduce the temperature to 220°C (425°F) and bake for around 20 minutes. The breads should be dark, almost burnt. The temperature can be increased at the end of the baking time.

Oatmeal bread

2 loaves

1 liter (4 cups) water
50 g (1 ¾ oz) fresh yeast
4 teaspoons salt
1 dl (½ cup) wheat germ
5 dl (2 cups) rolled oats
16-20 dl (6 ⅔ - 8 ⅓ cups) all-purpose flour

Prepare according to standard directions. Make 2 loaves. Wet the surface and roll in oatmeal before rising.

Sunflower seed bread
made in a bread machine
1 loaf

Place ingredients in the machine in the following order:
2 ½ dl (1 cup) water
1 tablespoon oil (optional)
1 tablespoon dark corn or sugar syrup or molasses
1 ½ teaspoons salt
1 ¾ dl (¾ cup) finely ground whole-wheat flour
4 ¼ dl (1 ¾ cups) all-purpose flour
1 dl (scant ½ cup) sunflower seeds
1 ½ teaspoons dry yeast (always dry yeast in a bread machine)

Bake according to directions for machine. Of course this recipe can be used for baking in a regular oven.

Mediterranean bread

with garlic and olives

2 loaves

Day 1:

5 dl (2 cups) water
3 ¹/₂ tablespoons yogurt or sour milk
25 g (1 oz) fresh yeast
2 dl (³/₄ cup) rye flour
2 dl (1 cup) all-purpose flour
2 teaspoons salt
Make according to general directions. Cover and let rest for 10-15 hours.

Day 2:
Uncover the dough and add

2 ¹/₂ dl (1 cup) rye flour
2 tablespoons olive oil
2-4 garlic cloves, minced
as many olives as you like, both green and black, sliced
a little liquid from the olives
around 1 liter (4 cups) all-purpose flour

Stir together and add enough all-purpose flour to make a relatively soft dough. Cover and let rise for 1 hour. Punch down and knead again. Cover and let rise for 1 hour. Form into 2 loaves. For pretty loaves, place the dough in floured baskets. Let rise at room temperature for around 30 minutes, if desired. Preheat the oven to 250°C (475°F). Just before baking, tip the loaves out onto a greased baking sheet. Remove the baskets and bake for 10 minutes. Lower the temperature to 200°C (400°F) and bake for 20 minutes.

Syrup cake

5 loaves

1 liter (4 cups) water
50 g (1 ³/₄ oz) yeast
4 teaspoons salt
1 liter (4 cups) rye flour
1 dl (scant ¹/₂ cup) molasses
3 ¹/₂ tablespoons soft margarine or butter

1 ¹/₂ - 2 teaspoons ground ginger
2 liters (8 ¹/₃ cups) all-purpose flour
150 g (5 oz) raisins

Follow general directions. Add the raisins at the end so they don't get crushed during kneading. All raisins on the surface of the bread should be removed before rising and baking or they will burn.

English milk bread

7 loaves

1 ¹/₃ liter (5 1/3 cups) full-fat milk
3 dl (1 ¹/₄ cups) water
2 eggs
2 tablespoons salt
60 g (¹/₄ cup) butter
4 liters (16 ³/₄ cups) all purpose flour

Homemade bread

4 loaves

1 liter (4 cups) skim milk
50 g (1 ³/₄ oz) fresh yeast
1 tablespoon salt
1 liter (4 cups) coarsely or finely ground whole-wheat flour
1 dl (scant ¹/₂ cup) light molasses
3 ¹/₂ tablespoons soft butter or margarine
1 liter (4 cups) rye flour
1 liter (4 cups) all-purpose flour

The dough should be quite stiff. Place the loaves 1-2 cm (¹/₂") apart and brush the sides with oil, so they separate easily after baking. Sprinkle a little flour on top and prick with a fork. Let rise and bake according to general directions, but do not add water to the oven during baking.

Mineral bread

4 loaves

1 liter (4 cups) water
2 teaspoons salt (preferably sea salt)
50 g (1 ³/₄ oz) fresh yeast
1 tablespoon dark corn syrup or molasses

5 tablespoons (¹/₃ cup) seaweed flour
10 dl (4 cups) whole-wheat flour
4 dl (1 ²/₃ cups) rye flour
8 dl (3 ¹/₃ cups) all-purpose flour

Flaxseed bread

4 loaves

7 dl (2 ³/₄ cups) water
3 dl (1 ¹/₃ cups) milk
50 g (1 ³/₄ oz) fresh yeast
1 tablespoon salt
2 dl (³/₄ cup) flaxseed
1 dl (¹/₂ cup) wheat bran
4 tablespoons (¹/₄ cup) oil
1 ³/₄ liters (7 ¹/₄ cups) all-purpose flour

Old-fashioned cottage loaf

An old-fashioned sweet wheat bread. It was originally made as a round loaf with a ball of dough on the top.

5 dl (2 cups) skim milk
5 dl (2 cups) orange juice
2 ¹/₂ teaspoons salt
50 g (1 ³/₄ oz) fresh yeast
8 dl (3 ¹/₃ cups) rye flour
2 dl (³/₄ cup) sugar
2 ¹/₂ liters (10 ¹/₂ cups) all-purpose flour

Homemaker's bread

This bread came about through cooperation between the Norwegian Association of Homemakers and the Bakers' Union and was an instant success.

4 loaves

1 liter (4 cups) water
4 teaspoons salt
50 g (1 ³/₄ oz) fresh yeast
1 ³/₄ dl (³/₄ cup) wheat germ
8 ¹/₂ dl (3 ¹/₂ cups) whole-wheat flour
5 dl (2 cups) rye flour
1 ¹/₃ liter (5 ¹/₂ cups) all-purpose flour
2 ¹/₂ tablespoons oil
2 tablespoons sugar (optional)

Sigdal bread

This bread was developed by engineer Johannes Erstad, head of the laboratory at A/S Vaksdal Mills, in cooperation with technical director Arne Schulerud at the Norwegian Technological Institute. It's both healthy and delicious.

4 loaves

Day 1:
12 dl (5 cups) whole-wheat flour
10 g (⅓ oz) fresh yeast
5 dl (2 cups) water (12-15°C/55-60°F)

Cover the dough and set in a warm place (25-27°C/77-80°F) for 18-24 hours.

Day 2:
Uncover the dough and add

6 ½ dl (2 ¾ cups) skim milk
30 g (1 oz) fresh yeast
4 teaspoons salt
7 ½ dl (3 cups) finely ground whole-rye flour
2 tablespoons dark corn syrup or molasses
3 tablespoons oil
16 dl (6 ¾ cups) all-purpose flour

Proceed according to standard directions.

Forest ranger bread

A lot of work and many ingredients, but worth the trouble.

4 loaves

1 liter (4 cups) water
1 ½ dl (⅔ cup) 2 % milk
1 ½ dl (⅔ cup) buttermilk or cultured milk
1 ½ tablepoons salt
75 g (2 ½ oz) fresh yeast
2 dl (¾ cup) whole rye (or wheat) kernels
2 dl (1 cup) coarsely or finely ground whole-rye flour
2 dl (¾ cup) flaxseed
3 dl (1 ¼ cups) wheat bran
1 dl (½ cup) toasted sesame seed
1 dl (½ cup) toasted oats
1 dl (⅓ cup) sunflower seeds, lightly crushed

27 dl (11 cups) all-purpose flour

Proceed according to standard directions. Roll the loaves in a mixture of sesame seeds, flaxseed and sunflower seeds and bake in loaf pans.

Nan bread

10 flat breads

500 g (3 ⅓ cups) all-purpose flour
1 tablespoon dry yeast
1 tablespoon sugar
2 ½ dl (1 cup) buttermilk or cultured milk
2 ½ dl (1 cup) full fat milk
3 tablespoons soybean oil

Combine all ingredients and let rise until double. Divide into 10 pieces of equal size and roll flat. Bake quickly on a grill, first on the one side, then on the other.

Gold medal bread

Norwegian bakers always travel with our sports teams to the Olympic games and to world championships, ready to supply fresh Norwegian bread at every meal. Here is a "gold-medal" recipe.

3 loaves

5 dl (2 cups) buttermilk or cultured milk
5 dl (2 cups) water
30 g (1 oz) fresh yeast
4 teaspoons salt
2 dl (¾ cup) wheat bran
2 ½ dl (1 cup) rolled oats
1 ½ dl (⅔ cup) whole rye flour
1 ½ dl (⅔ cup) whole wheat flour
20 dl (8 ⅓ cups) all-purpose flour
3 ½ tablespoons soft butter or margarine

If desired, soak the whole grain flour in half the water for a couple of hours first. Otherwise proceed according to standard directions. Knead the dough for around 10 minutes. Cover and let rise for 30 minutes, until double. Divide into three pieces of equal size. Form into loaves. Cover and let rise for 40 minutes. Preheat the oven to

Hamburger buns

240°C (450°F). Brush the loaves with water and throw half a cup of water into the oven just before baking. As soon as the loaves are in the oven, lower the temperature to 200°C (400°F) and bake for 40-45 minutes.

Hotdog or hamburger buns

Better than bought, and with no preservatives.

40 buns

1 liter (4 cups) skim milk
50 g (1 ¾ oz) fresh yeast
1 tablespoon salt
1 ¾ dl (¾ cup) sugar
125 g (4 oz) soft margarine
30 dl (12 ½ cups) all-purpose flour (up to ½ whole wheat flour, if desired)

Let the dough rise until double. Shape into a long sausage and cut into 40 pieces, 50-60 g (2 oz) each. Let rest for a few minutes, then shape into hotdog or hamburger buns. Brush with water and sprinkle with sesame seed. Place on a greased baking sheet. Cover and let rise for 20-30 minutes. Preheat the oven to 240°C (450°F). Bake for 8-10 minutes, until golden. These buns freeze well.

Variation

Make crescent rolls of the same dough. Brush with melted butter before baking.

Subject Index

Recipe Index

Omslag:
Eide, Per: Fish, sea and fjord
Grønli, Espen: Food pictures
Ove Bergersen: Cow
Løken, Bård: Lamb
Søby, Øystein: Rolling landscape

Other Photographers
Alfsen, Per / EFF page: 153, 3rd column
Barros / Image bank, page: 53
Bergersen, Ove / Samfoto, page : 73
Bratlie, Espen / Samfoto, page: 27, 54
Børjesson, Alf / EFF page:121 3rd column,125, 132 bottom, 133 top, 134, 146
Eide, Per, page: cover, fjord and sea, 4, 8, 9, 13, 18, 19, 30, 36, 38, 55, 1st column, 80 bottom, 84 bottom, 89 top, 95, 97, 104 bottom, 108, 112, 114, 115, 116, 137, 145, 148, 151, 152 top, 153 bottom, 158, 3rd column, 159, 1st column, 160, 1st column top, 163, 206, 213, 3rd column, 225, 228 bottom, 236 bottom, 243 top 3rd column, 246 bottom, 273
Fossland, Jon Terje / Fame Photo Company, page: 16, 3rd column, 17
Haga, Tom / EFF page: 126, 1st column, 131
Halsetrønning, Steve / Samfoto, page: 14
Helgestad, Asgeir / Samfoto page: 190
Henriksen, Anders, page: 43, 44, 45, 47
Holmberg, Bjørn-Owe / Samfoto, page: 34
Holthe, Kim / EFF page: 139, 3rd column, 147, 237
Juul, Arild / EFF, page: 15, 16, 1st column, 31
Koller, Lena / EFF page: 113
Løken, Bård / Samfoto, page: 12
Næss, Baard / Samfoto, page: 58
Møller, Mette / Dagbladet / ALL OVER PRESS, page: 7
Rørslett, Bjørn / Samfoto, page: 20, 21
Strand, Ragge / EFF page: 124, 3rd column, 132 top
Søby, Øystein / Samfoto, page: cover field, 75.
Wilson, Bengt / EFF page: 140
Wuttudal, Tore / Samfoto, page: 35
Wuttudal, Tore, page: 23, 37
Åsheim, Ole / Samfoto, page: 28

Picture sources:
Arcus, page: 51
Bread Facts, page: 26, 275, 277, 283
Export office for fish, page: 64 bottom, 117, 119, 122, 2nd column, 126 top, 128 bottom, 133, 3rd column, 156, 157, 161, 237.
Information office for eggs and white meat, page: 29, 67, 86, 87, 107 1st column, 165, 166, 167, 3rd column, 168, 174 bottom, 177, 257 top, 259, 260, bottom.

Information office for fruit and vegetables, page: 96, 98, 55, 3rd column bottom.
Information office for meat, page: 187, 188, 189, 192, 194 bottom, 199 bottom, 200 top, 203 bottom, 205, 207 top 2nd column, 211 top, 221, 223, 235, 236 top.
TINE, page: 59, 60, 61, 76-81, 83-85, 91, 238, 240, 241, 246, 3rd column, 248, 251, 252, 261-268, 271, 1st column, 279.
Vestlandske Sales Group, page: 22

Dishes and props in photos:
Til Bords, Sandefjord
Porsgrunn Porselen